FOOD *from* PLENTY

Good food made from
the plentiful, the seasonal
and the leftover

DIANA HENRY

MITCHELL BEAZLEY

Contents

Introduction

I started to write this book just before the current global recession. As soon as the downturn hit, publishers and newspaper and magazine editors went into credit crunch over-drive; they all wanted books and articles about cheap food. I thought this was missing the point. Before the credit crunch, a sea change in our attitude towards food was already taking place. We had known for ages – though we hadn't fully faced it – that we were not using what we have in the best way. In the developed world we were over-fishing, using too many of the world's resources to produce meat, and totally disconnected from the agricultural practices that put the food on our plates. Many of us were eating a dangerously unhealthy diet. Perhaps worst of all, we were wasting tonnes of food; literally throwing it out.

My response to the cry for articles on cheap food was that a desire for this had already brought about a tragic state of affairs: not only BSE, but also a world full of unhealthy, processed junk food that comes with a low price tag but at a high cost in other ways. And when people bemoaned how little we had, all I could think was how very much we had.

This book is about a thoughtful approach to food, one that is better for you in terms of money saved and pleasure gained, and for the world around you. By that I don't just mean the planet, but the people who produce our food.

I am not here to preach, though. The last thing I want to do is make you don a hair shirt before you go shopping. I am a food writer. I am essentially in the business of giving pleasure. But I believe that approaching food in a caring, thoughtful way will increase the pleasure you get from it. Knowing what to do with the leftover chicken in your refrigerator, how to deal with a glut of apples by making chutney, how to turn a load of inexpensive potatoes and winter greens into the most delicious, olive oil-rich supper (the dish is from Greece and it's on page 85) will bring you more joy than buying over-processed food, and make for a healthier, happier life.

A shift in emphasis

We are much more concerned, post-BSE, about where our food comes from and how it has been produced. We go to farmers' markets, we demand information about provenance, and we have even taken to growing our own vegetables. We want good food. But good food can come with a higher price tag. Intensively farmed meat is cheaper than meat from animals reared with care on a small farm. Artisan bread is more expensive than factory-made loaves.

I am not asking you to triple your food spend. The key to good eating is to buy better food and use it well. This means balancing the cost of good food by, for example, using all of a roast – making more meals from the leftovers and stock from the bones – and eating cheaper cuts of meat and inexpensive pulses, vegetables and grains at other times. The food that offers terrible value for money is that which is prepared for us: supermarket ready meals and the like. It lasts for only one meal and contains cheaper ingredients (such as meat produced under conditions – often in other countries – which we know nothing about).

The remains of the day

As I was growing up I learnt the art of dove-tailing meals: always using up leftovers. This was not out of poverty, but because a philosophy of using every bit of an animal and not throwing out food prevailed. This is good for the household budget, but it's also a sane way to think about the world's resources. The word 'leftovers' does not sound great. The French, more charmingly, call them '*les delicieux petits restes*'. They have the right approach: leftovers can produce some of the most imaginative and delicious dishes.

My favourite kind of cooking is not the showy-off sort, which takes days of planning and shopping, but the pottering, 'I-wonder-what's-in-the-fridge' kind. There's no grand plan: you just go where serendipity and improvisation take you. Monday, when there's a bit of weekend roast left, is the best day for this musing kind of approach. Chicken – if you can get your hands on it – is perfect (though we fight over cold roast chicken in our house). Fry the leftover nuggets with bacon, a couple of tablespoons of cream and a handful of frozen peas and you have a sauce for pasta. (Even half a cup of gravy, fried mushrooms and a dollop of cream are delicious on pasta.) You can toss shredded chicken with rice, strips of omelette and chilli to make a perfect hangover cure too.

Cold roast lamb, cooked nice and pink so that a bit more heat won't harm it, can form the basis of a Middle Eastern pilaf that will be just as enjoyable as yesterday's roast. If you have some preserved lemon to throw in, or a few dried apricots, so much the better. What of leftover veg? Potatoes are easy. Sauté slowly – maybe with some mushrooms – until the pan is covered with golden flakes, finish with garlic and parsley, and you have a dish that is perfect with duck or chicken.

And then there is stock. Get those bones into a pot. There is so much flavour still to be extracted, it is a shame to throw them away. It takes next to no effort and you can reduce the result by boiling, then freeze it in tubs. Soups and sauces are then yours for the making (and although it's great that you can now buy fresh stock, just look at its price; much better to make your own).

The art of using food up even goes as far as finding something to do with a bag of over-soft plums. They can easily be transformed into a pot of jam. You don't have to get out a preserving pan and go into full-scale production – it's very easy to make just one small pot and keep it in the refrigerator for eating on toast or with yogurt at breakfast.

What to do with '*les restes*' is a primary feature of my opening chapter, and one of the cornerstones of this book. But throughout the chapters you will find tips about what to do with leftovers. For me the path to contentment definitely wends its way past the stove, but it's always a good idea to go via the remains in the refrigerator.

Seasonal sustenance

Seasonality is the modern cook's mantra, so you hardly need me to repeat it, but eating food in season saves you money and makes you feel better. Why pay £3.50 for a punnet of tasteless strawberries in February? They'll be delicious in June, and by July they'll be relatively cheap too.

The mad practices employed to give us out-of-season produce are also bad for the planet. (I do make an exception for exotic fruit and vegetables; they're not cultivated in Britain and I'm glad to eat mangoes and pineapples when they are in season in the countries in which they are grown.)

To market, to market...

You have a lot of power. With every supermarket purchase you tell them how much you're prepared to pay for pork from a well-cared-for pig; you can save a great British apple variety; you can choose to support local food producers; and you can have an impact on whether a particular fish is fished to extinction.

I don't want the day to come when I tell my grandchildren about the fish we used to eat, or look at countryside that has been turned into a theme park and reminisce about the agriculture we once had. And I think it's brilliant that we have bakers and cheese makers who are so passionate about their product that they make it their life's work.

So buy local, buy British, support good farmers and artisan food producers and have a thought for sustainability. It doesn't have to cost the earth. With a bit of care, you can buy good food that will take you through the week for less than it costs to buy a weekful of ready meals.

Caring about ourselves

We are more anxious these days about what food is doing to our bodies. This is laudable, but has also led to a kind of craziness. Shopping for my children, I realized I felt guilty about not buying them food with added 'bonuses'. You know the kind of thing: drinks with extra vitamins, spreads that reduce cholesterol, bio yogurt that balances gut bacteria. Then two things happened. I saw that Coca-Cola appeared to be boasting about its healthiness (an 8oz serving of Diet Coke Plus provides, according to their website, 15 per cent of your RDI for niacin and vitamins B6 and B12). Then I interviewed an American journalist called Michael Pollan. Pollan had written a book called *In Defence of Food*, and it put my thinking straight. The book is about getting back to real food, forgetting about what nutritionists and marketeers tell us we should eat (as they so often get it wrong) and instead enjoying food with nothing added or taken out. As Pollan says, this food has no information on it and doesn't make extra money for those who sell it. A simple carrot cannot be labelled. But a carton of vegetable juice can, so you go for that option for the misguided sense of security it gives you. Pollan's mantra, and I urge you to follow it, is this: eat food, not too much, mostly plants. If you buy as much fresh and unprocessed stuff as possible, increase your intake of vegetables, grains and pulses, and don't overeat, you're going in the right direction. Happily, it will also save you money and treat the planet in a more responsible way.

Making life easier and more enjoyable

Where it seems appropriate, I have suggested cooking some ingredients – especially pulses – in larger quantities than you immediately need, so you can use them later in the week. Cooking for the week ahead makes sense economically and also makes life easier (you've expended both effort and fuel, so you might as well get the most out of it). Look out for tips on ingredients that you can cook and adapt to see you through several days.

There are also recipes for what I call 'long-term cooking': chutneys, jams and other preserves. For years I was a bit embarrassed about doing this kind of thing. Although it gave me enormous pleasure (there's a real thrill in stashing jars of food away), preserving was seen as the domain of old ladies or frumpy aunts. Now we're realizing that it saves you money and allows you to create a bit of luxury. French cherry wine, anyone? It's on page 256…

The recipes

This is a book for home cooks. None of the recipes requires a high level of skill. It also reflects a do-able approach to food. I'd love to be able to buy a whole animal from the butcher (it does save money) or cure my own ham (ditto) but I don't have a big enough freezer or, as I live in a city, the space or environment for doing these things. But most of us have room for a few jars of chutney in the kitchen cupboard, and the time occasionally to make our own pizzas or a loaf of bread. You don't have to move to the country or go part-time to get the most out of *Food from Plenty*.

All of the dishes are homely, and some are, in fact, humble, but that doesn't mean dull. There are dishes here from all over the world – from Sicily to Sweden, Ireland to Iran – all of them economical but indulgent too.

What it boils down to is taking more care. We need to value our planet, our bodies, the people who produce our food, the animals who provide it, and those we feed every day. It makes for a much happier life.

The roast and '*les restes*'

A roast, juicy, sweet and burnished from the oven, isn't just about good food, it's a way of living. It is a grand gesture, the pinnacle of home cooking, honouring both the animal and those you are feeding. It's also one of the most sensible meals you can cook, providing food that keeps on nourishing you in the coming days.

The art of looking in the refrigerator and pondering what you can do with bits of cooked meat (which the French, poetically, term '*les restes*') used to be something we learnt as children. Now we live in a 'one meal, one dish' culture. Food is finished and cleared (even scraped into the bin) on a daily basis. But this is a more expensive and less enjoyable way to cook and eat. If you begin the week with a roast, make stock from the bones for soup, then use the leftover meat for a pie or pilaf, the meat more than earns its place.

Even so, though I've given information on what to look for in the priciest joints of beef – such as sirloin – below, I haven't covered it in the recipes. I just find it too expensive.

What to buy

Scares about meat have had an upside: we are now more concerned about where our meat comes from, how it has been raised and what it has been fed.

Even if you don't care how animals are treated, your palate will benefit from taking it into consideration. A stressed animal means tougher meat. An animal reared at a normal rate (not fast-grown) and allowed to roam outdoors, foraging for whatever it fancies, will taste better than one that has undergone a standardized feeding regime and been fattened quickly. Also, slow-grown animals that are not densely stocked are more resistant to illness, so don't need regular antibiotics. And after slaughter they are more likely to be properly hung. The problem is that this meat costs more. I am not telling you always to buy the expensive option; I don't. Even going for the 'least bad' makes a difference. I just want you to know how to eat better, and in a way that is caring.

The supermarkets have smartened up their act lately. They now sell ranges that are organic or free-range, but read the labels carefully (they are good at obfuscation) and be aware that you could get more information from a butcher or farmer.

Where to buy it

It's getting harder to find a good butcher. Many have gone out of business because they cannot compete with supermarkets. But faced with plastic-wrapped packs in a supermarket, who do you ask for advice? A butcher can tell you where your meat comes from, what breed it is, and how it lived. He will source unusual cuts, bone a shoulder of lamb or joint a chicken. A good butcher will hang meat properly and he is unlikely to sell you poor meat, as he'll have to face you over the counter and apologize when you complain. Look for a member of the Quality Guild of Butchers. It isn't a guarantee, but it's a good start. An alternative is to buy from farm shops and farmers' markets. This cuts out the middle man and supports small farmers. Lastly, you can have home-delivery from a high-quality meat company or farm. But there's no point in me being holier-than-thou. I know that, because of time and cost, your only option may be the supermarket. If so, go for the best you can afford.

What to look for

PORK Pork is the meat on which I will not compromise. Pigs have been reared so cruelly in the past that I buy organic pork, or pork with the Freedom Food label (reared to the RSPCA's welfare standards). I avoid any that isn't British, as welfare conditions tend to be worse elsewhere, and British pig farmers need our support. But it's the flavour of properly reared pork that has won me round. I will fork out for pork from specific outlets and breeds. There has been much fanfare about Gloucester Old Spot, but I prefer Tamworth and Middle White; you will come to know what you like. There's a world of difference between pork from an old-fashioned breed that has grazed outside, eating windfall apples and roots, and pork that has been intensively farmed. Do yourself a favour and experience that difference.

BEEF Great beef comes from beef cattle, fed on grass and natural forage, not from 'dairy-cross' animals fed indoors on pellets. A good butcher will tell you which he is selling, and from what breed. Look out for Hereford, North Devon, Dexter, Highland and Welsh Black, among others. Good beef should not be 'aged' in vacuum packs, but dry-aged (hung). This breaks down the fibres, making it more tender and flavourful. It also dries the meat – making it better for cooking – and darkens the flesh. Beef should have a good covering of creamy white fat and clear 'marbling' – threads of fat running through it.

LAMB Finding good lamb presents fewer problems. Lamb is not usually intensively farmed and there's a range of taste and texture depending on the breed and where it has grazed. But there is semi-intensive rearing of lambs for the crazy 'spring' market. 'Spring lamb' is in fact from an animal born the previous autumn, and specially managed for autumn lambing. These lambs are usually reared indoors and given concentrated feeds. They grow fast and don't get enough exercise, so don't develop good flavour or enough fat. Lamb is really best eaten between May and October. It has good fat and is more likely to have been hung.

CHICKEN I am agog when I see a chicken for £1.99, less than you'd pay for a bag of spuds. But high-profile campaigning has had an impact. According to a survey for Compassion in World Farming, sales of 'standard' chicken fell by 11 per cent in 2008 while 35 per cent more free-range and organic birds were bought. This shows many shoppers will pay more for chickens reared with care, and many poultry farmers are happy to make changes as long as supermarkets don't try to drive down prices.

The multiplicity of labelling ('barn-reared', 'extensive indoor reared' and so on) makes it hard to know what's what. I home in on these:

Free-range They have access to the outdoors for at least half their life. They mustn't be packed more densely than 13 chickens per square metre. Birds cannot be killed before 81 days old.

Organic Both free-range and slower-grown, given an organic diet and no routine antibiotics. They are kept in smaller flocks, with more space to move inside and out, and are killed at 81 days.

Freedom Food Reared to the RSPCA's welfare standards. Chickens are more slowly grown and stocking densities are lower than for standard birds.

I won't lay down the law on what you should buy. I buy less, but better, chicken than I used to. Freedom Food costs only about £1 more than a standard chicken, so there's really no excuse not to choose that. I don't expect to pay a couple of quid for a chicken, but I'm glad I don't have to spend £15 (or more) either. What I will not buy is a ready-meal that contains chicken. That chicken is usually from countries whose welfare practices are unknown.

How to roast

We have become nervous about roasting. I myself have been in tears over lamb (when it wasn't cooked to the required pinkness), but experience has taught me two things: roast red meat for less time than you imagine it needs, and anybody can roast a chicken.

With all roasts, allow them to rest for 15–25 minutes after cooking, insulated well (I cover with foil, then a few thick towels kept for this purpose). It's better to undercook than overcook meat. Undercooked meat can be bunged back in the oven. If it's overcooked, all you can do is pretend it was deliberate…

You need to know your oven and how you like your meat, but here are my guidelines. Like Hugh Fearnley-Whittingstall, I believe in roasting prime cuts at a high heat for the first 15–30 minutes (what Hugh calls 'the sizzle'), though there are variations in this chapter.

After the initial sizzle:

For pink lamb, cook for 12 minutes per 500g (1lb 2oz) at 180°C/350°F/gas mark 4.

For rare beef, cook for 10 minutes per 500g (1lb 2oz) at 160°C/325°F/gas mark 3.

For pork (which should be thoroughly cooked, though not to dryness), cook for 25 minutes per 500g (1lb 2oz) at 180°C/350°F/gas mark 4.

Chickens are different. I don't do an initial 'sizzle'. Cook a chicken at 190°C/375°F/gas mark 5 for 20 minutes per 500g (1lb 2oz), plus an extra 10 minutes.

Simple roast chicken with herbs

There's nothing like roast chicken to make you feel hungry, happy and cared for. You can vary the herbs, though rosemary and sage are pretty powerful so use them carefully, and aniseedy chervil (if you can find it) is lovely in spring. My only rule is to roast for 20 minutes at 190°C/375°F/gas mark 5 for each 500g (1lb 2oz), plus an extra 10 minutes.

Serves 6

leaves from 4 thyme sprigs
1 tbsp chopped flat leaf parsley
50g (1¾oz) butter, softened
salt and pepper

2.2kg (5lb) chicken
1 glass (150ml/¼ pint) dry white wine
   or water

1 Preheat the oven to 190°C/375°F/gas mark 5. Mash the herbs with the butter and season. Carefully lift the skin of the breast of the bird, starting from the neck end, so that you have a pocket into which to stuff the butter. Ease the skin from the legs in the same way. Push in as much butter as you can without tearing the skin, then set the chicken in a roasting tin and smear the remaining butter on the outside. Season.

2 Roast for about 1 hour 50 minutes, pouring the wine or water into the tin halfway through. To check if it's cooked, plunge a skewer between the leg and the body; the juices that run out should be clear, with no trace of pink.

3 Cover the bird with foil, then insulate it (I keep old towels for this) and leave to rest for 15–20 minutes. Put the bird on a heated platter (or just take it to the table in the roasting tin) and serve.

GRAVY

I must admit I hardly ever make gravy, preferring instead simply to spoon out the wonderful cooking juices, but if you want to make it properly, let the bird rest, insulated, and put the roasting tin on the hob. Skim off the excess fat. Add chicken stock or water (about 400ml/14fl oz) to the tin and bring to the boil, scraping up all the juices and sediment from the bottom as you do so. Boil until you have a flavour and texture you like. You don't need to use a thickener: there's nothing wrong with thin gravy. Just make sure you don't reduce it so much that it is unpalatably salty.

ALSO TRY...

Leave out the herbs used above and mix the butter with torn basil and chopped sunblush tomatoes, or chopped black olives and anchovies, or grated Parmesan cheese and crushed garlic. These butters should be stuffed under the skin, or their ingredients will burn, so use plain butter to smear on the outside.

MORE WAYS TO ROAST CHICKEN

Corfu roast chicken with sweet potatoes and cayenne Season the chicken inside and out and place a lemon half and 2 bay leaves into the cavity, sprinkle with ½ tbsp cayenne and drizzle with olive oil and lemon juice. Cook as for Simple Roast Chicken (see page 16). Cut 2 red onions into wedges and cut 900g (2lb) sweet potatoes (no need to peel) into chunks. Toss with another ½ tbsp cayenne, salt, pepper and 2 tbsp olive oil. Put these round the chicken when there's 45 minutes cooking time left. Turn the vegetables a couple of times and sprinkle with chopped parsley and mint before serving.

Roast chicken with autumn fruits Cook as for Simple Roast Chicken (see page 16), but use only thyme in the butter and put the bird into a tin large enough for the fruit as well. You'll need 2 pears, quartered, 2 apples, cut into wedges, 4 plums, halved and stoned, 2 red onions cut into wedges and 30g (1¼oz) dried cranberries or dried sour cherries (soaked in boiling water for 15 minutes and drained). Add 6 thyme sprigs. Sprinkle with 2 tbsp light brown sugar, season and dot with butter. Toss in the fruit 45 minutes before the end of the cooking time and stir a couple of times for even browning.

Smoked paprika roast chicken with aioli Mix 6 tbsp olive oil, salt, pepper and 2½ tbsp smoked paprika. Paint this on the chicken. Cook as for Simple Roast Chicken (see page 16). Meanwhile, crush 2 garlic cloves with a little salt in a large mortar and pestle or bowl. Stir in 2 egg yolks. Add 300ml (½ pint) olive oil drop by drop, very slowly at first, beating as you do so. Only add more oil once the previous lot has been incorporated and the mixture has thickened. (If it splits, add the curdled mixture to a new yolk a little at a time, beating as before, but go easy this time.) Taste and season with more salt, pepper and lemon juice or white wine vinegar or both. Keep in the refrigerator, covered, until ready to serve with the chicken.

Roast chicken with preserved lemon and bay An idea from my friend, chef Matt Tebbutt. Put a whole preserved lemon (drained), a handful of coriander sprigs, 6 bay leaves and 2 heads of garlic, halved horizontally, inside the chicken. Season inside and out, put into a roasting tin and drizzle with olive oil. Roast as for Simple Roast Chicken (see page 16). Toast sourdough or French bread, then squeeze the softened garlic from inside the bird on to the toasts with some of the preserved lemon, diced. Carve at the table and moisten the toasts with the cooking juices.

Greek lemon roast chicken with potatoes and oregano Season the chicken inside and out and put into a very large roasting tin (you'll be adding vegetables later). Put half a lemon and a few bay leaves inside. Drizzle on some olive oil, squeeze on the other half of the lemon and roast as for Simple Roast Chicken (see page 16). Cut 2 large, peeled red onions into wedges (you should get 5 wedges from each half), halve 1kg (2lb 4oz) of small waxy potatoes, cut 2 lemons into wedges and break 2 heads of garlic into separate cloves (no need to peel). Toss with olive oil, salt and pepper, ½ tbsp dried oregano and the juice of ½ lemon. When the chicken still has 45 minutes roasting to go, put the vegetables round the chicken, sprinkle 2 tsp dried oregano on top and return to the oven. By the time the chicken is ready, the vegetables will be cooked.

Buttermilk-dressed roast chicken with gooseberry sauce, potatoes and leaves
Smear butter all over the chicken and season inside and out. Cook as for Simple Roast Chicken (see page 16). Meanwhile, cover 500g (1lb 2oz) gooseberries with cold water in a saucepan and put them on a high heat. By the time the water has come to the boil, the gooseberries will have softened a little. Immediately drain them. Put 125g (4½oz) caster sugar and 2 tbsp water in a frying pan (it must be a frying pan so that the liquid evaporates rapidly) and heat until the sugar has completely dissolved. Toss in the gooseberries and quickly heat them through. Some gooseberries will collapse, others stay whole. Stir in 1 tbsp white wine vinegar. Leave to cool. To make a dressing, combine 375ml (13fl oz) buttermilk with 6 tbsp whipping cream, 1 garlic clove, crushed, salt and pepper, a pinch of sugar and a small bunch of mint leaves, chopped. Once the chicken is cooked, cover it with foil, insulate and leave to rest for 15–20 minutes. Boil 600g (1lb 5oz) waxy potatoes and toss them with a little butter, salt and pepper. Put the potatoes and the leaves of 3 baby Little Gem lettuce into a bowl and drizzle over some of the dressing. Serve the salad with the chicken, offering the gooseberry sauce and the rest of the dressing on the side.

Malaysian roast chicken Prick the skin of the chicken all over with a fork so that the flavourings can penetrate the flesh. Mix together 6 tbsp oyster sauce, 4 tbsp soy sauce, 4 tbsp light brown sugar, 4 garlic cloves, crushed, 2 tsp chilli sauce, and a 2cm (¾in) square piece of fresh root ginger, peeled and very finely chopped. Taste for the balance of hot, sour, salty and sweet. Paint this all over the chicken, and rub it inside as well. Cover with foil and refrigerate for a couple of hours, or overnight if you can. Put into a roasting tin lined with fresh foil (to save your roasting tin) and roast as for Simple Roast Chicken (see page 16). After 15 minutes, pull the foil up around the chicken, then uncover the bird again in the last 15 minutes of cooking time – this stops the sugars in the marinade burning. Cover and insulate the chicken with fresh foil for 15–20 minutes so that it can rest before serving. Serve with the cooking juices. Rice and stir-fried green veg are good on the side.

Cherry and goat's cheese-stuffed chicken

In the summer you can use fresh cherries, pitted, instead of dried ones.

Serves 6

1.8kg (4lb) chicken
salt and pepper
15g (½oz) butter, softened

FOR THE STUFFING
25g (1oz) butter
1 onion, finely chopped

3 garlic cloves, crushed
100g (3½oz) white breadcrumbs
150g (5½oz) creamy goat's cheese, in chunks
4 tbsp chopped fresh dill
75g (2½oz) dried sour cherries, soaked in
     hot water for 15 minutes then drained

1 Preheat the oven to 190°C/375°F/gas mark 5. Wash the chicken inside and out and pat dry with kitchen paper. Season inside and out.

2 Melt the butter for the stuffing in a frying pan and cook the onion until soft but not coloured. Add the garlic and cook for another minute. Tip into a bowl and add the other stuffing ingredients. Gently mix (don't squash the cheese) and season well. Stuff the bird, place in a roasting tin and smear the butter on the outside. Roast for 1½ hours or until cooked through.

3 Spoon the stuffing into a serving bowl. Serve the chicken with the stuffing, lemon wedges, a cucumber salad and a big bowl of bulgur wheat.

ALSO TRY...

Pelopponese chicken with bread, feta and tomato stuffing Sauté 1 onion, finely chopped, in 4 tbsp olive oil until soft. Add 4 garlic cloves, finely chopped, for 2 more minutes. Add 250g (9oz) cherry tomatoes, chopped, and sauté until soft. In a bowl put 300g (10½oz) bread (such as ciabatta) in chunks, 75g (2½oz) feta cheese, crumbled, and 20g (¾oz) dill, parsley or mint, chopped. Add 1 tbsp tomato purée mixed with 2 tsp olive oil, a small beaten egg, the onion and tomatoes and seasoning. Mix well, then use to stuff the chicken. Season the outside of the bird, drizzle with olive oil and roast as above.

Saffron roast chicken with Azerbaijani stuffing Adapted from a Margaret Shaida recipe. Preheat the oven as above. Rinse 75g (2½oz) basmati rice. Parboil in lightly salted water for 10 minutes. Drain. Chop 50g (1¾oz) each dried figs and apricots and mix with 25g (1oz) dried barberries or cranberries and 50g (1¾oz) dried cherries. Put in a bowl and cover with just-boiled water. Leave for 15 minutes, then drain. Sauté an onion, chopped, in 25g (1oz) butter until soft, then add the rice and stir to coat. Add the fruit with 50g (1¾oz) walnuts or almonds, chopped. Season and cook for 2 minutes, stirring. Dissolve ½ tsp saffron threads in hot water and add 100g (3½oz) melted butter and the juice of 1 lemon. Season the chicken and stuff with the rice. Put a piece of foil, big enough to tent the chicken, into a roasting tin. Place the chicken on top and pour over the saffron mixture. Pull the foil together and scrunch the edges to make a good seal. Roast for 1 hour. Open the foil and cook for another 30 minutes. Serve with the juices, green salad and a bowl of chopped cucumber mixed with yogurt and mint.

Restorative chicken and parsley risotto

Sometimes I long to have leftover chicken just so that I can make this risotto. It isn't authentically Italian but seems to me to be the Italian equivalent of that great Jewish penicillin, chicken soup. You can make the risotto without the chicken – a lemon and parsley risotto is lovely – and you don't have to add the embellishment of the egg yolk or, indeed, the cream. But there's nothing wrong with making the most of your leftovers: life's too short to make them into the kind of food that feels puritan and austere.

Serves 4

1.2 litres (2 pints) chicken or vegetable stock
75g (2½oz) butter
1 tbsp olive oil
1 small onion, finely chopped
300g (10oz) risotto rice
½ unwaxed lemon
250g (9oz) leftover cooked chicken, in chunks

1 egg yolk
5 tbsp freshly grated Parmesan cheese, plus more to serve
2 tbsp finely chopped flat leaf parsley
salt and pepper
4 tbsp double cream

1 Heat the stock to a simmer and keep it simmering throughout the cooking time. Heat half the butter and all the oil in a heavy-bottomed saucepan and add the onion. Cook on a medium heat until soft but not coloured. Add the rice and turn it round in the fat and juices until translucent.

2 Start to add the stock, a ladle at a time, stirring continuously. Don't add any new stock until the last addition has been absorbed. You are aiming for rice with the faintest hint of bite in the centre of the grains. This should take about 20 minutes.

3 Finely grate the lemon zest and stir it in two-thirds of the way through the cooking. Add the chicken for the last 5–10 minutes, making sure it is heated through thoroughly. Squeeze the juice from the lemon half and mix it in a small bowl with the egg yolk, Parmesan, parsley, salt and pepper and cream.

4 When the risotto is ready, take it off the heat, add the lemon juice mixture and the rest of the butter and stir gently but thoroughly. Taste for seasoning. Cover and leave to rest for 2 minutes, then serve immediately. Offer extra grated Parmesan, if you want.

Vietnamese chicken with Nuoc Cham

This is a quite ordinary dish in itself, basically an eastern pilaf, the rice absorbing the stock in which it is cooked. But it is the accompaniment that makes it special. Hot, sour, salty, sweet, this dish ends up being much more than the sort of food you expect to throw together with leftovers. It is literally a blast for the tastebuds. I do add other ingredients I have to hand, perhaps mushrooms, green beans or julienned carrot. But no sweetcorn, please!

Serves 4

FOR THE NUOC CHAM
4 garlic cloves, chopped
2 red chillies, halved, deseeded
  and chopped
good pinch of salt flakes
juice of 1 lime
2 tbsp fish sauce
4 tsp caster sugar

FOR THE CHICKEN AND RICE
350g (12oz) long-grain rice
700ml (1¼ pints) chicken stock

4 slices fresh root ginger
salt and pepper
1 tbsp groundnut oil
3 shallots, very finely sliced
400g (14oz) leftover cooked chicken,
  shredded or in small chunks
6 spring onions, chopped on the diagonal
generous handful of mint leaves, torn

1 To make the Nuoc Cham, put the garlic and chillies in a mortar and pestle with the salt and grind until you almost have a paste. (It doesn't have to be perfectly smooth.) Add everything else and mix. Taste and adjust the balance of hot, sour, salty and sweet to taste. It's very powerful, so let it down with a little water if you like, but remember it's going to be eaten with something starchy.

2 Put the rice into a saucepan and pour on the stock. Bring to the boil. Add the ginger and season. Boil until the rice starts to look 'pitted' (about 4 minutes), then cover the pan and reduce the heat to very low. There will still be liquid left underneath the rice; it will be absorbed – and the steam will cook the rice – in about 15 minutes. Don't stir as this makes the rice sticky, but make sure it isn't sticking at the bottom (check gently with a fork) and add a little more boiling water if it is. The rice should be tender, light and fluffy. Remove the bits of ginger. Keep the rice warm.

3 Heat the oil in a frying pan and quickly fry the shallots until pale gold. Add the chicken and cook until hot through. Carefully fork these into the rice with the spring onions and mint. Serve with the Nuoc Cham – either drizzle it on top or let people help themselves.

Chiang Mai chicken noodles

A great change from Thai chicken curry, which I seem to make rather a lot. You can also make this with leftover pork.

Serves 4

FOR THE NOODLES
groundnut oil
1 onion, sliced into crescent moon shapes,
   or 6 shallots, sliced
4 garlic cloves, sliced
1 tsp ground turmeric
2 tbsp red Thai curry paste
400ml can coconut milk
200ml (7fl oz) chicken stock
350g (12oz) leftover cooked chicken,
   in chunks

½ tsp soft light brown sugar, or to taste
2 tsp fish sauce, or to taste
juice of ½ lime, or to taste
400g (14oz) egg noodles

TO SERVE
2 spring onions, chopped on the diagonal
1 red chilli, halved, deseeded and shredded
2 tbsp chopped coriander
wedges of lime

1 Put 1 tbsp of the oil into a saucepan and sauté the onion or shallots until golden. Add the garlic and cook for 2 minutes, then add the turmeric and curry paste. Stir for 1 minute until the spices become fragrant. Add the coconut milk and stock and bring to a simmer. Cook for 15 minutes. Add the chicken and heat through thoroughly. Season with the sugar and fish sauce and adjust it to your taste; you may want lime or more sugar.

2 Cook the noodles according to the packet instructions. Divide them between four bowls, spoon over the chicken curry and sprinkle over the spring onions, chilli and coriander. Offer wedges of lime to serve.

West Country chicken and ham pie

This is a perfect post-Christmas dish when you have leftover turkey and ham.

Serves 4

60g (2oz) butter
3 leeks, cleaned and sliced
60g (2oz) flour, plus more to dust
425ml (¾ pint) milk
salt and pepper
1 tsp English mustard
300g (10oz) leftover cooked chicken,
  cut into chunks

150g (5½oz) cooked ham, cut into chunks
2 tbsp chopped flat leaf parsley
freshly grated nutmeg
300g (11oz) puff pastry
1 egg yolk, mixed with a little water
  and salt

1 Melt the butter in a heavy pan and add the leeks. Cook gently for 5 minutes, add a splash of water, reduce the heat, cover the pan and sweat for 10 minutes. Add the flour and stir for 1 minute. Take the pan off the heat and gradually add the milk. Return to the heat and bring to the boil, stirring; reduce the heat and simmer for 5 minutes. Season, add the mustard, chicken and ham. Heat through, then add the parsley and nutmeg to taste. Cool.

2 Preheat the oven to 200°C/400°F/gas mark 6. Spoon the chicken into an enamel pie dish (measuring about 20x25cm/8x9in). On a floured surface, roll the pastry out to the thickness of a 50 pence piece. Cut off a strip, wet it and place it on the lip of the pie dish. Lay the rest of the pastry on top, pressing down firmly. Trim off the excess. Crimp the edges and use pastry scraps to decorate. Make 3 cuts in the middle to let the steam escape.

3 Brush with the egg yolk and bake for 30–40 minutes, or until golden.

ALSO TRY...

Russian chicken, mushroom, soured cream and dill pie Cook 125g (4½oz) rice until *al dente*. Set aside. Sauté 250g (9oz) button mushrooms and 150g (5½oz) oyster mushrooms, both roughly chopped, with 1 onion, chopped, in 50g (1¾oz) butter until golden. Season, add 2 garlic cloves, finely chopped, and cook for 2 minutes. Stir in 30g (1¼oz) flour and cook for 1 minute. Remove from the heat and gradually add 300ml (½ pint) milk. Return to the heat, bring to the boil and stir until thickened. Stir in 425g (15oz) cooked chicken, cut into chunks, the juice of ½ lemon, 150ml (¼ pint) soured cream and 15g (½oz) dill, finely chopped and heat through. Spread the rice in a buttered dish (measuring roughly 26x22cm/10½x8½in and 6cm/2½in deep), then pour on the sauce. Leave to cool. Roll out 375g (13oz) puff pastry, wet the edges of the dish and press it down. Trim off the excess and crimp the edges. Make a few little slits in the pie to let steam escape, then brush with beaten egg yolk. Bake in a preheated oven at 200°C/400°F/gas mark 6 for 10 minutes, then reduce the heat to 180°C/350°F/gas mark 4 for a further 20–25 minutes, until golden.

Greek chicken, pumpkin and feta pie

You can make this in advance if you butter the top well and cook it at the very last minute.

Serves 8

1.2kg (2lb 12oz) well-flavoured pumpkin or butternut squash
6 tbsp olive oil
¾ tsp ground cinnamon
salt and pepper
700g (1lb 9oz) spinach, washed and tough stalks removed
2 onions, finely chopped
2 garlic cloves, finely chopped
generous grating of nutmeg

75g (2½oz) Parmesan cheese, grated
250g (9oz) ricotta cheese
2 eggs, lightly beaten
175g (6oz) feta cheese, crumbled
1½ tbsp chopped parsley
50g (1¾oz) butter
250g (9oz) filo pastry
350g (12oz) leftover cooked chicken, cut into chunks

1 Preheat the oven to 200°C/400°F/gas mark 6. Cut the pumpkin into slices, discard the seeds and fibres and put in a roasting dish. Brush with oil. Scatter with the cinnamon and season. Roast for 20–25 minutes, or until tender. Remove the skin.

2 Put the spinach into a large saucepan with the water clinging to it after washing. Cover and set over a low heat. Let it wilt for 5 minutes, turning. Leave to cool. Squeeze out all the water, using your hands.

3 Heat the remaining oil in a frying pan and sauté the onions until soft and golden, then add the garlic and cook for another 2 minutes. Add the spinach. Season, add the nutmeg and half the Parmesan. Set aside. In a bowl mix the remaining Parmesan, the ricotta, eggs, feta and parsley. Season.

4 Take a 22cm (8½in) springform tin. Melt the butter. Keep the filo under a slightly damp tea towel as you work, otherwise it will become brittle and break. Brush the tin with butter and line with two-thirds of the filo. Lay overlapping sheets on the base first, then place sheets like the spokes of a wheel, radiating from the centre of the base with each hanging over the edge. Brush with butter as you go.

5 Lay in the spinach, then half the pumpkin and all the chicken. Put the cheese and egg layer on and top with the remaining pumpkin. Pull the overhanging filo over the filling, brushing with butter as you go. Use the remaining filo to cover the top, overlapping the sheets and tucking them down the sides. Brush liberally with butter. Don't worry about the pie looking neat – filo is very forgiving.

6 Cook in the oven for 45–50 minutes, until golden. If the pastry is getting too dark, cover it with foil, as it takes this amount of time for the egg layer to set. After baking, leave for 10 minutes, then carefully remove the tin and slide the pie on to a hot plate or serving dish.

Chicken and toasted bread salad with raisins, pine nuts and capers

This is based on a dish I had in Sicily, and on Californian chef Judy Rodger's famous roast chicken with bread.

Serves 4

FOR THE SALAD
75g (2½oz) raisins
about 5 tbsp olive oil
200g (7oz) country bread, roughly torn
400g (14oz) leftover cooked chicken, torn into pieces
40g (1½oz) pine nuts
2 tbsp capers, rinsed
125g (4½oz) salad leaves (baby spinach and rocket are good)

FOR THE DRESSING
2 tbsp medium-dry sherry
1 garlic clove, finely chopped
1½ tbsp sherry vinegar
½ tsp Dijon mustard
salt and pepper
good pinch of sugar
5 tbsp extra virgin olive oil

1 Pour boiling water over the raisins and leave them to plump up for 15 minutes or so. Mix together all the ingredients for the dressing, except the oil. Using a fork, whisk these while steadily pouring on the oil. Set aside.

2 Heat half the oil for the salad in a frying pan and sauté the bread pieces all over until golden and crisp. Throw these into a broad shallow bowl. Heat the remaining oil in the pan, season the chicken pieces and heat through thoroughly. Toss on top of the bread.

3 Toast the pine nuts in the frying pan: they don't need oil – just cook them while agitating the pan a little, until golden (it takes about 30 seconds, so watch they don't burn). Put these into the salad bowl and add the drained raisins and the capers. Throw in the salad leaves, add the dressing and toss. Serve immediately.

ALSO TRY...

Chicken, watercress and potato salad with herb and preserved lemon dressing To make the dressing, put 5 canned anchovy fillets, 10 basil leaves, 15 mint leaves, the leaves of a small bunch of parsley, 2 garlic cloves, 1 tbsp capers, rinsed, 2 tbsp preserved lemon juice and some pepper into a blender. Pulse-mix, adding 150ml (5fl oz) extra virgin olive oil as you do so. Discard the fleshy bit from a preserved lemon. Chop a quarter of the rind and add to the dressing. Shred the rest and set aside. Boil 350g (12oz) small waxy potatoes until tender, drain, add a knob of butter and keep warm. Cook 150g (5½oz) green beans until *al dente*. Toss the potatoes, beans and 200g (7oz) watercress with a little of the dressing, fresh lemon juice and 2 tbsp extra virgin olive oil, then put 500g (1lb 2oz) cooked chicken, torn into pieces, on top and drizzle over more dressing. Scatter the preserved lemon shreds over. Serve, providing the remaining dressing in a bowl.

Chicken, wild rice and blueberry salad

A mixture of wild and brown or basmati rice is fine, or you can buy a bag with wild, brown basmati and Camargue red rice all in one, which looks great.

Serves 6–8

300g (10oz) wild, red and basmati
  rice mixture
600ml (1 pint) chicken stock
salt and pepper
750g (1lb 10oz) leftover cooked chicken,
  cut into broad strips
60g (2oz) toasted, flaked almonds, or
  chopped, unsalted pistachios
4 tbsp chopped flat leaf parsley

200g (7oz) rocket, watercress or baby
  spinach
4 handfuls blueberries
FOR THE DRESSING
1 tbsp cider vinegar
½ tbsp Dijon mustard
1 tbsp runny honey
4 tbsp groundnut oil
4 tbsp light extra virgin olive oil

1 Put the rice into a saucepan and cover with the stock. Bring to the boil, season, then reduce the heat to a simmer. Cook until all the stock has been absorbed and the rice is tender. If it gets too dry, add a little water. It will take 25–30 minutes. Remember, wild rice never goes soft; it remains firm and nutty. Meanwhile, make the dressing by simply whisking everything together. Taste for seasoning.

2 As soon as the rice is ready, pour on half the dressing and mix well so it absorbs the dressing while still warm. Leave to come to room temperature.

3 Toss in everything else, together with the rice and the remaining dressing. Taste for seasoning; rice dishes need a lot. This is also good the next day, but let it come up to room temperature once you've taken it out of the refrigerator.

ALSO TRY...

You can make a version of this salad with dried apricots and pistachios (it's very pretty) or dried cranberries and chopped pecans instead of fresh blueberries.

Roast lamb with sherry, thyme and red onions

Time accompanying dishes to be ready when you carve, not when the lamb comes from the oven.

Serves 8

FOR THE LAMB
6 garlic cloves
salt and pepper
leaves from 8 thyme sprigs
olive oil
3kg (6lb 8oz) leg of lamb
300ml (½ pint) medium
  sherry

FOR THE ONIONS
8 red onions, halved
3 tbsp olive oil
6 tbsp sherry vinegar
250ml (9fl oz) sweet sherry
about a dozen thyme
  sprigs

1 Preheat the oven to 220°C/425°F/gas mark 7. Crush the garlic with the salt, pepper and thyme leaves in a mortar and pestle. Add enough oil to make a loose paste. Rub over the lamb, place in a roasting tin and roast for 20 minutes, then reduce the heat to 180°C/350°F/gas mark 4 for a further 70 minutes. Halfway through cooking, add half the medium sherry. Now baste the lamb at intervals, adding the remaining medium sherry and 150ml (5fl oz) water, watching that the dish does not dry out or the juices will burn.

2 Meanwhile, put the onions in a heatproof gratin dish, or small roasting tin, where they fit snugly in a single layer. Drizzle with the oil, season, then add the vinegar and sweet sherry. Scatter the thyme sprigs on top. When the lamb has 30 minutes cooking time left, put the onions in the oven for 50 minutes, basting occasionally. The sweet sherry should be absorbed by the onions. If they become too dry, add another good slug.

3 Take the lamb out of the oven, insulate with foil and towels and rest for 20–25 minutes. Put on a heated platter, surrounded by the onions. Serve immediately with the juices.

4 If you want gravy, pour the cooking juices into a jug and spoon off the fat. Set the roasting tin over a medium heat and add 250ml (9fl oz) water or white wine. Bring to the boil, scraping up the bits stuck to the pan, and taste. Adjust with more wine, sherry, even a splash of balsamic vinegar, if you like.

ALSO TRY...

Roast lamb, Castilian style Make incisions all over the lamb and stuff with slivers of garlic. Rub with olive oil, salt, pepper and 2 tsp paprika. Roast as above. Put 300ml (½ pint) water in a saucepan with the juice of 1 lemon, 2 tbsp sherry vinegar, 2 bay leaves, ½ tsp each ground cumin and dried oregano, 2 rosemary sprigs and 3 whole peeled garlic cloves and bring to the boil. When the lamb has roasted for 20 minutes, ladle half the liquid over. Add the remainder at intervals during the cooking time. Rest as above, then serve with the juices.

Lamb with caper, parsley and preserved lemon stuffing

A great way to stretch a leg of lamb.

Serves 6

2 onions, finely chopped

2 garlic cloves, crushed

75g (2½oz) butter

40g (1½oz) white breadcrumbs

40g (1½oz) capers, rinsed

40g (1½oz) flat leaf parsley, finely chopped

2 tsp preserved lemon juice

¾ large homemade or 2 small commercial preserved lemons

2 tbsp olive oil, plus more for the joint

flaked sea salt and pepper

1.4kg (3lb 3oz) boned leg of lamb

60ml (2¼fl oz) white wine

300ml (½ pint) lamb or chicken stock

1 Preheat the oven to 220°C/425°F/gas mark 7. Put the onions, garlic and 50g (1¾oz) of the butter in a pan and cook for 4 minutes, until the onions are soft. Put the breadcrumbs, capers, parsley and lemon juice in a bowl and add the onions. Discard the lemon flesh. Cut the rind into slivers and add, with the oil and pepper. The mixture should be neither soggy nor dry; add oil or breadcrumbs as needed.

2 Spread out the lamb and season. Pat on the stuffing. Roll up and tie at intervals with kitchen string. Dribble over a little oil and season. Place in a roasting tin and roast for 15 minutes, then reduce the temperature to 180°C/350°F/gas mark 4 and cook for 40 minutes for pink lamb.

3 Put the lamb on a platter, cover and rest for 20 minutes. Deglaze the tin with the wine, scraping up the juices. Add the stock, boil and reduce until thickened slightly. Strain into a clean saucepan, heat and whisk in the remaining butter. Serve with the lamb.

ALSO TRY...

Pack these stuffings into a boned leg and cook as above:

Orange, mint and watercress Add 150g (5½oz) watercress, chopped, to wilt with the sautéed onions. Mix with the breadcrumbs, the grated zest of 1 orange, 2 tbsp orange juice, 4 tbsp chopped mint and 25g (1oz) almonds, chopped. Add 15g (½oz) butter, in chunks, and season. Make the gravy with a little added orange juice.

Aubergine and date Fry 1 aubergine, cubed, in 4 tbsp olive oil until soft. Separately soften ½ onion, chopped, in 1 tbsp oil. To the onion, add 2 garlic cloves, chopped, 1½ tsp ground cumin, 1 tsp ground cinnamon and cook for 2 minutes. Add 50g (1¾oz) dates, chopped, and 1½ tbsp pistachios. Add a handful of chopped mint and some grated lemon zest, then mix with the aubergine. Eat with tahini dressing (see page 82).

Chorizo and olive Sauté 1 onion, chopped, 150g (5½oz) chorizo, chopped, and 150g (5½oz) waxy potatoes, diced, in 2 tbsp olive oil. When the onion is soft, add 60g (2oz) pitted black olives, 25g (1oz) parsley, chopped, the grated zest of 1 lemon and ½ tsp cayenne. Season and cook for 1 minute.

Lamb and roast pepper salad with garlic and anchovy cream

Cooked lamb loves strong flavours, but it needs to be cooked rare to work in salads and the fat must be trimmed.

Serves 4

FOR THE SALAD
3 red peppers
salt and pepper
olive oil
400g (14oz) small waxy potatoes
75g (2½oz) watercress and baby spinach
2 tbsp extra virgin olive oil
good squeeze of lemon juice
600g (1lb 5oz) rare-cooked lamb, sliced

FOR THE CREAM
50g can anchovies in olive oil
2 garlic cloves
55g (2oz) pine nuts
100ml (3½fl oz) extra virgin olive oil
lemon juice, to taste
1 tbsp very finely chopped flat leaf parsley

1 Preheat the oven to 200°C/400°F/gas mark 6. Halve and deseed the peppers and put them into a small roasting tin. Rub with oil, season and roast for 30 minutes. Slice and leave them in their juices. Steam or boil the potatoes until tender.

2 To make the cream, put the anchovies, garlic and pine nuts into a food processor. Turn it on and add the oil in a steady stream. Add the lemon juice and parsley. Set aside.

3 Put the leaves, potatoes and peppers (with their juices) into a bowl. Add the extra virgin olive oil and lemon juice, and season. Toss. Put on to a platter. Arrange the lamb on top and spoon over the garlic and anchovy cream.

ALSO TRY…

Use the same amount of sliced, rare lamb in these salads:

…with roast peppers, labneh, chickpeas and sumac To make the labneh, put 250g (9oz) Greek yogurt in a sieve lined with a new J-cloth or muslin. Pull the cloth up round the yogurt to make a bag and gently squeeze. Place over a bowl and refrigerate for 4–24 hours, squeezing every so often. When firm, peel off the cloth and break into walnut-sized chunks. Roast 4 red peppers as above and slice. Mix with 125g (4½oz) watercress or baby spinach, a handful of coriander leaves, the lamb, and a can of chickpeas, drained and rinsed. Whisk ¾ tbsp white wine vinegar with 4 tbsp extra virgin olive oil and seasoning; toss most of this with the salad. Dot in the labneh and drizzle on the remaining dressing. Sprinkle with sumac and serve.

…with flageolet and French beans and anchovies Cook 200g (7oz) French beans until tender. Toss with a 400g can flageolet beans, drained and rinsed, and 4 tbsp extra virgin olive oil. Add the juice of half a lemon, half a 50g can anchovies, drained and finely chopped, a garlic clove, crushed, and 3 tbsp chopped flat leaf parsley. Arrange the lamb on top and drizzle with more oil and grind on salt and black pepper.

Lamb pilaf with figs, pomegranate, feta and pistachios

Pilafs are great for using up leftover meat. This works well with chicken, too. Just stick to the same quantities for rice and stock. You don't need homemade stock for this: a good commercial one is fine.

Serves 4

1 onion, roughly chopped
olive oil
1 red chilli, deseeded and finely sliced
½ tsp ground allspice
2 garlic cloves, crushed
350g (12oz) basmati rice
700ml (1¼ pints) chicken or lamb stock
salt and pepper
50g (1¾oz) dried cherries, cranberries
   or barberries, soaked in hot water for
   15 minutes and drained

50g (1¾oz) dried figs, quartered
500g (1lb 2oz) leftover cooked lamb,
   in chunks
75g (2½oz) feta cheese, crumbled
2 tbsp chopped flat leaf parsley or mint,
   or a mixture
35g (1¼oz) unsalted pistachios or toasted
   almonds, chopped
seeds from ½ pomegranate
Greek yogurt, to serve (optional)

1 Cook the onion in a little oil in a saucepan until soft and golden. Stir in the chilli, allspice and garlic and sauté for another minute. Add the rice and stir briefly to coat in the oily juices. Now add the stock, seasoning and dried fruit. Bring to the boil, then immediately reduce the heat to a simmer. Cover the pan and cook for 20 minutes until the liquid has been absorbed and the rice is tender. Don't stir the rice while it's cooking. If the rice isn't yet tender, pour in a little boiling water, replace the lid and cook for a further 4–5 minutes. If the stock hasn't been completely absorbed, whack the heat up and quickly boil off whatever remains.

2 Heat 1 tbsp oil in a frying pan and quickly cook the lamb until heated through. Season and gently fork through the rice along with the feta, herbs and nuts. Shower with pomegranate seeds at the last minute and serve immediately. Plain Greek yogurt is good on the side.

ALSO TRY...

You can make an everyday version of the rather jewelled dish above with lamb, raisins or sultanas and dried apricots, or with chunks of sautéed aubergine and chopped dates. In both cases, you can bulk out the pilaf with tinned chickpeas (drained and rinsed) or lentils. The spices can also be changed according to what you have around: ground cinnamon is good, as is cumin.

Middle Eastern shepherd's pie with spiced parsnip crust

Don't be put off by the long ingredients list. This is very simple.

Serves 6

FOR THE MEAT

5 tbsp olive oil

800g (1lb 12oz) leftover cooked lamb, in small chunks

2 onions, roughly chopped

2 celery sticks, finely chopped

2 carrots, diced

6 garlic cloves, crushed

2 tsp ground cumin

2 tsp ground mixed spice

3 tsp ground cinnamon

2 tbsp plain flour

300ml (½ pint) chicken or lamb stock

grated zest and juice of 1 orange

75g (2½oz) raisins, soaked in boiling water for 15 minutes and drained

6 tbsp tomato purée

75g (2½oz) pine nuts, toasted

FOR THE PARSNIP CRUST

450g (1lb) floury potatoes, cut into even chunks

950g (2lb 2oz) parsnips, chopped

50g (1¾oz) butter

1 tsp ground cinnamon

2 tsp cayenne pepper

50ml (2fl oz) whipping cream

salt and pepper

FOR THE SPICED ONION TOPPING

2 onions, very finely sliced

15g (½oz) butter

1½ tsp olive oil

½ tsp ground cinnamon

1 red chilli, deseeded and finely sliced

3 tsp soft dark brown sugar

good squeeze of lemon juice

small bunch coriander or mint, roughly chopped (optional)

1 Heat the oil in a large broad casserole and brown the lamb. Transfer the lamb to a bowl. In the same pan cook the onions, celery and carrots until golden. Add the garlic and spices and cook for 1 minute. Put the lamb back and add the flour. Stir for 1 minute, then add the stock, zest, juice, raisins and tomato purée. Bring to the boil, reduce the heat and simmer for 45 minutes, stirring. Add the pine nuts.

2 Meanwhile, preheat the oven to 180°C/350°F/gas mark 4. Boil the potatoes and the parsnips separately until soft. Drain the potatoes and keep them in the saucepan in which they were cooked. Put a tea towel on top, then cover with a lid. Let these sit for a few minutes on a very low heat to dry out. Drain the parsnips and add to the potatoes. Heat the butter for the crust in a large saucepan with the spices. Add the potatoes and parsnips and mash, adding the cream and seasoning.

3 Spoon the lamb into a pie dish, spread the mash on top and put into the oven for 20–25 minutes until golden. Meanwhile, fry the onions for the topping in the butter and oil until golden. Increase the heat and allow some to become crisp. Add the cinnamon, chilli, salt, pepper and sugar. Cook until slightly caramelized. Squeeze on some lemon juice and mix in the herbs, if using. Pile the onions on the pie and serve.

Roast pork loin, porchetta style

Get your butcher to remove the skin from the pork and leave about 1cm (½in) fat.

Serves 6

2kg (4lb 8oz) loin of pork, off the bone
6 garlic cloves, sliced
3 tsp fennel seeds, crushed
4 rosemary sprigs, leaves chopped, plus
   more for the roasting tin

olive oil
salt and black pepper
about 8 bay leaves

1 Lay the pork on a board, flesh side up. Make incisions all over with a sharp knife and fill with the slivers of garlic. Rub the fennel and rosemary all over the flesh, along with olive oil to lubricate, pushing bits down inside the slits, and season generously. Make a bed in a roasting tin with rosemary sprigs and the bay leaves and lay on the pork, fat side down. Cover and refrigerate overnight. Bring to room temperature before cooking.

2 Preheat the oven to 220°C/425°F/gas mark 7. Tie the loin at intervals with kitchen string (not too tightly; it should hold its shape but not look like a sausage). Put into the roasting tin fat side up on top of the herbs (make sure these are under the pork or they will scorch) and cook for 25 minutes. Reduce the oven temperature to 180°C/350°F/gas mark 4 and cook for 1 hour 40 minutes, basting every so often.

3 Check to make sure it is properly cooked; the juices should run clear with no trace of pink when the flesh is pierced. Because I worry about pork I also cut into the underside (so I don't ruin the appearance) to check the flesh is white. Take the pork out of the oven, cover with foil, insulate and allow to rest for 15–20 minutes. Serve hot or at room temperature.

ALSO TRY...

Honey and mustard roast pork loin Lay the same-sized cut of pork as above on a board, flesh side up. Make incisions all over with a sharp knife. Stuff the chopped leaves from 3 rosemary sprigs into the incisions and season. Mix 4 tbsp Dijon mustard, 7 tbsp runny honey and the juice of ½ lemon and pour three quarters of it over the joint, making sure it goes down into the incisions. Refrigerate for a few hours, but bring to room temperature before cooking. Preheat the oven to 220°C/425°F/gas mark 7. Tie the loin with kitchen string as above. Put into a roasting tin with it's marinade. Cook as above, basting. Add the remaining honey and mustard mix 10 minutes before the end of the cooking time. If the joint is becoming too dark (if the honey begins to burn), cover with foil. When it is cooked, take it from the oven and cover with foil, insulate and rest for 15 minutes. Serve hot or at room temperature.

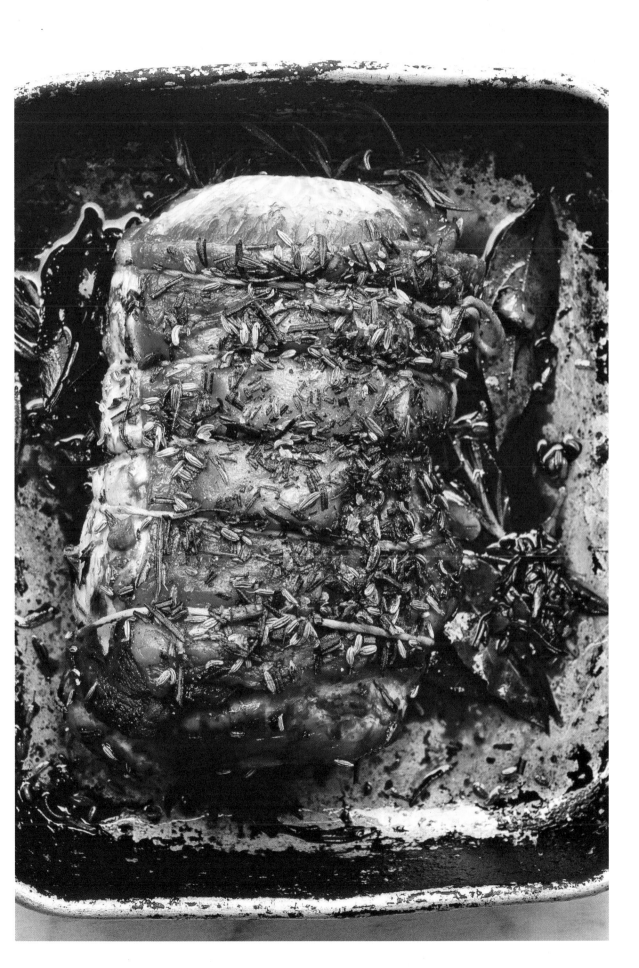

Pork, roast squash, apple and chestnut salad

This shows just what you can make out of a bit of leftover roast: it's earthy, colourful, spicy and very more-ish.

Serves 4

FOR THE SALAD
50g (1¾oz) butter
4 tbsp olive oil
½ tsp ground cinnamon
½ tsp ground ginger
1kg (2lb 4oz) squash or pumpkin, in peeled wedges
salt and pepper
2 tsp caster sugar
2 apples, halved, cored and cut into wedges
100g (3½oz) cooked chestnuts (vacuum-packed are fine)

100g (3½oz) spicy butcher's pork sausage, in chunks
200g (7oz) leftover cooked pork, in chunks
25g (1oz) hazelnuts, toasted
150g (5½oz) watercress or baby spinach, or a mixture

FOR THE DRESSING
1½ tbsp balsamic vinegar
smidgen of Dijon mustard
4 tbsp olive oil
3 tbsp hazelnut oil

1 Preheat the oven to 190°C/375°F/gas mark 5. Melt 25g (1oz) of the butter in a saucepan. Add 3 tbsp of the olive oil, the cinnamon and ginger. Put the squash in a roasting tin, pour the spicy mixture over and toss to coat. Season, then sprinkle on half the sugar. Roast for 25 minutes, until tender and slightly caramelized.

2 Make the dressing by simply whisking everything together and season.

3 Melt the remaining butter in a large frying pan and sauté the apples until golden. Add the chestnuts to heat through, then set aside. Add the remaining oil to the pan and sauté the sausage until cooked and brown, then add the pork and heat through. Season. Toss the warm squash with all the salad ingredients and the dressing.

ALSO TRY...

Pork, squash and mushroom salad with caramelized peanut and chilli sauce
Roast the squash (or pumpkin) as above. Sauté a 4cm (1½in) chunk of fresh root ginger, a red chilli and a garlic clove, all finely chopped, in 2 tbsp groundnut oil until pale gold. Add 2 tsp soft light brown sugar and 4 shallots, finely chopped, and cook for 2 minutes. Add 3 tbsp peanuts and cook for 4 minutes; the sugar and shallots should caramelize. Tip it all into a mortar and pound to a coarse paste. Stir in 2 tbsp groundnut oil, 1 tbsp sesame oil, 1 tbsp soy sauce, the juice of 1 lime and a generous handful of finely chopped coriander. Dilute with water, to taste. Season the same amount of leftover pork and sausage as above and fry in 1 tbsp groundnut oil. Set aside and sauté 125g (4½oz) mushrooms in another 1 tbsp oil. Toss the meat and mushrooms with the squash, 125g (4½oz) baby spinach, 2 tbsp light olive oil, the juice of ½ lime and seasoning. Drizzle a little sauce over the salad and serve the rest on the side. Use this sauce with roast pork belly and stir-fried greens, too.

Saigon crêpes

Vietnamese street food: there they use minced pork, but this is a perfect vehicle for leftover roast meat. It's a good party dish; there's something celebratory about street food when it's cooked at home, and it's perfect for a casual supper for friends.

Serves 4–6

FOR THE BATTER
115g (4oz) rice flour
3 tsp ground turmeric
4 tsp curry powder
2 tsp soft light brown sugar
good pinch of salt
300ml (½ pint) tinned coconut cream
4 spring onions, finely chopped
groundnut oil, for frying

FOR THE TOPPING
3 tbsp groundnut oil
150g (5½oz) mushrooms (button, chestnut, oyster or shitake), sliced
salt and pepper
1 onion, finely sliced

2 garlic cloves, crushed
2 red chillies, deseeded and finely sliced
100g (3½oz) raw or cooked prawns (optional)
300g (10½oz) leftover cooked pork, in little chunks
200g (7oz) beansprouts
1½ tbsp fish sauce

TO SERVE
juice of 1 lime
leaves from a small bunch of coriander, roughly chopped
Nuoc Cham (see page 23) if you have it, or wedges of lime

1 To make the batter, put all the dry ingredients into a bowl, make a well in the centre and gradually pour on the coconut cream and 300ml (½ pint) water, mixing in the dry ingredients as you go. Add the spring onions. Leave to stand for about 30 minutes.

2 For the topping, heat half the oil in a frying pan and fry the mushrooms until dark gold. Season and set aside. Heat the remaining oil in a large frying pan or wok and cook the onion over a medium heat until soft and golden, about 10 minutes. Add the garlic and chillies and cook for another 2 minutes. Add the raw prawns now if you are using them, with the pork. Toss everything together, then add the beansprouts (and the cooked prawns if you are using those) and mushrooms. Season, add the fish sauce and make sure everything is well amalgamated. Cover to keep warm.

3 To make the crêpes, heat ½ tbsp oil in a large nonstick frying pan. Add about 100ml (3½fl oz) of the batter and swish it around to the edges. In Vietnam they add the filling now and cook it with the batter but I think the crêpes taste better if they are made the French way, so cook each crêpe on both sides until golden. Keep in a low oven until you have cooked all the crêpes. To serve, spoon the filling on to the top, squeeze over some lime and scatter on coriander. Provide a bowl of Nuoc Cham (see page 23) if you have it.

Nasi goreng

This can be made with fresh meat – pork, chicken or beef – but is a great dish for dealing with leftovers. It is basically a simple egg-fried rice and it's best not to fancy it up too much, but you can adapt the main idea: leave out the prawns, for example, or add mushrooms or sugar snap peas.

Serves 4

2 tbsp groundnut oil

1 onion, cut into crescent moon shapes about 1cm (½in) thick at their widest

3 garlic cloves, finely sliced

2 red chillies, halved, deseeded and cut into slivers

300g (10oz) leftover cooked pork, in little chunks or shreds

400g (14oz) cooked rice

4 spring onions, sliced on the diagonal

3 eggs, beaten

100g (3½oz) cooked, shelled prawns

4 tbsp dark soy sauce, or to taste

salt and pepper

1 Heat 1½ tbsp of the oil in a large frying pan, sauté pan or wok. Add the onion and cook over medium-high heat until softish (though still with bite) and golden, even slightly singed at the tips. Add the garlic, chillies and pork and cook for another couple of minutes (it's good to get a bit of colour on the pork). Toss in the rice and spring onions and mix everything together lightly – it's important not to press the rice or it will become stodgy – and cook until the rice is heated through.

2 Meanwhile, quickly heat the remaining oil in a nonstick frying pan and add the eggs. Cook as if you are making an omelette, rather than scrambled eggs: don't stir the egg but drag the bits which are set round the side into the centre, then tip the pan to allow runny egg to set around the outside. Continue until it is all cooked. With a sharp knife, cut the egg into ribbons.

3 Add the egg to the rice along with the prawns, soy sauce, salt and pepper. Continue cooking for 2 minutes until heated through. Even though the soy sauce is salty you may still want to add a bit of salt, as starchy dishes always need a lot of seasoning.

Pork and apple pie

Pies made using a béchamel sauce to bind the filling can be heavy, so it's good to have a recipe in your repertoire without it. This filling is chunky, and thickened with breadcrumbs (great thickeners for braises and stews, but you do need to season again after you've added them). To make this slightly more luxurious, add 50ml (2fl oz) double cream to the filling. You can vary the filling, using mushrooms instead of apples, or cooked pumpkin instead of leeks. Try it, too, with cooked chicken instead of pork.

Serves 6

2 leeks

25g (1oz) unsalted butter

1 onion, roughly chopped

6 streaky bacon rashers, chopped

2 small or 1 medium eating apple (I like Cox for this)

450g (1lb) leftover cooked pork, in chunks

200ml (7fl oz) apple juice or cider

300ml (½ pint) chicken stock

2 tsp Dijon mustard (or more, to taste)

salt and pepper

3 tbsp flat leaf parsley, chopped

25g (1oz) brown or white breadcrumbs

350g (12oz) puff pastry

plain flour, to dust

1 egg, lightly beaten

1 Remove and discard any of the tough outer leaves from the leeks and trim the base. Cut the leeks into 3cm (1in) lengths. Melt the butter in a sauté pan and add the leeks, onion and bacon. Cook over a medium heat until there's some colour on the onion and bacon. Halve and core the apple(s) and slice. Add to the pan and cook until they are also colouring a little.

2 Toss in the pork, juice or cider, stock and mustard. Season and bring to the boil. Reduce the heat, add the parsley and breadcrumbs and stir. Preheat the oven to 200°C/400°F/gas mark 6.

3 Put the mixture into a pie dish and leave to cool a little. Roll out the pastry on a lightly floured surface. Cut strips that you can stick all the way round the edge of the pie dish (so the pastry lid has something to stick to). Lightly wet one side and press down all the way round. Now lay the remaining pastry on top and press down. Trim off the excess and crimp the edges. Use the leftover pastry to make decorations for the top. Make a few little slits in the centre through which the steam can escape. Using a blunt knife, knock up the sides of the pastry all the way round; this helps it to rise. Brush with egg and bake for 20 minutes, or until golden and puffy.

4 Serve hot. This is pretty much a meal in itself. I tend not to serve potatoes on the side (more starch) but offer watercress or spinach salad, or a big bowl of buttery cabbage.

Vegetable love

The weather, as I write, has changed dramatically. Yesterday we were enduring a long, harsh winter, today we have a bright blue-skied spring. Last week's vegetable dishes – a gratin of potatoes, parsnips and onions with dried cranberries and chestnuts, a cauliflower and blue cheese risotto and a Vietnamese pumpkin curry – won't get another outing until autumn. Now I'm planning Greek olive oil-braised leeks with dill and daydreaming about what I'll do with broad beans when they arrive.

Cooking more vegetables has been the biggest change in my kitchen during the last five years. I now eat meat or fish only three times a week. This wasn't deliberate and I'm not alone. Friends who used to bring chocolates or wine now offer gifts of asparagus, bearing them like bunches of flowers, or squashes from the allotment. Is this vegetable love due to straitened finances? Health concerns? I think there's another reason. My theory is that the popularity of farmers' markets and growing your own is about connecting. Cooking vegetables is very grounding (some, after all, arrive covered in soil). I love even walking past my greengrocer's. There's always something to slot into the week's food: crimson globes of beetroot, wild heads of frisée, slender stems of purple-headed broccoli. And they have produce I wouldn't find in the supermarket, such as ruby chard. Just looking at vegetables makes you feel healthy, gladdened by the colours, amazed at the abundance.

It's lucky that our increasing interest in vegetables has coincided with a need to take them more seriously. We know they're good for our health, but they're also a better way of using the planet's resources as it takes much more energy to produce meat. Eat more vegetables and you're in a win-win situation.

So, what to buy? Eat seasonally. Vegetables in season taste better, cost less and won't have been flown halfway round the world. Of course, I also buy what we can't grow well here (aubergines, for example) but try to find Mediterranean ones that have benefited from the sun.

Going on flavour alone, I buy organic when I can and *always* organic carrots, green beans and potatoes (they taste so different). Avoid packaging – apart from its being wasteful, most vegetables suffer, sweating under plastic rather than breathing – and bags of prepared salad. Even if they haven't been washed in chlorine they're no bargain; better to buy whole lettuces and use them up (cooked as well as in salads). Anything you have to wash yourself will be cheaper.

Vote with your purse and give business to those who care about flavour. Don't buy tomatoes that taste of cotton wool. Be demanding. And, to ensure particular vegetables don't disappear, buy a broad range. Kale may be 'in' at the moment but if its popularity dwindles it will become harder to find. Support greengrocers (they are disappearing at an alarming rate), farm shops and farmers' markets; that way you can talk to people who actually know about what they're selling.

Go cultivate some vegetable love. It will improve your life immeasurably.

Pinzimonio

Oh, the Italians do things with style. This starter is both simple and very chic. Don't offer the clumsy, faded crudités supermarkets sell to dip in pots of bad guacamole. You need fresh stuff. Use an extra virgin olive oil you particularly like: Tuscan will be bitter and grassy; Ligurian sweet and buttery... there's no 'right' choice. Offer good bread and flaked sea salt as well.

Serves 4

300g (10½oz) French breakfast radishes, with leaves
200g (7oz) young carrots
1 fennel bulb
juice of ½ lemon
300g (10½oz) young peas in the pod

150g (5½oz) young broad beans (podded weight)
150g (5½oz) cherry tomatoes on the vine
200ml (7fl oz) extra virgin olive oil
sea salt flakes and crushed black pepper
country bread, to serve

1 Wash the radishes, keeping the leaves attached if really fresh. Wash the carrots and trim the tails if long. Remove the tough outer leaves from the fennel and cut into slim wedges (keep the core, or the slices fall apart). Squeeze over some lemon to stop it discolouring.

2 Take some peas from their pods and leave the rest. There's no need to cook either peas or beans if young and sweet. Divide the vegetables between four plates, or put them all on a platter. Provide each diner with a small tumbler of oil. Serve with salt, pepper and good bread.

ALSO TRY...

Cold-weather vegetables with bagna cauda A more hearty, Piedmontese starter that also showcases the loveliness of good, simple things: vegetables with a warm bath of anchovy-flavoured oil. Prepare a selection of vegetables – whatever's in season – and put on a platter. Cut carrots and celery into slender sticks (keep the celery leaves if possible) and cauliflower into florets. Trim purple-sprouting broccoli shoots, cut fennel into slim wedges and separate radicchio or chicory into leaves. Melt 75g (2½oz) butter in a small, heavy saucepan over the lowest heat. Add 6 garlic cloves, finely sliced, and sauté very gently until soft, not coloured. Add 15 canned anchovies and pour in 300ml (½ pint) olive oil very gradually, stirring and pressing the anchovies and garlic with the back of a wooden spoon. Both the heat and the pressure help the anchovies 'melt'. Cook for 7 minutes, on the lowest heat, stirring constantly, until well amalgamated and smooth. Keep it hot over a spirit lamp or candle, or just get it to the table as quickly as possible and let diners dip their vegetables into the bagna. Serve bread on the side. Serves 8.

LEFTOVERS...

...Bagna cauda is also great on toast. Top – or not – with mozzarella.

Herbed ricotta with summer veg

Another variation on the theme of plain, raw vegetables. Fresh ricotta can be hard to get but the UHT stuff sold in tubs in the supermarket just doesn't cut it here. Go to a good Italian deli or cheese shop to seek out the fresh version. It is milky, sweet-smelling and almost crumbly.

Serves 4–6 as a starter or light lunch dish

FOR THE RICOTTA
450g (1lb) fresh ricotta cheese
1 garlic clove, crushed or grated
1 tbsp snipped chives
2 tbsp finely chopped flat leaf parsley
1 tbsp finely chopped mint leaves
finely grated zest of 1 lemon, plus a good
  squeeze of lemon juice
3 tbsp extra virgin olive oil, plus more
  to serve
salt and pepper

FOR THE VEGETABLES
A selection from:
raw peas
raw broad beans
French breakfast radishes with fresh,
  perky leaves, trimmed
baby carrots, trimmed
cherry tomatoes on the vine
high-quality black olives
toasted ciabatta, to serve

1 Mash the ricotta together with all the other ingredients, cover with clingfilm and put in the refrigerator to allow the flavours to mingle (it needs at least an hour). Bring it out before you want to serve it to allow it to get to room temperature.

2 Divide the ricotta between 4–6 plates (or put in a bowl or mound on a wooden board and surround with the vegetables and olives).

3 If it's early in the season and the broad beans are young, serve them podded but not cooked. If it's a little later, cook the podded beans until tender and slip them out of their skins so you can see their beautiful colour. Arrange the vegetables and olives beside the ricotta and drizzle olive oil over everything. Serve with toasted ciabatta.

ALSO TRY...

Lou cachat An old French dish created to use up bits of leftover cheese. Deliciously strong, it is lovely with toasted croûtes, radishes and black olives. Just mash together 200g (7oz) goat's cheese and 100g (3½oz) Roquefort with 5 tbsp crème fraîche and 3 tbsp brandy. Add pepper; it should be salty enough because of the Roquefort. The mixture should be slightly chunky. Leave, covered, in the refrigerator overnight, or even for a few days, so that the alcohol can infuse the cheese.

Claqueret Another French cheese dish – this one is light and herby rather than strong and boozy – that goes with all sorts of spring and summer vegetables. You can also add crumbled goat's cheese. Mix 400g (14oz) thick fromage blanc with 6 tbsp crème fraîche, 3 shallots, finely chopped, 3 garlic cloves, crushed, 1 tbsp white wine vinegar, 1 tbsp extra virgin olive oil, 2 tbsp dry white wine, 3 tbsp each finely chopped chives, parsley and chervil and some salt and pepper.

Purple-sprouting broccoli with mozzarella, chilli and anchovies

Purple-sprouting broccoli tastes sweet and is so good for you. It arrives when we really need it – at the brighter end of winter when we're dying for new ingredients. I steam it as you would asparagus, standing with the heads out of the water. You may need to trim the stalks (they dry out quickly) but don't remove the leaves.

Serves 4 as a starter or 2 as a main course

500g (1lb 2oz) purple-sprouting broccoli
300g (10½oz) mozzarella cheese
2 x 50g cans anchovies in oil
6 tbsp extra virgin olive oil, plus more
  to drizzle
4 garlic cloves, finely sliced

1 red chilli, deseeded and finely sliced
juice of 1 lemon
freshly ground black pepper
1 tbsp chopped flat leaf parsley or
  torn basil

1 Trim the broccoli and steam until just tender (4–5 minutes). Slice the mozzarella into rounds, or tear into chunks.

2 Drain the anchovies. Gently heat the oil in a small frying pan. Add the garlic and chilli and cook for a few minutes until the garlic is very pale gold. Add the anchovies and press with the back of a wooden spoon to break them up (they melt into a sauce).

3 Put the hot broccoli on plates and top with the mozzarella. Add the lemon juice, pepper and parsley to the anchovy oil and spoon over. Drizzle with more oil, grind on more pepper and serve.

ALSO TRY...

As a side dish Omit the mozzarella and halve the amount of anchovies. Very good with roast lamb.

With cumin, chilli, mint and yogurt Heat 6 tbsp groundnut oil in a wok. Add 700g (1lb 9oz) trimmed broccoli. Stir-fry for a few minutes. Add 3 tsp cumin seeds, 2 red chillies, deseeded and very finely sliced, and 3 garlic cloves, finely sliced. Cook for 2 minutes, tossing. Splash in some water, season, cover and cook on low heat for a minute, until just tender. Drizzle with plain yogurt and chopped mint.

With ginger, chilli and soy Stir-fry as above, but add fresh root ginger, peeled and grated, to the chillies and garlic and omit the cumin. Replace the water with sherry. Splash on soy sauce at the end and let it bubble away to glaze.

With ricotta, lemon, olive oil and Parmesan Steam 450g (1lb) broccoli until just tender. Divide between plates and quickly top with 125g (4½oz) ricotta cheese, broken into chunks, the finely grated zest of 1 lemon and the juice of ½, salt and pepper, a really generous slug of extra virgin olive oil and 50–75g (1¾–2½oz) Parmesan cheese, shaved.

Lebanese runner beans with tomatoes

I wasn't brought up with runner beans – I have no idea why they never seemed to be around in Ireland – and when I came to live in England I found most people scorned them. Fresh from someone's garden or allotment, though, they are delicious. If you don't have runner beans, French beans are just as good. And this is definitely a dish to use up a glut of ripe tomatoes.

Serves 4

6 tbsp olive oil

1 onion, roughly chopped

4 garlic cloves, finely sliced

4 tsp ground cumin

800g (1lb 12oz) tomatoes, roughly chopped

salt and pepper

½ tbsp tomato purée

½ tbsp soft light brown sugar

good squeeze of lemon juice or slug of
  white wine vinegar

500g (1lb 2oz) runner beans, cut into strips
  lengthways or in 5cm (2in) lengths

extra virgin olive oil, to serve

2–3 sprigs of mint (optional)

1 Heat the olive oil in a heavy pan and sauté the onion until soft and golden. Add the garlic and cook for another couple of minutes, until soft, then add the cumin, tomatoes, salt and pepper. Stir everything around so that the tomatoes get coated in the oil.

2 Add 75ml (2½fl oz) water and the tomato purée, sugar and lemon juice or vinegar. Keep on a medium heat, cover and let the tomatoes sweat. You need to turn them over every so often, pressing them to help them disintegrate as they cook. The sauce shouldn't be too wet.

3 After about 15 minutes, stir in the beans and allow them to cook for about 12 minutes. They will become really soft but you can cook them for a shorter time if you prefer. Add more water or olive oil if you find the mixture becomes too dry. Taste for seasoning and add the extra virgin olive oil and some mint leaves, if you like.

ALSO TRY...

Runner beans are lovely just stewed in olive oil, so cook as above without the cumin, tomatoes or sugar – just add more olive oil and about 50ml (2fl oz) water and cook until tender. The water will evaporate (but don't let the pan boil dry) and the beans will become rich with the oil. They need good seasoning, too.

Green beans with feta, chilli and tarator

Mediterranean and Middle Eastern people cook green beans for longer than we do. While that mutes their colour, it does wonders for flavour. You don't have to cook them to death, just make sure they're not undercooked.

Serves 4–6 as a side dish

FOR THE TARATOR

25g (1oz) coarse country bread

4 tbsp milk

50g (1¾oz) blanched almonds or hazelnuts

1 fat garlic clove

85ml (3fl oz) extra virgin olive oil

juice of ½ lemon, or to taste

FOR THE BEANS

500g (1lb 2oz) green beans

175g (6oz) feta cheese, crumbled

2 tbsp chopped flat leaf parsley, coriander or mint

1 red chilli, deseeded and shredded

salt and pepper

generous squeeze of lemon juice

3 tbsp extra virgin olive oil

finely grated zest of 1 lemon

1 To make the tarator, soak the bread in the milk for 30 minutes. Purée in a food processor with the nuts and garlic, adding the oil and lemon juice. Add water if you want it thinner. Season to taste with salt and pepper.

2 Top the beans. Steam or boil until just tender. Toss in a shallow bowl with the feta, half the herbs, half the chilli, salt, pepper, lemon juice and olive oil. Drizzle with the tarator and scatter with the lemon zest, remaining herbs and chilli.

ALSO TRY...

Green and flageolet beans with mustard and herb crumbs These crumbs are also good on courgettes, broccoli and cauliflower. Preheat the oven to 180°C/350°F/ gas mark 4. Melt 25g (1oz) butter with 1½ tbsp olive oil. Mix with 1½ tbsp Dijon mustard, 2 tsp thyme leaves, ½ tbsp finely chopped parsley and the finely grated zest of 1 lemon. Put 75g (2½oz) coarse white breadcrumbs into a roasting tin and stir in the butter-mustard mixture. Cook in the oven for 10–12 minutes, until toasted, shaking occasionally. Cook 250g (9oz) green beans, topped, in boiling, lightly salted water until just tender. Rinse. Drain a 410g can flageolet beans and rinse. Heat 2 tbsp olive oil and sauté 4 chopped spring onions until soft. Add both kinds of beans, season and heat through. Scatter with the toasted crumbs and serve.

Potatoes, beans and pesto Put 60g (2oz) basil, 50g (1¾oz) pine nuts, 20g (¾oz) grated Parmesan cheese, 1 garlic clove, 125ml (4fl oz) extra virgin olive oil and salt and pepper into a food processor. Whizz. Check the seasoning. Scrape into a bowl and stir in 15g (½oz) grated Parmesan. Cook about 20 waxy potatoes in boiling salted water until almost tender, then add 250g (9oz) French beans, topped, and cook for 4 minutes. Drain (add 2 tbsp of the water to the pesto) and season. Carefully toss the potatoes and beans with the pesto. Serve immediately. Serves 4 as a side dish.

Peas, broad beans and chorizo with mint

A Spanish combination very good with fish (toss in quickly fried squid for a delicious supper), rabbit and chicken (see the recipes below). Chopped spring onions – cooked with the chorizo – are a good addition.

Serves 4–6

250g (9oz) fresh or frozen peas (podded weight if fresh)
salt and pepper
250g (9oz) fresh or frozen baby broad beans (podded weight)

2 tbsp olive oil
150g (5½oz) chorizo sausage, cut into chunks
good squeeze of lemon juice
leaves from 5 mint sprigs, torn

1 Cook the peas in boiling salted water until tender. Do the same with the beans. Drain. If the beans aren't young, slip off the skins so the lovely emerald colour is revealed.

2 Heat the oil in a frying pan and fry the chorizo until golden. Add the peas and beans and heat through. Season, add the lemon juice and put into a warm, broad, shallow bowl. Add the mint and serve.

ALSO TRY...

Adding the above to a sauté of rabbit or chicken. Brown seasoned bone-in chicken thighs or rabbit joints, add 500ml (18fl oz) chicken stock and cook until tender and cooked through (about 40 minutes). Remove the meat and reduce the cooking liquid by half. Make the above dish and add it to the liquid with the meat, heat through and serve.

Peas and beans with dill Cook beans and peas until tender then add a slosh of double cream, a squeeze of lemon juice, chopped dill and a smidgen of Dijon mustard, if you like. Beautiful with salmon, trout, roast lamb or chicken.

French peas with lettuce Sauté shredded lettuce – I like slightly bitter, milky baby Gems – and chopped spring onions in abundant butter until just soft, then throw in cooked peas, salt and pepper. Toss. Add mint, parsley or chervil.

Raw broad beans with cured ham or cheese Serve young, raw beans with Parma, Serrano or even an expensive Iberico ham (worthwhile a couple of times a year when beans are in their prime). The young, green freshness of broad beans goes exceptionally well with sweet, salty pork. Slices of hard goat's or sheep's cheese are also good accompaniments.

Toasts with crushed broad beans Roughly mash cooked broad beans (slip off the skins first) with plenty of extra virgin olive oil, salt and pepper and a bit of lemon juice. Add chopped dill, parsley, mint or chervil. Pile on bits of toasted ciabatta, baguette or sourdough bread and top with shaved Parmesan or hard goats' cheese. Alternatively top with cooked white crab meat or prawns. Great for a lunch or an informal starter.

Beetroot, fennel and radish salad

This is great with salmon, trout or mackerel (both fresh and smoked) or with a hunk of cheese (goat's cheese and Lancashire work well). I even like it the next day, when the salad is soft and stained with beetroot juice.

Serves 4

FOR THE DRESSING
½ tsp grain mustard
1 tsp runny honey
salt and pepper
2½ tsp cider vinegar
4 tbsp extra virgin olive oil
½ globe of preserved ginger, very
  finely chopped, plus 1 tsp syrup
1 garlic clove, crushed
1 small red chilli (not too hot), deseeded
  and finely shredded

FOR THE SALAD
10 radishes, trimmed
1 fennel bulb
lemon juice
½ red onion
½ green apple
2–3 small raw beetroot
handful of mint leaves, chopped

1 To make the dressing, put the mustard, honey, salt, pepper and vinegar into a small jug or cup and, using a fork, whisk in the olive oil in a steady stream. Add all the other ingredients.

2 Slice the radishes very finely, lengthways, to get thin, teardrop-shaped slices and toss into a bowl.

3 Halve and quarter the fennel and trim the tops (discard the dried-out tips, but reserve the tufty fronds for tossing with the salad). Core each quarter. Using a very sharp knife, cut into wafer-thin slices, lengthways. Add to the bowl and squeeze on some lemon juice to keep the fennel from discolouring.

4 Cut the onion so finely that it's almost shaved. Halve the apple and remove the core. Cut each piece into matchstick-like lengths. Add these to the bowl too and toss in more lemon juice. Peel the beetroot and, using a mandolin or a very fine, sharp knife, cut the flesh into wafer-thin slices. Toss these into the bowl too, along with the mint. Add any fennel fronds. Pour on the dressing, toss and serve.

ALSO TRY...

Indian spiced carrot and beetroot salad This is the most spectacular colour. It's worth making for that alone but its sweetness is lovely against the starchiness of houmous or the subtlety of sliced avocado. It's good, too, with spicy roast chicken. Peel 1 carrot and 1 small beetroot and grate coarsely into a bowl. Add 1 tsp ground cumin, a drop of chilli sauce, 2 tbsp rapeseed oil, 1 tsp red wine vinegar, a couple of good squeezes of lemon juice, 15g (½oz) chopped blanched almonds, ½ tbsp sesame seeds, ½ tbsp pumpkin seeds, 1½ tbsp raisins, plumped up in boiling water and drained, and 2 tbsp chopped coriander. Mix carefully and check the seasoning.

Spanish tomato and bread salad

I like *panzanella*, the Tuscan bread and tomato salad, but, in truth, usually find it a bit soggy. The bread chunks here are made as Spanish *migas*, soft in the middle but crunchy outside. I like them warm, so there's a contrast of temperatures in the salad. Use a range of tomatoes: little yellow ones, round ones, oval ones, baby plums, and so on, to look as lovely as possible. This salad is good with *bocconcini* or, if you leave out the anchovies, little chunks of cold ricotta dropped in at the last minute. It looks best in a shallow bowl where you can see the array of tomato colours and shapes.

Serves 4

200g (7oz) bread (such as ciabatta)
5 tbsp milk
700g (1lb 9oz) mixed tomatoes
20 canned anchovies
2 tbsp tiny capers, rinsed
5 tbsp extra virgin olive oil

1½ tbsp balsamic vinegar
salt and pepper
1 tsp caster sugar
leaves from 1 bunch basil (about 15g/½oz),
   torn
3 tbsp olive oil, for frying

1 Tear the bread into chunks and put into a bowl with the milk. Turn the bread over in the milk and leave for 15 minutes or so. Halve the small tomatoes and cut the large ones into quarters or eighths; you may want to leave some of the tomatoes whole if they are really tiny; you just need a good selection of colour and shape. Put into a broad, shallow serving bowl with all the other ingredients except the basil (which is better tossed in at the last moment) and the oil for frying.

2 Squeeze the milk out of the bread. It doesn't matter if some chunks seem to be falling apart: just reform them by squeezing with your hand. Heat the olive oil for frying and cook the bread pieces in batches, so that they become a lovely golden colour all over the outside.

3 Add the basil to the salad along with the bread, toss well and serve.

ALSO TRY...

Pa amb tomàque A great Catalan snack. Toast a piece of sourdough or good country bread on both sides (if you do it under a grill, fine; if you do it on a barbecue, you're in for a big treat). Immediately rub with garlic – this is much easier if you use half a head, halved horizontally – mucking about with a clove will only make you cross. Now cut a ripe, well-flavoured tomato in half and rub that on, squeezing out the juices and squishing the flesh so it soaks into the bread. Drizzle with your favourite extra virgin olive oil and sprinkle with sea salt and black pepper.

Tomato and basil tart

Large, scarlet, fragrant with basil, this is a gorgeous tart and, in terms of cooking, is not much more than an assembly job. Do make sure your tomatoes are finely sliced or they won't become cooked through and slightly caramelized in the cooking time.

Serves 6

1.2kg (2lb 12oz) plum tomatoes
200g (7oz) mascarpone
1 garlic clove, crushed
100g (3½oz) Parmesan cheese, grated
75g (2½oz) Gruyère cheese, grated

40g (1½oz) basil leaves, torn, plus more
  to serve
salt and pepper
500g (1lb 2oz) ready-made puff pastry

1 Preheat the oven to 200°C/400°F/gas mark 6. Slice the tomatoes about 5mm (¼in) thick. Discard the slice that has the core (you can use this and the other end piece for a tomato sauce); you need only the clean slices for this. Mash the mascarpone with a fork and add the garlic, cheeses and basil. Season.

2 Roll the pastry out to make a 33cm (13in) circle and put it on a floured baking sheet. Spread the mascarpone mix over this, leaving a 5cm (2in) rim round the outside. Now place the tomatoes on the pastry, starting from the outside edge. Place them in overlapping concentric circles, ending up with one slice in the middle of the tart. Season the tomatoes with salt and pepper.

3 Put into the oven and cook for 30 minutes. Reduce the heat to 150°C/300°F/gas mark 2 and cook for a further 35 minutes. The tomatoes should be slightly caramelized. Scatter with some basil leaves and serve immediately.

ALSO TRY...

Tomato, thyme and mature Cheddar tart Make the tart as above, but replace the Parmesan with really strong Cheddar cheese and leave out the basil. Scatter the tomatoes with the leaves from about 5 thyme sprigs before cooking.

Caramelized onion, pear and blue cheese tarts with walnuts and rosemary

Tarts are very comforting – the buttery pastry and the faint rustle as you cut a slice – and look as though they take more effort than they do.

Serves 4

75g (2½oz) unsalted butter
4 tbsp olive oil
3 large onions, very finely sliced
salt and pepper
leaves from 1 rosemary sprig, chopped
plain flour, to dust

1kg (2lb 4oz) puff pastry
3 pears, peeled, cored and sliced
 lengthways
2 tsp caster sugar
275g (9¾oz) gorgonzola cheese, in chunks
75g (2½oz) walnut pieces, toasted

1 Preheat the oven to 220°C/425°F/gas mark 7 and put in two baking sheets.

2 Heat 50g (1¾oz) of the butter and the oil in a large saucepan. Add the onions and turn to coat. Add 1 tbsp water, cover and sweat over a very low heat, stirring occasionally. After 30 minutes, uncover and cook for a further 30 minutes, stirring. The onions will darken and caramelize. Season and add the rosemary. Set aside.

3 On a lightly floured surface, roll the pastry into 4 x 23cm (9in) rounds. Top with the onions, leaving a rim. Transfer to the baking sheets, putting a sheet of baking parchment under each tart. Bake for 8 minutes. Melt the remaining butter and quickly sauté the pears. Sprinkle with the sugar and cook for 30 seconds, until golden.

4 Scatter the tarts with cheese and pears and bake for 3–4 minutes. Sprinkle with the walnuts and serve with a leafy salad.

ALSO TRY...

Goat's cheese, onion and spinach tart with pine nuts and raisins Preheat the oven to 190°C/375°F/gas mark 5. Heat 6 tbsp oil in a pan and add 4 onions, finely sliced. Add 2 tbsp water and sweat for 25 minutes. Wilt 1.2kg (2lb 12oz) spinach, drain and squeeze out the water. Chop and mix with the onions. Season and add grated nutmeg. Roll out 500g (1lb 2oz) puff pastry very thinly. Put on to a floured baking sheet, prick with a fork and bake for 20 minutes. Remove and gently flatten. Turn the heat up to 200°C/400°F/gas mark 6. Spoon on the spinach, leaving a rim. Top with 250g (9oz) goat's cheese, crumbled, 2 tbsp pine nuts and 3 tbsp raisins (plumped in boiling water, then drained) and bake for 10–15 minutes. Serves 4 as a starter.

Bacon, potato and onion galette Roll out and bake 500g (1lb 2oz) puff pastry as above. Slice 500g (1lb 2oz) cooked potatoes thinly. Sauté 1 large onion, sliced, in 15g (½oz) butter over a low heat. Lay the potatoes and onions on the pastry, brush with melted butter and season, leaving a rim. Bake for 15 minutes. Sauté 400g (14oz) bacon lardons until gold. Scatter on the tart when it has 5 minutes cooking time left. Serves 4 as a starter.

Courgettes with raisins, pine nuts and mint

This is based on a recipe in Claudia Roden's *Book of Middle Eastern Cookery*. I've been making it for years as it behaves very well (it's good the day after, and hot, warm or at room temperature). Leave out the onions if you prefer a more purely courgette dish. Lovely with lamb or as part of a Middle Eastern mezze.

Serves 4 as a side dish

500g (1lb 2oz) courgettes
olive oil
1 red onion, in crescent moon-shaped slices
2 garlic cloves, finely sliced
50g (1¾oz) raisins, soaked in boiling water
  for 15 minutes and drained

1½ tbsp pine nuts or chopped blanched
  almonds, toasted
juice of ½ lemon
torn leaves from 8 mint sprigs

1 Slice the courgettes to about the thickness of a pound coin. Heat 2 tbsp olive oil in a large frying pan and cook the courgettes in batches until golden on both sides and soft. Season as you go and add more oil as you need it (courgettes soak up quite a lot but that only makes them more delicious). Put each batch into a shallow bowl as they finish cooking.

2 Now add another 1 tbsp oil and cook the onion until completely soft and golden (even slightly singed at the tips). Add the garlic and cook for another 2 minutes, until pale gold and soft. Toss the onion and garlic with the courgettes, raisins, nuts, lemon juice and mint. Taste and adjust the seasoning. You may find you want more lemon; there should be a balance of sweetness from the raisins and sourness from the lemon.

ALSO TRY...

Courgettes with hazelnut tarator Sauté the courgettes in olive oil as above – with the onion, if preferred – and, once they are soft, drizzle with tarator (see page 58). Scatter with chopped parsley, mint or coriander and grated lemon zest.

Slow-cooked garlic courgettes Deliciously rich. Heat 15g (½oz) unsalted butter and 3 tbsp olive oil in a very large frying pan and gently cook 6 garlic cloves, very finely sliced, until soft but not coloured. Now add 500g (1lb 2oz) courgettes sliced to the thickness of a pound coin, and turn over to coat. Increase the heat a bit so the courgettes get a little bit of colour, then reduce the heat, season and cook slowly (you almost 'stew' them in the butter and oil) until completely soft, almost collapsing. This tastes purely of courgettes and doesn't need anything else. I can eat a plateful on their own.

Radish, olive, anchovy and parsley salad

Lovely with a chunk of chalky goat's cheese and absolutely fantastic with cold roast beef or lamb: the strong flavours go so well with meat. You don't have to use white balsamic vinegar – I know not everyone has it – but it means the lovely white and pink radishes aren't tainted.

Serves 4

400g (14oz) radishes, preferably with really
    fresh leaves attached
150g (5½oz) black olives
30g (1oz) flat leaf parsley, roughly chopped
10 cured anchovies, drained and
    finely chopped
1 small garlic clove, crushed

½ red chilli, deseeded and shredded
    (optional)
4 tbsp extra virgin olive oil
3 tsp white balsamic vinegar (or dark if
    white isn't available)
freshly ground black pepper

1 Wash the radishes, trim and, if they have good leaves, carefully pat these dry and set aside to go into the salad. Cut the radishes into thin slices (if you have French breakfast radishes, cut them lengthways: this makes lovely teardrop shapes).

2 Pit the olives, or slice the flesh off the stones if they are hard to pit, and chop. Toss everything together in a shallow bowl along with any reserved leaves and serve immediately. Don't be tempted to add salt – the ingredients are salty enough.

Turkish carrots and lentils with herbs

This shows just how delicious frugality can be.

Serves 4–6 as a side dish, 3 as a main course

4 tbsp olive oil	2 tbsp tomato purée
1 onion, in slim crescent moon slices	2 tsp caster sugar
4 garlic cloves, finely chopped	275ml (9½fl oz) vegetable stock or water
1½ tsp coriander seeds, crushed	salt and pepper
¼–½ tsp dried chilli flakes	2 tbsp chopped mint, parsley or dill
100g (3½oz) green or Puy lentils	good squeeze of lemon juice
6 large carrots, sliced	extra virgin olive oil, to serve

1 Heat the oil in a saucepan and sauté the onion until soft and pale gold. Add the garlic and spices and cook for 2 minutes. Now add everything else except the herbs, lemon juice and extra virgin olive oil.

2 Bring to the boil and cook until tender and the liquid has been absorbed. It should take 30 minutes.

3 Taste, add the herbs and lemon juice, then adjust the seasoning. Add a generous slug of extra virgin olive oil. Serve hot, warm or at room temperature.

ALSO TRY...

Moroccan spiced carrots Heat 1½ tbsp olive oil in a heavy saucepan and sauté 2 garlic cloves, finely chopped, and 1 red chilli, deseeded and shredded, until the garlic is pale gold. Add 2 tsp ground cumin and 1 tsp cayenne and cook for another minute, then add 500g (1lb 2oz) carrots, in batons, and turn to coat. Add 75ml (2½fl oz) orange juice, a pinch of soft light brown sugar, seasoning and water to cover. Bring to the boil, reduce the heat and cook until tender. The carrots should absorb the liquid. Stir in 2 tbsp chopped coriander. Serve hot, warm or at room temperature as a side dish or part of a Middle Eastern mezze. Serves 4 as a side dish.

Uzbeki carrots Cook 500g (1lb 2oz) carrots (in batons or chunks) in water until tender, then drain. Heat 1 tbsp olive oil and 15g (½oz) butter in a frying pan and add 2 tsp caraway seeds, 2 tsp sweet paprika and ½ tsp dried chilli flakes. Cook for 30 seconds, then toss in the carrots. Stir them around, season and serve. Serves 4 as a side dish.

The recipes above are quite exotic, but also consider: Cook 500g (1lb 2oz) carrots (in batons or slices) in chicken stock or water with a knob of butter, seasoning and a little sugar until the liquid has been absorbed and the carrots are tender and glazed. Or add chunks of fried bacon and parsley or mint. A slug of double cream is lovely, too. Or go luxurious and toss the cooked carrots with butter-fried wild (or cultivated) mushrooms, adding a dollop of cream and a generous grating of nutmeg or scattering of parsley.

Kaye korma curry

Use this as a blueprint for a mild vegetable curry, with whatever is abundant. I sometimes make it with aubergines, courgettes, or squash, and don't always add beans or peas. It is very good-tempered and reheats well.

Serves 4

2 tbsp sunflower or groundnut oil

1½ tsp black mustard seeds

2 onions, finely chopped

4 garlic cloves, crushed

4cm (1½in) fresh ginger root, peeled and finely chopped

1 red chilli, deseeded and finely chopped

½ tsp ground turmeric

1 tsp ground coriander

200g (7oz) tomatoes, cut into chunks

250g (9oz) carrots, cut into chunks

350g (12oz) potatoes (waxy or floury; if waxy, there's no need to peel), cut into chunks

250ml carton coconut cream

salt and pepper

100g (3½oz) French or dwarf beans, topped and halved

100g (3½oz) frozen peas

juice of ½–1 lime, to taste

1 tbsp chopped coriander

1 Heat the oil in a flameproof casserole and add the mustard seeds. As soon as they pop, add the onions. Fry over a medium heat until the onions are good and brown, but not burnt. Add the garlic, ginger and chilli and cook for 5 minutes, then add the ground spices and cook for another minute to release their fragrance.

2 Add the tomatoes, carrots and potatoes. Stir and cook for 4 minutes to soften the tomatoes, then add enough water just to cover, followed by the coconut cream. Season and bring to just under the boil. Reduce to a steady simmer and cook until almost tender (add more water if it looks dry). The sauce should just coat the vegetables.

3 The beans and peas need to cook for only about 3–4 minutes, so add them towards the end of cooking. Taste and add half the lime juice, then taste again, adjust the seasoning and decide whether you want to add more. Stir in the chopped coriander just before you serve the curry.

ALSO TRY…

Vietnamese sweet potato curry On the table in about 20 minutes. Heat 1 tbsp groundnut oil in a saucepan and cook 2 onions, cut into crescent moon shapes, over a medium heat until golden. Add 1 red chilli, deseeded and shredded, 1 tbsp ground coriander and ½ tbsp ground turmeric and cook for another minute, stirring. Add a 400g can coconut cream, 1½ tbsp soft light brown sugar and 1.2kg (2lb 12oz) sweet potatoes, peeled and cubed. Bring to just under the boil, reduce the heat and cook until the sweet potato is tender. To thicken, press some of the potato with the back of a spoon so it disintegrates. Add 2 tbsp fish sauce and the juice of 1 lime, then taste for seasoning and a balance of hot, sour, salty and sweet flavours. Stir in a generous handful of torn basil. Serve with boiled rice.

Moroccan seven-vegetable couscous

This is a great dish for a crowd. Use whatever vegetables are in season – just make sure you add each at the right time so it doesn't overcook.

Serves 8

6 tbsp olive oil

2 onions, halved and cut into wedges

2.5cm (1in) fresh root ginger, peeled and chopped

3 garlic cloves, finely chopped

¾ tsp ground turmeric

500g (1lb 2oz) butternut squash, deseeded, peeled and cut into chunks

3 potatoes, sliced

3 large carrots, cut into chunks

1.5 litres (2½ pints) chicken stock or water

good pinch of saffron threads

1 cinnamon stick

2 generous handfuls raisins

salt and pepper

2 small fennel bulbs

4 courgettes, thickly sliced

3 tomatoes, quartered

1 bunch coriander, stalks chopped, leaves roughly chopped

400g can chickpeas, drained and rinsed

400g (14oz) couscous, to serve

1 tbsp harissa, or to taste

1 Heat 2 tbsp olive oil in a large saucepan and add the onions. Cook until softening and slightly singed. Reduce the heat, add the ginger, garlic and turmeric and cook for 2 minutes. Add the squash, potatoes, carrots and stock or water. Once it heats, crumble in the saffron and add the cinnamon and raisins. Season and bring to the boil.

2 Remove any tough outer leaves from the fennel, trim the tips (keep any fronds to serve), quarter and core. Once the vegetables in the pot have cooked for 10 minutes, add the fennel, courgettes, tomatoes and coriander stalks. Cook for 15 minutes, stirring, until completely soft. Add the chickpeas for the last 5 minutes.

3 Pour 350ml (12fl oz) boiling water or stock over the couscous plus 4 tbsp olive oil. Cover and leave for 15 minutes, then fork through to separate the grains.

4 Remove a ladleful of broth and mix with the harissa in a warmed jug so people can help themselves. Sprinkle with the coriander leaves and serve.

ALSO TRY...

Cauliflower, aubergine, chickpea and date tajine Heat 1½ tbsp olive oil in a large, heavy saucepan and sauté 1 onion, cut into wedges, until it softens and browns. Heat 1 tbsp olive oil in a large frying pan and sauté 2 aubergines, cut into chunks, until coloured on all sides. To the onions add ½ tsp ground ginger, ½ tsp dried chilli flakes, 1½ tsp ground cumin, ½ cinnamon stick and 3 garlic cloves, finely chopped, and cook for 1½ minutes over a medium heat. Add the aubergines to the onions with 1 litre (1¾ pints) stock or water, a good pinch of saffron, 50g (1¾oz) stoned dates, halved, and a 400g can chickpeas, drained and rinsed. Bring to the boil, then cover and simmer for 10 minutes. Stir in the florets from 1 small cauliflower and cook until tender (10–15 minutes). Mix in the chopped zest of 1 preserved lemon, taste for seasoning, add 4 tbsp chopped coriander and serve with couscous.

Mediterranean potato, tomato and goat's cheese gratin

This recipe shows gratins can be light and fresh. You can simplify it – you don't have to include aubergines or olives – but if you leave out something substantial, increase the amount of potatoes. Perfect with roast lamb.

Serves 4 as a main course with salad, 6 as a side dish

2 aubergines, thinly sliced

olive oil

salt and pepper

2 red onions, very finely sliced

2 garlic cloves, crushed

500g (1lb 2oz) waxy potatoes, very, very finely sliced

4 large tomatoes, very thinly sliced

leaves from 6 thyme sprigs

6 tbsp finely chopped flat leaf parsley

grated zest of ½ lemon

100g (3½oz) black olives (preferably Niçoise), chopped

150g (5½oz) goat's cheese, crumbled

1 Preheat the oven to 190°C/375°F/gas mark 5. Brush the aubergines with olive oil, put on baking sheets and roast for 15 minutes. They should be soft, coloured and cooked through. Season well.

2 Using a little more oil, sauté the onions in a frying pan until soft but not coloured. Add the garlic and cook for a minute.

3 Brush a gratin dish with a little oil. Add a layer of potatoes, then a layer of aubergines, one of onions, one of tomatoes and then begin again with the aubergines. Sprinkle on the herbs, lemon zest, olives and goat's cheese and season as you go. End with a layer of potatoes, arranged in neat slices. Brush with olive oil and cook in the oven for 45 minutes, or until the potatoes are cooked through. Cover with foil if the gratin is getting too dark. Serve immediately.

ALSO TRY...

Gratin savoyard Preheat the oven to 200°C/400°F/gas mark 6. Authentic Savoie gratin does not contain leeks, but I don't think it pays to be too purist. Do use Beaufort, though, if you can get it. Wash 300g (10½oz) trimmed leeks really well and slice thinly. Melt 35g (1¼oz) butter in a heavy pan and sweat the leeks, covered, until soft. It will take about 15 minutes. Add a tiny splash of water every so often to make sure they don't catch and burn. Butter a gratin dish and sprinkle with 1 garlic clove, chopped. Slice 800g (1lb 12oz) potatoes very finely, using a mandolin or very sharp knife. Lay these in the dish in layers, alternating with the leeks and 200g (7oz) Gruyère or Beaufort cheese, grated. Season well as you go along. Finish with a layer of potatoes in neat overlapping slices, sprinkled with cheese. Heat 400ml (14fl oz) chicken stock and pour over the vegetables. Bake for 1 hour, or until the potatoes are tender and the liquid has evaporated.

Creamy white vegetable, chestnut and cranberry gratin

A dish from an inspiring American cook called Jody Adams (it really is worth tracking down her book, *In the Hands of a Chef*). It seems festive because of the cranberries, but I start making it in October.

Serves 4 as a main course, 6 as a side dish

400g (14oz) potatoes	2 garlic cloves, very finely sliced
300g (10½oz) parsnips	leaves from 2 thyme sprigs
300g (10½oz) celeriac	salt and pepper
425ml (15fl oz) double cream	butter, for the dish
140ml (4½fl oz) soured cream	50g (1¾oz) dried cranberries
85ml (2¾fl oz) full-fat milk	100g (3½oz) cooked chestnuts, sliced

1 Preheat the oven to 180°C/350°F/gas mark 4. Slice the potatoes, parsnips and celeriac very finely – a mandolin is the best tool for this. In a large saucepan, mix together the creams and milk and bring to just under the boil. Add the sliced vegetables, garlic and thyme and cook gently for 5 minutes.

2 Season really well and spoon half the vegetables into a buttered gratin dish. Sprinkle the cranberries and chestnuts on top, then add another layer of the vegetables. Bake for 1 hour, or until completely tender. You may need to cover with foil after 45 minutes to stop the gratin becoming too dark in colour.

ALSO TRY...

The recipe above is one of the most useful in the book as it lends itself to so many variations. Stick to the basic quantities of root vegetables or potatoes, cream and milk and you can improvise to your heart's content. If you end up with a stash of wild mushrooms, they are delicious sautéed then layered in a gratin of potatoes and parsnips, or potatoes and Jerusalem artichokes. Cheese can be sprinkled between the layers (Parmesan, Gruyère or Cheddar are all good) and sautéed onions, bacon or ham are good too.

Potato and horseradish gratin Wonderful with roast beef. Make as above but use only potatoes and omit the garlic. Spread a third of the potatoes in a gratin dish and dot 3 tbsp creamed horseradish on top. Repeat to make another layer, then top with the remaining potatoes. Cook as above.

Beetroot and potato gratin Make as above but use 500g (1lb 2oz) each of potatoes and cooked beetroot. You can also add horseradish (great with salmon or beef). Another good addition is flaked smoked mackerel (layer between the slices and bake).

Cauliflower, bacon and Cashel blue gratin

This makes a lovely main course. The main recipe shows a gratin with cheese sauce, the pumpkin recipe below a gratin with cream (more expensive but less time-consuming). Make sure your vegetables aren't too wet; it produces a watery gratin.

Serves 4 as a side dish

FOR THE GRATIN

1 large cauliflower, in florets
salt and pepper
100g (3½oz) bacon lardons
50g (1¾oz) Cashel or other soft blue cheese, in small chunks
2 tbsp coarse white breadcrumbs

FOR THE CHEESE SAUCE

50g (1¾oz) butter
50g (1¾oz) plain flour
500ml (18fl oz) milk
75g (2½oz) mature Cheddar cheese, grated
3 tsp English mustard
squeeze of lemon juice

1 Preheat the oven to 200°C/400°F/gas mark 6. Cook the florets in lightly salted boiling water until just tender, then drain really well (water collects easily in cauliflower).

2 To make the sauce, melt the butter in a heavy saucepan and add the flour. Over a low heat, stir for a couple of minutes. Remove from the heat. Gradually add the milk, beating well after each addition, and adding more only when the mixture is completely smooth. Return to the heat and bring to the boil, stirring, until thickened. Reduce the heat and cook for 4 minutes. Add the Cheddar and mustard and stir to melt the cheese. Add a squeeze of lemon juice and taste for seasoning.

3 Fry the bacon in its own fat. You want a pale golden colour but not to cook it through. Put the cauliflower into a gratin dish, season and sprinkle with the bacon. Pour on the sauce, then dot with the blue cheese. Sprinkle with the breadcrumbs. Bake for 20 minutes, or until golden, bubbling and toasted. Serve immediately.

LEFTOVERS...

This makes a gorgeous soup. Just add chicken stock and milk (in a 2:1 ratio) and heat gently. Purée. Check the seasoning and bring to the boil again before serving.

ALSO TRY...

Make the gratin above with leeks or broccoli (cook until tender and drain very well), or add a layer of leeks, cooked Savoy cabbage or spinach to the cauliflower.

Pumpkin, tomato and Gruyère gratin Preheat the oven to 200°C/400°F/gas mark 6. Peel, deseed and cut 1kg (2lb 4oz) squash into wedges. Put into a large roasting tin with 800g (1lb 12oz) plum tomatoes, halved. Add 6 tbsp olive oil and season. Turn to coat. The tomatoes should end cut-side-up. Roast for 40 minutes. Put into a gratin dish, season and pour over 150ml (5fl oz) double cream. Sprinkle on 25g (1oz) of both Parmesan and Gruyère or Cheddar cheese, grated, and some dry breadcrumbs. Bake for 20–25 minutes, until golden and bubbling.

Roast squash and spinach lasagne

Everybody loves lasagne – you can almost hear the sighs of satisfaction as you place it on the table – and you can adapt this at will, adding roasted mushrooms (roasted to drive off the moisture), or sautéed fennel.

Serves 8

FOR THE LASAGNE

2.3kg (5lb) butternut or Crown Prince squash, peeled and deseeded

4 tbsp olive oil

salt and pepper

1.2kg (2lb 10oz) spinach, washed

50g (1¾oz) butter

generous grating of nutmeg

8 fresh lasagne sheets

125g (4½oz) Parmesan cheese, grated

FOR THE TOMATO SAUCE

2 x 400g cans tomatoes (ideally cherry)

1 large onion, finely chopped

4 garlic cloves, finely chopped

2 tbsp olive oil

4 tsp soft light brown sugar

FOR THE BÉCHAMEL SAUCE

1.5 litres (2½ pints) full-fat milk

10 peppercorns

½ onion

1 bay leaf

150g (5½oz) butter

150g (5½oz) plain flour

grated nutmeg

1 Preheat the oven to 190°C/375°F/gas mark 5. Slice the squash, put into a roasting tin, drizzle on the oil and season. Toss and roast until tender and slightly charred. It can take 40 minutes. Increase the oven temperature to 200°C/400°F/gas mark 6.

2 Meanwhile, make the tomato sauce. Put all the ingredients in a saucepan, bring to the boil, reduce the heat and simmer, uncovered, for 30 minutes. Season to taste.

3 For the béchamel, put the milk in a saucepan with the peppercorns, onion and bay and bring to the boil. Remove from the heat and leave for 45 minutes to infuse. Strain. Melt the butter in a heavy saucepan and add the flour. Over a low heat, stir for 2 minutes. Remove from the heat. Gradually add the milk, beating well after each addition and adding more only when completely smooth. Bring to the boil, stirring, until thick. Reduce the heat and cook for 4 minutes, then season well, adding the nutmeg.

4 Put the spinach in a saucepan with the water that clings to it after washing. Cover and put over medium heat. Wilt for about 4 minutes, turning. Squeeze out the water, chop the spinach and put it in a frying pan with 15g (½oz) of the butter. Heat gently, tossing, season and add the nutmeg.

5 Use the remaining butter to grease a pie or gratin dish (about 1.4 litre/2½ pint capacity). Add a layer of squash, then a layer of tomato sauce. Lay lasagne sheets on top, cut so they don't overlap. Add a layer of béchamel, half the spinach and half the cheese. Now put in another layer of lasagne and the remaining spinach. Add a layer of squash, a layer of tomato sauce and a final layer of béchamel. Sprinkle on the remaining cheese. Bake for 35–40 minutes, or until golden and bubbling.

Moroccan spiced roast squash and chickpeas with minted onions

It's probably obvious that I'm a big fan of roast squash and pumpkin. It's partly because I used to yearn for them – they have those lovely fairy-tale connections and look as if they would be sweet and velvety – but they were difficult to get hold of so I'm making up for lost time. This particular recipe is splendid-looking, especially if the tomatoes are on the vine.

Serves 6

2kg (4lb 8oz) well-flavoured squash or pumpkin
salt and pepper
olive oil
2 x 410g cans chickpeas, drained
225g (8oz) cherry tomatoes
2 red chillies, deseeded and very finely sliced

4 star anise
3cm (1¼in) fresh root ginger, peeled and grated
4 garlic cloves, very finely sliced
3 onions, very finely sliced
juice of ½ lemon
leaves from 5 mint sprigs, torn

1 Preheat the oven to 190°C/375°F/gas mark 5. Deseed and peel the squash and cut into wedges. Put it into a roasting tin where the pieces can lie in a single layer with room for the tomatoes later. Season and drizzle with 5 tbsp olive oil. Turn with your hands to coat. Roast for 20–30 minutes.

2 Add the chickpeas, tomatoes, chilli, star anise, ginger and garlic. Toss to distribute the flavourings evenly. Roast for 15–20 minutes, or until tender and slightly singed.

3 Add 3 tbsp oil to a frying pan and cook the onions over a medium heat until soft. Season and increase the heat to brown the onions. Add the lemon juice and the mint. Serve the dish with the onions strewn on top. Couscous is great on the side. For those who want the dish hotter, offer a little bowl of harissa let down with boiling water.

ALSO TRY…

Roast pumpkin with spinach and tahini dressing Preheat the oven to 190°C/375°F/gas mark 5. Slice 1kg (2lb 4oz) pumpkin or squash about 2cm (¾in) thick. Put into a roasting tin. Mix 7 tbsp olive oil with 2 tsp ground ginger, ½ tsp ground cinnamon and ½ tbsp caster sugar. Pour over the wedges, season and toss. Roast for 20–30 minutes, until tender and slightly caramelized. Beat 150ml (5fl oz) Greek yogurt with 150ml (5fl oz) tahini, then add the juice of 2 lemons, 4 tbsp extra virgin olive oil and 4 garlic cloves, crushed. Add enough water to make a sauce a bit thicker than double cream. Taste and season; it needs quite a lot of salt. You may also want more oil to thin it out. Toss some baby spinach with enough extra virgin olive oil and lemon juice to make them glossy. Season, put in a broad, shallow bowl and set the squash on top. Squeeze over some lemon juice, drizzle on the tahini dressing and serve.

Sicilian braised vegetables with saffron, pine nuts, raisins and capers

I have played fast and lose with Italian influences here, but the dish is delicious nevertheless. You can serve it without the gremolata or olives. Lovely with roast lamb or veal, and a main course in it's own right.

Serves 4

FOR THE VEGETABLES
3 tbsp olive oil
500g (1lb 2oz) small waxy potatoes, halved lengthways
250g (9oz) baby onions
3 garlic cloves, crushed
½ tsp dried chilli flakes
400ml (14fl oz) dry white wine
good pinch of saffron threads
salt and pepper
2 small fennel bulbs, halved
1 small cauliflower, in florets (keep any good, fresh leaves)

55g (2oz) raisins, soaked in boiling water and drained
600ml (1 pint) vegetable or chicken stock
1½ tbsp capers, rinsed
1½ tbsp pine nuts, toasted
2 tbsp chopped mint
good drizzle of extra virgin olive oil

FOR THE GREMOLATA (OPTIONAL)
25 good-quality green olives in oil
1 small orange
2 garlic cloves, very finely chopped
2 tbsp chopped mint

1 Heat the oil and gently brown the potatoes and the onions until pale gold. Add the garlic and chilli and sauté for another minute, then add the wine. Bring to the boil, add the saffron, salt and pepper and reduce to a simmer. Cook until the potatoes are starting to become tender, about 10 minutes. You'll find that a lot of the liquid has evaporated.

2 Add the fennel and cauliflower (including any cauliflower leaves), the raisins and stock. Stir well and bring to the boil. Reduce the heat and cook until everything is tender, another 12–15 minutes. Carefully stir every so often to make sure everything is well coated in the juices.

3 Add the capers and pine nuts and stir gently; be careful not to break up the vegetables. Taste for seasoning. Sprinkle on the mint and drizzle with extra virgin olive oil.

4 For the gremolata, pit the olives and chop the flesh roughly. Remove the orange zest with a zester and mix with everything else. Scatter on top of the vegetables, then drizzle with extra virgin olive oil.

Greek potatoes, curly endive, spinach and leeks with dill, mint and garlic yogurt

Greece truly makes the most of vegetables. This is a complete, delicious one-pot meal; you won't miss meat. Curly endive cooks to softness and the bitterness is pacified. Rocket can also be used.

Serves 6 as a side dish

60ml (2fl oz) olive oil	3 tbsp chopped dill
5 leeks, cut into chunks	leaves from 6 mint sprigs, torn
550g (1lb 4oz) small waxy potatoes, halved	good squeeze of lemon juice
salt and pepper	extra virgin olive oil, to serve (optional)
250g (9oz) spinach	2 garlic cloves, crushed
150g (5½oz) curly endive leaves, torn	200g (7oz) Greek yogurt

1 Put half the oil into a heavy saucepan and add the leeks and potatoes. Season, add a splash of water, cover and sweat for 20 minutes. Add a bit of water every so often and stir.

2 Once the potatoes are almost tender, add the spinach, endive and remaining oil and turn gently. Add another splash of water, season, cover and cook until the leaves have wilted – about 4–5 minutes. Add the herbs and lemon juice, put into a serving dish and drizzle with the extra virgin olive oil, if you want.

3 Mix the garlic into the yogurt and serve with the vegetables.

LEFTOVERS...

Make these into soup. Add chicken stock, heat, mash to break down the potatoes and leave chunky or purée. Top with Greek yogurt and a drizzle of olive oil.

ALSO TRY...

Turkish potatoes with tomatoes and black olives Heat 4 tbsp olive oil in a large, heavy pan and sauté 1 large onion, sliced, until soft and golden. Add 4 garlic cloves, crushed, 2 green chillies, deseeded and chopped, and ½ tbsp ground cumin. Cook for 2 minutes, then add 700g (1lb 9oz) waxy potatoes, cubed. Stir to coat in the spices and add 2 x 400g cans tomatoes (preferably cherry, in thick juice), 1 tbsp tomato purée, ½ tbsp soft light brown sugar, 1 tbsp red wine vinegar, 200ml (7fl oz) water, ½ tbsp dried oregano and 2 tbsp roughly chopped parsley. Stir and bring to the boil. Season. Reduce to a simmer and cook, uncovered, until the vegetables are tender and the sauce is thick. Add 100g (3½oz) good-quality black olives (in oil, not brine), pitted, 4 minutes before the potatoes are ready. If the sauce isn't thick enough, whack up the heat; if it is too thick, add water. Taste for seasoning (add harissa if you want it hotter). Stir in 2 tbsp chopped flat leaf parsley and serve drizzled with olive oil. Serves 6–8 as a side dish.

Niçoise vegetable stew with rouille

This is like a Provençal fish soup without the fish. It has a really gutsy flavour. If you want to make it fishy, you can poach some fish in the soup at the end; or you can cook fish separately and put some on top of each serving. If you don't like rouille you can serve this stew with aioli (garlic mayonnaise, see page 18) instead.

Serves 4 as a main course, 6 as a side dish

FOR THE STEW

4 tbsp olive oil

500g (1lb 2oz) small waxy potatoes, halved lengthways

150g (5½oz) baby onions

3 leeks, trimmed, washed and cut into chunks

2 garlic cloves, crushed

¼ tsp dried chilli flakes

700ml (1¼ pints) vegetable or chicken stock

good pinch of saffron threads

1 strip of orange zest

3 thyme sprigs

salt and pepper

2 small fennel bulbs, sliced lengthways

6 plum tomatoes, quartered

grated Gruyère cheese and baguette croûtes, to serve (optional)

FOR THE ROUILLE

3 garlic cloves, roughly chopped

2 egg yolks

150ml (5fl oz) olive oil

4 tsp tomato purée

lemon juice

½ tsp cayenne pepper

1 Heat the oil and gently sauté the potatoes, onions and leeks for about 15 minutes. It's nice if the potatoes get a little golden. Stir from time to time to make sure nothing is sticking. Add the garlic and chilli and sauté for another minute, then add half the stock.

2 Bring to the boil, add the saffron, orange zest, 2 of the thyme sprigs, salt and pepper and reduce to a simmer. Cook until the potatoes are just becoming tender, about 10 minutes.

3 Add the fennel and the tomatoes. Stir well and cook until the vegetables are tender, another 10 minutes or so. Stir carefully every so often to make sure everything's well coated in the saffron juices, but try not to break up the potatoes.

4 For the rouille, put the garlic and a little salt into a mortar and grind to a purée. (Or crush the garlic and put into a bowl with some seasoning.) Mix in the yolks, then add the oil drop by drop, beating all the time (with a wooden spoon or electric hand beater). The mixture should thicken. Don't add the next drop of oil until the previous drop has been incorporated fully and the mixture has thickened. Add the tomato purée, lemon juice to taste and the cayenne, then adjust the seasoning.

5 Strip the leaves from the remaining thyme sprig and add to the stew. Serve in soup plates with rouille spooned on top. I sometimes also serve grated Gruyère and croûtes, as you would with Provençal fish soup.

Fried kale and turnip with bacon bits and black pepper

Kale has made a come-back. It's slightly chewy and a bit bitter – both in a good way – and you can feel it making you healthier as you eat it. It's also a joy to handle: those big leaves spring back when squeezed, they're so full of life.

Serves 4

700g (1lb 9oz) turnip or swede, cut into
    chunks
salt and pepper

500g (1lb 2oz) kale
35g (1¼oz) butter
175g (6oz) bacon, in chunks or cubes

1 Boil the turnip in lightly salted water until tender, then drain. It can take 45 minutes.

2 Remove the ribs from the kale and tear or shred the leaves. Put into a large saucepan, cover with boiling water. Add salt and cook for about 4 minutes, then drain.

3 Melt the butter in a pan and fry the bacon until coloured, then add the turnip. Increase the heat and fry until golden. Add the kale to heat through. Season, adding lots of pepper, and serve.

ALSO TRY...

Stir-fried kale with ginger, garlic and chilli Prepare, cook and drain 400g (14oz) kale as above. Heat 2 tbsp oil in a wok and fry 1 red chilli, deseeded and sliced, 2 garlic cloves, sliced, 2cm (¾in) fresh root ginger, peeled and chopped, and 4 spring onions, chopped, for 2 minutes (don't let the garlic burn). Add the kale. Cook for 1½ minutes, turning to absorb the flavours. Season, squeeze over fresh lime juice and serve.

Warm salad of bacon, egg and kale with fried potatoes and mustard dressing Prepare, cook and drain 400g (14oz) kale as above. Whisk together 4 tbsp extra virgin olive oil, ½ tbsp balsamic vinegar, 1 tsp grain mustard, ½ tsp honey and seasoning. Cut 300g (10½oz) cooked potatoes into 5mm (¼in) slices. Heat 3 tbsp olive oil and fry 350g (12oz) bacon lardons and the potatoes. When they are golden, add the kale. Season and carefully toss with most of the mustard dressing. Fry 4 eggs in a little oil. Divide the salad between four plates, then top with a fried egg and the remaining dressing.

Penne with kale, roast onions and Gorgonzola Preheat the oven to 190°C/375°F/gas mark 5. Prepare, cook and drain 350g (12oz) kale as above. Toss 3 large onions, cut into wedges, into a roasting tin with 6 tbsp olive oil, 2 tbsp balsamic vinegar, salt and pepper. Roast for 30–35 minutes, until tender and slightly charred. Meanwhile, cook 300g (10½oz) penne until *al dente*. Drain and return to the saucepan. Add the kale, 2 tbsp olive oil and seasoning and cook until everything is warmed through. Stir in the onions and 150g (5oz) Gorgonzola cheese, crumbled, to melt.

Savoy bubble and squeak with mature Cheddar and fried egg

Food like this is irresistible, and gives leftovers a good name. You can obviously use leftover cabbage but I never seem to have any (leftover mash is another matter). Make four smaller cakes if you prefer. Grated Gruyère, in place of Cheddar, produces long, melting strings which add to the yum factor.

Serves 4

300g (10½oz) Savoy cabbage	400g (14oz) cooked mashed potato
40g (1½oz) butter	1 onion, roughly chopped
salt and pepper	150g (5½oz) mature Cheddar cheese, grated
groundnut oil, for frying	4 eggs

1 Trim the cabbage and take out the coarse ribs. Cut into broad strips. Melt 15g (½oz) of the butter in a saucepan and add the cabbage, seasoning and a splash of water. Cover and cook for 3 minutes, shaking a couple of times, or until wilted.

2 Heat the remaining butter and ½ tbsp groundnut oil in a large frying pan. Tip in the potato and onion and fry, turning and seasoning well. As you turn, bits will brown and almost char. Break it up so you get brown bits mixed in. Stir in the cabbage, then the cheese. When the cheese starts to melt, leave it fairly undisturbed – just press it down every so often with a palette knife – and cook on low heat until golden. Flip it over if you can manage (I find it too heavy) or slide it on to a board, turn over and slide back into the pan.

3 In a separate frying pan, heat 2 tbsp oil and fry the eggs. Serve them on top of the bubble and squeak. If you really want to make a silk purse out of a sow's ear, make some creamy mustard sauce (see page 155) and pour it over the egg. Delicious.

ALSO TRY...

Savoy and leek colcannon Cook 800g (1lb 12oz) floury potatoes in boiling salted water. Meanwhile, trim 4 leeks and slice finely. Melt 75g (2½oz) butter in a heavy saucepan. Stir in the leeks, add a splash of water, season and cover the pan. Let them sweat for 10 minutes, stirring occasionally, then stir in 200g (7oz) Savoy cabbage, shredded, add another splash of water and cover. Leave to sweat for 5 minutes until soft and buttery. Drain the potatoes, return them to the saucepan and set a clean tea towel on top. Cover and set over low heat for 4 minutes to 'dry out' the potatoes and give a better mash. Mash. Heat 150ml (5fl oz) milk and gradually add it to the potatoes, mashing until there are no lumps. Finally add the cabbage and leeks with their juices, plus another 25g (1oz) butter. Season really well. Serve immediately.

Roussillon baked potatoes

You can make two kinds of baked potato. The simpler way is just to bake them. The second, learnt years ago at school, is to bake the potatoes, scoop out the flesh and mash it with other ingredients before returning to the skins and baking a little more. The second type needs a recipe, so here it is.

Serves 2

2 baking potatoes
sea salt flakes and pepper
30g (1oz) butter
4 streaky bacon rashers, 2 chopped
¼ onion, finely chopped

30g (1oz) blue cheese, such as Roquefort, crumbled
1 small egg, beaten
½ tbsp finely chopped parsley (optional)
freshly ground black pepper

1 Preheat the oven to 200°C/400°F/gas mark 6. Wash the potatoes and pat with salt flakes, then bake for 50 minutes. Test with a knife to check they're tender. They will have lovely crisp skin.

2 Meanwhile, melt the butter in a frying pan until foaming, then add the chopped bacon and onion. Cook until the onion is soft but not coloured.

3 Halve the potatoes, scoop out the flesh and mash with the fried onion and bacon, cheese, egg, parsley (if using) and pepper (the cheese and bacon make this salty so you shouldn't need to add any more). Pile into the potato skins, top with the 2 uncooked bacon rashers and bake for 10–15 minutes, until golden and bubbling.

ALSO TRY...

Bacon and egg baked potatoes Make 2 Roussillon baked potatoes as above but omit the beaten egg and use Cheddar, grated, instead of blue cheese. When you have returned the mash to the potato skins, make a hollow in each and break in a small egg. Season, add a knob of butter, and bake for 15 minutes to set the egg.

Smoked haddock and mature Cheddar baked potatoes Bake 2 potatoes as above. Put 50g (1¾oz) smoked haddock into a small pan and pour over some milk. Bring to the boil, reduce the heat, cover and poach for 4 minutes. Break the haddock into large flakes (discard any skin). Halve the potatoes and scoop out the flesh. Mash with 15g (½oz) butter, 1 egg, 40g (1½oz) mature Cheddar cheese, grated, and seasoning. Loosely fold in the haddock. Pile into the potato skins, sprinkle with more cheese and return to the oven for 10–15 minutes.

Baked sweet potato with goat's cheese and olive-hazelnut salsa Bake 1 sweet potato as above for 40 minutes or until cooked. Meanwhile, put 25g (1oz) blanched hazelnuts, 1 garlic clove and ½ tbsp parsley into a mortar and pestle and pound, gradually adding 1 tbsp extra virgin olive oil. Add 60g (2oz) pitted black olives, chopped, and pound again. Stir in a good squeeze of lemon juice and season. Split the potatoes, spoon the relish inside and sprinkle on 60g (2oz) goat's cheese. Serves 1.

Criques de Gramat

These are from the Lot Valley. Add chopped onion (sauté before mixing with the potatoes) if you fancy, or use bacon instead of ham.

Serves 3 as a main course, 6 as a side dish

700g (1lb 9oz) floury potatoes

200g (7oz) Gruyère cheese, grated

125g (4½oz) cooked or cured ham,
  in little chunks

4 garlic cloves, very finely chopped

3 tbsp finely chopped flat leaf parsley

2 large eggs

salt and pepper

plain flour, to coat

oil, for frying (groundnut or light olive)

1 Grate the potatoes coarsely and put into a clean tea towel. Squeeze the excess moisture out really well. Put the potatoes into a bowl and mix in all the other ingredients except the flour and oil. Season well.

2 Cover a plate with flour. Take a fistful of the mixture and shape it into a cake (about 9cm/3½in across). Press into the flour on both sides. Shake off the excess (too much flour spoils both taste and texture). Put on a baking sheet.

3 Heat 2 tbsp oil in a large frying pan and cook 2–3 cakes at a time over a medium heat. The outside should be golden and crisp. Reduce the heat and cook until meltingly soft within (taste one to check). It takes 15 minutes. Keep them warm while you make the rest. If serving as a main course, offer green salad as well.

ALSO TRY…

Pommes de terre sarladaises Slice 750g (1lb 10oz) waxy potatoes about 2mm (¹⁄₁₆in) thick; don't wash. Heat 3 tbsp goose fat in a heavy frying pan with a lid. When it is hot, add the potatoes and sauté over medium-high heat. Turn for 5–7 minutes to colour all over, and season. Cover and reduce the heat to medium-low. Cook for 25 minutes, turning occasionally; it doesn't matter if the slices fall apart. Some bits will become crispy, others soft. Add more fat if they stick and burn. Stir in 2 garlic cloves, chopped, and 2 tbsp chopped parsley. Serve immediately. Serves 4.

Boxty Irish potato pancakes with a buttermilk tang, good with sausages and apple jelly, or smoked fish and beetroot relish. Grate 75g (2½oz) raw potatoes and mix with 125g (4½oz) fresh mashed potatoes, 75g (2½oz) plain flour, ½ tsp bicarbonate of soda and enough buttermilk to make a thick batter (about 150ml/¼ pint). Season. Heat a frying pan and melt a knob of unsalted butter – enough to coat the pan. When it is really hot, spoon the batter in to make 9cm (3½in) diameter cakes. Cook for 5 minutes on each side, until golden brown. Put on kitchen paper and keep warm while you make the rest.

Viennese potatoes with pickled cucumber, caraway and soured cream

Chunks of leftover pork or sausage (especially smoked sausage) are lovely added to this. It's also a good side dish with sausages, pork, mackerel or salmon. If you're eating it in winter, heat the soured cream with the cucumber before serving.

Serves 6

1½ tbsp groundnut oil

500g (1lb 2oz) cold, cooked waxy potatoes, cut into chunks

2 tsp caraway seeds

1½ tsp hot paprika

1½ tsp sweet paprika

salt and pepper

50ml (2fl oz) soured cream

1½ tbsp chopped pickled fat cucumbers (preferably sweet and sour)

1 tbsp chopped dill

1 Heat the oil in a wide frying pan and add the potatoes. Fry over a medium heat until they begin to turn gold. Add the caraway, paprikas and seasoning and cook for another 2 minutes, tossing the potatoes around so they get coated with the spices.

2 Put the potatoes into a serving bowl, spoon the soured cream over and scatter with pickled cucumber and dill.

ALSO TRY...

It sometimes seems mad not to cook extra potatoes just to have the pleasure of making new dishes. Sauté chopped or sliced potatoes in a mixture of unsalted butter and olive oil until golden, adding garlic at the end for a couple of minutes more. Add chopped parsley, thyme or rosemary, with finely grated lemon zest or even shredded preserved lemon. Don't forget the seasoning.

Batata harra (hot Middle Eastern fried potatoes) Heat 2 tbsp olive oil in a large frying pan. Add 700g (1lb 9oz) cold cooked potatoes, cut into chunks, and fry over a medium-high heat until golden brown. Add seasoning, 2½ tsp ground coriander and 1½ tsp cayenne and cook for 2 minutes. Toss in 3 tbsp fresh coriander, chopped, squeeze on lemon juice and serve. For a Spanish spin, use smoked paprika instead of ground coriander and cayenne.

Fried potatoes and wild mushrooms Heat 1 tbsp light olive oil with 25g (1oz) unsalted butter in a nonstick frying pan. Cook 100g (3½oz) wild mushrooms (or mixed wild and cultivated), sliced if large, until golden. They must have exuded their moisture – and it should have evaporated – or the dish will be soggy. Set aside. Put another tbsp oil in the frying pan and add 500g (1lb 2oz) halved, cooked waxy potatoes; fry until golden. Return the mushrooms to the pan, season, heat through and add finely chopped parsley. Serve immediately. These are very popular in southwest France, where they sometimes use a bit of walnut oil for the frying.

Racing pulses

Beans take time, and we don't have so much of that these days. We're all in too much of a hurry, in thrall to the 'dinner in a dash' approach to food that precludes simmering pots of pulses. Beans aren't part of our culinary heritage, either. The French have cassoulet, the Americans have Boston baked beans, Middle Eastern cooks mash chickpeas into houmous and we Brits open a tin of Heinz. It's a pity, as nothing quite provides the culinary comfort that beans give, they're good for you and they cost next to nothing. Simmered long and slow, beans are transformed into a melting mass imbued with the flavours – bacon, lamb, olive oil, duck fat, garlic, onion or herbs – with which you've cooked them.

You do need to think ahead to have your beans ready to cook (stick them in a bowl, cover with water and leave overnight), though the quick-soak method (bring beans up to the boil, take them off the heat and leave them to soak for 2 hours) means you can enjoy them on the same day as you get the urge to eat them. You should allow about 55g (2oz) dried weight of pulses per person. Once soaked and cooked, they'll at least double in weight. I always cook more beans than I need for a given dish, as they are great for salads and keep in the refrigerator for several days. (Cover tightly, though, as they are also like sponges for soaking up other flavours.)

Beans may look similar, but they are all distinct and you'll get to know your favourites. I love haricots. Small, white and not too starchy, they are used for baked beans and cassoulet. Cannellini beans are similar, but a bit bigger with a fluffier texture, and flageolets – which are not the semi-dried version of haricot beans as some people think, but a distinct variety – are pale green with a creamy texture and a delicate flavour. Borlotti beans are large, pink-speckled, and have a hammy, slightly sweet flavour. Black-eyed beans are small and creamy with a black 'scar' where they were joined to the pod, and the pinto beans that dominate South American cookery are an orange-pinky colour with rust-coloured specks and quite a sweet flavour. Kidney beans – the scourge of badly made bean salads – are used in chilli con carne, Mexican bean soups and Caribbean dishes.

Butter beans are large, starchy and thick-skinned with a potato-like taste, and are good with assertive ingredients and big flavours such as mustard and chorizo. Chickpeas are nutty and firm (in fact they never soften to collapsing) and – though I may well be pilloried for saying this – I can never detect much difference between home-cooked and canned, so rarely cook them from scratch.

There are a few things to watch out for when dealing with dried beans. Make sure that they're not more than six months old – older than that and they take longer to cook, in fact very old ones will never soften at all – and keep checking them during cooking. Age, soaking time and variety all affect the length of time they need to soften, so it is impossible to give an exact cooking time. The softness to which you cook them depends on what you are going to use them for: salads need a firm bean; for puréed soups you can cook them further until they are disintegrating; for stews you may want to cook them along with the other stew ingredients, so rescue them when they still retain plenty of bite.

Always throw away the bean-soaking liquid and use fresh water for cooking them. With kidney beans, you need to boil them vigorously in fresh water for 10 minutes to destroy any toxins. Drain and continue to simmer them in fresh water for 45 minutes (no other beans need this treatment).

Lastly, beans need plenty of seasoning. Whether it comes from salt or stock, they require a little help on this front. Not everyone agrees, but I am of the school of thought that thinks that salt added to beans before they are cooked toughens the skins, so I add it only towards the end.

Lentils have an image problem just as much as beans do. We associate them with sandal-wearing hippies and brown vegetarian food. Not one passed my lips until I was 15 years old. Then, as I sat at a simple meal with my French exchange family (all we were eating was bowls of salad, crudités and baguette, but it stands out as one of the best meals of my life), a big platter of lentils, glossy with olive oil, was set before us. Tossed while still warm in a mustardy vinaigrette, the pulses, with their starchy nuttiness, contrasted beautifully with the sharpness of the dressing. This is still one of my favourite salads and if I'm cooking lentils I always do a big batch so I have some to eat later in the week. Cooked quite plainly and dressed while still warm, lentils absorb the flavours of any dressing, becoming imbued with oil, lemon, garlic, whatever you put with them. Cooked lentils make a wonderful base for all sorts of other salads. Try them with smoked haddock or sausage, roast pumpkin with goat's cheese, celeriac and walnuts, or shreds of ham hock and leaves of bitter chicory. Dressings made with nut oils are good too, and lentils work very well in creamy and spicy vinaigrettes (a creamy curry version is delicious).

Along with beans and potatoes, lentils can truly be described as earthy; in fact they almost taste of soil. They're starchy, prone to collapsing into a purée, and deeply comforting. They don't need to be soaked, and they cook more quickly than beans (they are ready in anything from 20 to 40 minutes, depending on their age and type). There are quite a few varieties to choose from and they all behave slightly differently. The orangey red lentils make a great side dish for Middle Eastern or Indian main courses. Cook them in stock or water with onions, garlic, cumin and maybe a little chilli for a dish which provides a low hum of spiciness. Make it hotter and add tomatoes and peppers and you have a great mid-week veggie main course (a staple in my house) to eat with rice and a bowl of raita. Red lentils cook really quickly (in only about 15 minutes) and make a superb soup (have a look in the soup chapter, page 218, for a delicious bowlful).

Then there are the large green or brown lentils. They are whole and unskinned, and therefore retain their shape after cooking. I tend to go for the more expensive versions of these lentils (because even when lentils are 'expensive' they're still relatively cheap) and buy those from Puy. These are small and a beautiful green-grey colour, the 'grand cru' of the lentil world. They have a nuttier flavour and a less starchy texture than regular green lentils. They're great as a side dish with sausages, roast cod or salmon, or thick slices of ham (banish the idea of potatoes as your starch and think lentils instead). I usually cook them as I do for salads, with sautéed onion, carrot, celery and perhaps some chunks of bacon in a light chicken stock, though they also take well to being cooked in wine, or having cream or mustard added at the end. Reckon on 20–35 minutes (depending on how old they are) for cooking whole, unskinned lentils.

Split peas, which can be yellow or green (the yellow ones have a sweeter flavour), take just slightly longer to cook than lentils. In 45 minutes you will have a sloppy, starchy purée. They are good in soups (especially when made with a strongly flavoured stock, such as ham) and the yellow variety make a lovely Greek mezze – thick with olive oil and flavoured with garlic.

If long soaking and cooking seem like too much of a palaver, there's always canned, though canned beans are more successful than canned lentils (which can tend to be mushy). You can make a great puréed white bean soup with canned beans, and tinned flageolets tossed with butter, garlic and parsley are a great store-cupboard standby to serve with lamb. They're more expensive than the dried variety, though, and you will miss out on the comfort of a warm kitchen as they cook. Most important, you don't get the opportunity to flavour them by simmering them along with herbs, spices and fats. Perhaps the cheapness of beans and lentils has done them no favours. It really is worth cooking your own. Try to free them from their nut-roast image; they can be lip-smackingly good.

Lentil, red pepper and goat's cheese salad

You can cook lentils this way for other salads too, topping with warm smoked haddock, duck breast or roast beetroot with mackerel. Be sure to dress the lentils while warm, so they stay moist and absorb the vinaigrette.

Serves 6 for lunch

FOR THE SALAD

5 large red peppers, halved and deseeded

olive oil

balsamic vinegar

salt and pepper

½ onion, very finely chopped

1 celery stick, very finely chopped

1 garlic clove, finely chopped

250g (9oz) Puy lentils, rinsed

3 thyme sprigs

1 bay leaf

600ml (1 pint) light chicken or vegetable stock, or water

good squeeze of lemon juice

2 tbsp chopped flat leaf parsley

125g (4½oz) watercress or rocket

200g (7oz) goat's cheese, crumbled

FOR THE VINAIGRETTE

¼ tbsp sherry vinegar

¾ tbsp balsamic vinegar

5½ tbsp extra virgin olive oil

1 Preheat the oven to 190°C/375°F/gas mark 5. Put the peppers in a roasting tin and drizzle with a little olive oil and a slug of balsamic vinegar. Season. Roast for 40 minutes. Cut the flesh into fairly broad strips. Leave these in the tin with their juices.

2 Heat 1 tbsp olive oil and gently sauté the onion, celery and garlic until soft but not coloured. Add the lentils and turn to coat. Chuck in the thyme and bay leaf. Pour on the stock, season, bring to the boil, then reduce the heat and simmer, uncovered, until just tender. This could take 20–35 minutes depending on the age of the lentils, so watch carefully; they turn to mush very quickly. They should absorb all the stock.

3 Make the vinaigrette by mixing everything together. Pick the bay and thyme from the lentils, add the lemon juice and stir in 2 tbsp vinaigrette and the parsley. Mix with the peppers and their juices. Check the seasoning.

4 Toss the leaves with 2 tbsp dressing and put all the vegetables in a large, shallow bowl or on a platter. Scatter over the goat's cheese. Drizzle with a little more dressing and serve.

ALSO TRY...

Lentil and bacon salad with poached egg Prepare the lentils as above but sauté 1 small carrot, diced, with the onion. Make the dressing as above but add another 1 tbsp olive oil and ½ tsp Dijon mustard. Toss the lentils with half the dressing and the juice of ½ lemon. Sauté 150g (5½oz) bacon lardons in their own fat and poach or fry 4 eggs. Toss 125g (4½oz) spinach or watercress with 2 tbsp dressing and mix gently with the lentils. Divide between 4 plates and throw on the bacon. Top each serving with an egg. Drizzle with more dressing. Serves 4 for lunch.

Austrian sweet-and-sour lentils

The French do lentils, the Italians do lentils and – joy of joys – the Austrians do too, in their own inimitable way. If you have some home-cooked ham (and its stock), this dish is a knock-out: you can flake some and stir it into the lentils instead of bacon. Just make sure your stock isn't too salty (sometimes it's unusable, in which case use chicken stock). This makes a great old-fashioned supper with sausages and buttered cabbage, and it's very good with roast pork for Sunday lunch.

Serves 8 as a side dish

FOR THE LENTILS
1 tbsp vegetable oil
150g (5½oz) bacon lardons
1 onion, finely chopped
1 carrot, diced
1 tbsp caraway seeds
2 tsp hot paprika
2 tsp sweet paprika
450g (1lb) brown or green lentils
800ml (1 pint 7fl oz) ham (for preference)
  or chicken stock
3 thyme sprigs
2 bay leaves

3 tbsp white wine or cider vinegar
good squeeze of lemon juice
salt and pepper
1 tbsp caster sugar, or to taste
2 tbsp chopped parsley

TO SERVE
soured cream
milk
paprika (optional)
2 tsp caraway seeds (optional)
15g (½oz) butter (optional)

1 Heat the oil in a large, heavy saucepan and add the bacon, onion and carrot. Sauté until the bacon is well-coloured and the onion soft and golden. Add the caraway and paprikas and cook over a medium heat for another minute, to release the fragrance. Now stir in the lentils, making sure they get well coated, then add the stock, thyme and bay leaves. Bring to the boil, reduce the heat and simmer for 25–35 minutes, until the lentils are tender and the stock has been absorbed (brown lentils lose their shape more quickly than green ones so make sure they aren't overcooking).

2 Add the vinegar, lemon juice and seasoning (you won't know until now how salty your lentils will be, as it depends on your stock and bacon). Add sugar to taste; the dish should have a good balance of sweet and sour, so go carefully. Stir in the parsley.

3 Serve with soured cream drizzled over the top (let it down with a little milk so it's a bit thinner). Either scatter the cream with a little paprika or fry the caraway seeds in the butter and drizzle that over.   •

LEFTOVERS...

Any extras can easily be made into soup (it's a good idea to plan leftovers so you can make this). Simply add water or stock and purée. If you prefer a chunky soup, add diced carrots, stock and – later – frozen peas or canned drained and rinsed white beans. Lovely with a swirl of soured cream and a big handful of chopped fresh dill.

Creamy lentils and pumpkin with ginger and cumin

A satisfying vegetarian stew with the flavours of India. Pumpkin or squash is brilliant paired with lentils – you get both the sweet and the earthy. This is lovely topped with very finely sliced onion, fried until dark brown.

Serves 8 as a main course

1.8kg (4lb) pumpkin or butternut squash
olive oil
salt and pepper
2 large onions, sliced into crescent moons
6 garlic cloves, finely chopped
½ tbsp ground cumin
½ tbsp ground coriander
3 tsp ground ginger

2 red chillies, deseeded and shredded
200g (7oz) green or brown lentils
600ml (1 pint) chicken or vegetable stock
50ml (2fl oz) double cream
squeeze of lemon juice
4 tbsp chopped coriander
2 tsp garam masala (optional)
2 tbsp toasted flaked almonds

1 Peel the pumpkin, discard the seeds and cut into large chunks. Heat 4 tbsp olive oil in a frying pan or large saucepan and add the pumpkin (you will need to do this in batches to get it all cooked). Season and cook over a high heat until golden on the outside and caramelized in parts (you can do this bit by roasting instead; see page 28 for instructions). Season and set aside.

2 Heat 2 tbsp more olive oil in a large saucepan and cook the onions until softening and golden (rather charred at the tips is good too). Add the garlic and cook for another couple of minutes, then add the dried spices and chillies. Cook for a couple of minutes to release their flavours, then add the lentils and season. Stir to make sure the lentils get well coated in the cooking juices and spices. Add the stock and bring to the boil. Reduce the heat and cook for about 15 minutes.

3 Add the pumpkin, with any cooking juices, to the lentils and cook until the pumpkin is tender. Stir in the cream. Heat through, add the lemon juice and coriander and check the seasoning; this can take quite a lot of salt because of the pulses, but it depends how salty your stock was. Stir in the garam masala, if using, and scatter over the almonds. Serve with rice or barley.

Lentils with spring cabbage and peperoncino

I could eat this simple dish by the plateful, with no other accompaniment. Do use a good extra virgin olive oil; it takes basic food to great heights. And season judiciously.

Serves 4

250g (9oz) Puy lentils
1 pointed spring cabbage or ½ small Savoy
olive oil
4 garlic cloves, finely sliced
1 tsp dried chilli flakes, or to taste

2 tbsp coarsely chopped flat leaf parsley
juice of ½ lemon
4 tbsp extra virgin olive oil
2 tsp balsamic vinegar
salt and pepper

1 Cook the lentils in enough water to cover until they are tender but haven't fallen apart, about 20 minutes.

2 Meanwhile, remove the hard core and any tough ribs from the cabbage and cut the leaves into strips. Heat 2 tbsp oil in a large frying pan or wok and stir-fry the greens for a couple of minutes over a medium heat. Add the garlic and chilli and cook until the garlic is pale gold and the cabbage has wilted, about 4 minutes. Drain the lentils and immediately toss them with the cabbage.

3 Add the parsley, lemon juice, extra virgin olive oil, balsamic vinegar and plenty of salt and pepper (lentils take a lot of seasoning). Taste and adjust the seasoning or the amount of oil or lemon as necessary. Serve hot, warm or at room temperature.

Lentils and purple-sprouting broccoli with anchovies and parsley

Serves 4

1 tbsp olive oil
1 small onion, finely chopped
1 red chilli, deseeded and chopped
2 garlic cloves, finely sliced
250g (9oz) Puy or green lentils
salt and pepper

7 tbsp extra virgin olive oil
juice of ½ lemon
2 tbsp finely chopped flat leaf parsley
10 canned anchovies, drained and finely
    chopped
350g (12oz) purple-sprouting broccoli

1 Heat the olive oil in a saucepan and sauté the onion until soft, then add the chilli and garlic and cook gently for a minute. Add the lentils and stir in the juices, then add water to cover by 5cm (2in). Season. Bring to the boil, reduce the heat and simmer until tender. Immediately drain and stir in 4 tbsp of the extra virgin olive oil, with half the lemon juice, parsley and anchovies. Put into a shallow serving bowl.

2 Boil or steam the broccoli until just tender and put on top of the lentils. Season and drizzle with the remaining extra virgin olive oil, lemon juice, parsley and anchovies. Serve warm.

Split pea purée with Greek lemon and oregano chicken

Split peas in the starring role, with herby, lemony chicken on the side. Dress with good olive oil (a punchy Greek if you can – they're gutsy and terrific value for money).

Serves 4

FOR THE CHICKEN
8 skin-on chicken thighs
finely grated zest of 1 and juice of 2 lemons
8 tbsp olive oil
salt and pepper
2 tbsp dried oregano
8 thyme sprigs

FOR THE PURÉE
200g (7oz) split peas
1 small onion, finely chopped

1 chilli (red or green), deseeded and
 chopped
2 tsp ground cumin
2 tbsp olive oil
juice of 1 lemon

TO SERVE
½ small red onion, sliced wafer-thin
2 tbsp chopped flat leaf parsley
extra virgin olive oil

1 Mix the chicken with the lemon zest and juice, oil, salt and pepper, oregano and the leaves from half the thyme. Cover and leave for 2 hours (or longer) in the refrigerator. Turn over every so often.

2 Put the peas in a saucepan and cover with 1.2 litres (2 pints) water. Bring to the boil, skimming off any froth. When the water looks clear, add the onion, chilli and cumin and simmer, uncovered, until the peas collapse into a thick puree, about 30 minutes. Cool, then mash with the oil, lemon juice, salt and pepper. Taste – it needs good seasoning.

3 Meanwhile, preheat the oven to 200°C/400°F/gas mark 6. Put the chicken in a roasting tin with the remaining thyme. Cook for 45 minutes, or until the juices run clear when the chicken is pierced. Serve the hot chicken with the pea purée, lukewarm or at room temperature; top with the red onion and parsley and a drizzle of extra virgin olive oil.

ALSO TRY…

This pea purée is a mezze in Greece, served with other little starters such as roast peppers, baked beetroot and tzatziki; it is particularly lovely against sweet things. Try it topped with warm hard-boiled eggs and sliced onions and served with pitta bread.

For a more Indian dish, add 2 tsp ground coriander and a chunk of fresh root ginger, peeled and finely chopped, with the cumin. Add chopped fresh coriander at the end.

Omit the cumin and stir a little double cream and a dollop of Dijon mustard into the peas before they collapse; delicious with pork chops.

Add chicken or vegetable stock and make a soup. This is good with really dark, caramelized onions on top, chopped fresh coriander and a good slug of olive oil.

Lamb, beer and black bean chilli

I came across this recipe in the wilds of Nevada about 20 years ago, when I was snowed in, leafing through my host's stash of ancient *Gourmet* magazines for the most warming dishes.

Serves 6

4 tbsp sunflower, groundnut or olive oil
750g (1lb 10oz) shoulder of lamb, cubed
1 large onion, roughly chopped
4 garlic cloves, crushed
2 green chillies, deseeded and finely
  chopped
½ tbsp ground cumin
2 x 400g cans tomatoes in thick juice
600ml (1 pint) American or Mexican lager
1 tbsp tomato purée
1 tbsp soft dark brown sugar

3 tsp dried oregano
salt and pepper
2 x 400g cans black beans, drained and
  rinsed
juice of ½–1 lime
3 spring onions, finely chopped
2 tbsp chopped fresh coriander

TO SERVE
soured cream or Greek yogurt
avocado slices
grated Lancashire or Wensleydale cheese

1 Heat the oil in a flameproof casserole and brown the lamb well all over. Remove the lamb and set it aside. Add the onion to the pan and cook until soft and golden, then add the garlic and chillies and cook for 2 minutes. Add the cumin and cook for another minute. Return the lamb to the pot along with the tomatoes, lager, tomato purée, sugar, oregano and lamb, season well and bring to the boil.

2 Immediately reduce the heat to a very gentle simmer and cook – uncovered – for 1½–2 hours or until the lamb is completely tender. Stir in the beans halfway through.

3 Taste, add the lime juice, spring onions and fresh coriander, stir and taste again. Adjust the seasoning. Serve with soured cream or Greek yogurt, avocado slices and grated cheese.

ALSO TRY...

Sausage and black bean chilli Make as above but, instead of lamb, use sausages – lamb, pork or venison – and cook for 1 hour.

Turkish black-eyed peas with spicy sausage Heat 2 tbsp olive oil in a flameproof casserole and fry 1 onion, roughly chopped, and 400g (14oz) spicy lamb sausage, cut into chunks. When these are golden, add 4 garlic cloves, chopped, 1 red chilli, deseeded and chopped, ½ tsp each ground cinnamon and allspice and 2 tsp cumin. Cook for 2 minutes, then add a 400g can chopped tomatoes in thick juice, a 400g can black-eyed peas (drained and rinsed), 250ml (8fl oz) stock or water and seasoning. Stir in 2 tbsp chopped flat leaf parsley, ¼ tbsp dried oregano and 2 tsp soft light brown sugar. Bring to the boil, reduce the heat and simmer for 35 minutes until thick. Check the seasoning (you may want more sugar or chilli), stir in more parsley and serve with rice or bulgur wheat. Serves 4.

Spanish white beans with black pudding and chorizo

Serve with rice, or wedges of coarse country bread, and some greens. It's fantastic as a side dish with fish as well (try it with fillets of bream or with farmed cod).

Serves 4

3 tbsp olive oil

1 onion, roughly chopped

2 tsp smoked paprika

350g (12oz) white beans, soaked overnight and drained

150g (5½oz) piece of bacon

1 bay leaf

salt and pepper

150g (5½oz) chorizo

150g (5½oz) morcilla or black pudding

4 tbsp chopped fresh coriander or flat leaf parsley

1 Heat 2 tbsp of the oil and sauté the onion until golden. Add the paprika to the onion and stir over a gentle heat for a minute, then add the beans. Remove and reserve the bacon rind and cut the bacon into chunks. In a separate pan, sauté the bacon in its own fat until browned.

2 Add water to come 5cm (2in) above the beans and add the bacon, rind and bay leaf. Bring to the boil, then reduce the heat to a gentle simmer. Cook until the beans are almost completely tender, about 2 hours, depending on their age. Keep covered and watch the level of liquid: you want the beans to become stewy and thick, so remove the lid after 1¼ hours or so, but make sure the beans don't become dry. Once they are soft, remove the bay leaf and bacon rind, season and partly mash some of the beans so they disintegrate.

3 Remove the skin from the chorizo and morcilla or black pudding and slice. Heat the remaining olive oil and sauté. Add to the beans with the coriander or parsley. Stir, heat through and serve.

ALSO TRY...

The cheapness of white beans (and convenience of canned) makes them invaluable. That creamy starchiness is great with strong flavours. Make a salad version of the above, tossing drained cooked beans with chunks of cooked chorizo, strips of roast red pepper and lots of fresh coriander. Or make as above with either chorizo or black pudding (both would be too much) and serve with roast cod on top. White beans make a great base for quick salads: toss with dressing, shaved red onions, lots of chopped parsley and canned tuna, or chopped black olives, tomatoes and anchovies.

Butterbeans with sausages, leeks and cider Make as above, but instead of chorizo and morcilla, use 8 good pork sausages (leave whole, brown, and add with the bacon) and omit the smoked paprika. Replace half the water with cider, add 6 thyme sprigs, 2 bay leaves and 2 leeks, cut into chunks and sautéed.

Chickpea, potato and anchovy salad with preserved lemon and garlic cream

Not a subtle dish but a delicious one. Get a good can of anchovies; it will make a huge difference. I don't pre-soak the anchovies as I like the saltiness but, if you prefer, soak in milk for 15 minutes, drain and pat dry. If you use bought preserved lemons (which tend to be smaller than homemade), use half instead of a quarter.

Serves 4 as a starter or side dish

FOR THE SALAD
225g (8oz) baby waxy potatoes
250g (9oz) cooked chickpeas, drained
25 canned anchovy fillets, drained (reserve the oil) and halved
¼ preserved lemon

FOR THE DRESSING
3 garlic cloves
40g (1½oz) pine nuts
85ml (3fl oz) extra virgin olive oil
juice of ½ lemon
salt and pepper
handful of flat leaf parsley or coriander

1 Boil the potatoes until tender and put in a bowl with the chickpeas and anchovy fillets. Moisten with a little anchovy oil. Cut the preserved lemon rind into fine slivers and discard the flesh. Add the rind to the bowl.

2 To make the dressing, put the garlic and pine nuts into a food processor and, with the motor running, pour in the oil. Add the lemon juice, salt and pepper and check for seasoning. Add the herbs and pulse-blend. Drizzle over the salad and serve.

ALSO TRY...

Chickpea, cauliflower and roast pepper salad with feta and smoked paprika
Preheat the oven to 200°C/400°F/gas mark 6. Brush 2 halved, deseeded red peppers with oil, put into a roasting tin and season. Roast for about 30 minutes, or until completely tender, then slice and put into a flat, broad serving bowl. Break a small cauliflower into florets, put into a saucepan and cover with water. Salt, bring to the boil and cook until just tender – it must still have bite. Drain well. Add 2 tbsp olive oil to a frying pan and sauté 1 onion, sliced in crescent moon shapes, until soft and pale gold. Add 2 garlic cloves, finely sliced, and 1½ tsp smoked paprika. Season and cook for another minute. Scrape into the serving bowl and add another 1 tbsp oil to the frying pan (don't clean it). Heat the oil and add the cauliflower. Fry quickly to get colour and heat through. Add the cauliflower and a 400g can chickpeas, drained and rinsed, to the serving bowl. Pour 2 tsp white wine vinegar into a cup and season. Whisk in 4 tbsp extra virgin olive oil to make a dressing. Pour over the salad, add a generous handful of chopped coriander and 150g (5½oz) feta cheese, broken into chunks, and gently mix. Serves 6–8 as a side dish.

Good grains

At university I shared a house with a guy we called Brown Man. His part of the kitchen cupboard was full of foods in shades of taupe, beige and putty. Chefs and savvy cooks have now fully embraced everything on his shelves; they were weighed down with grains.

Grains are as cheap and healthy as ever, but we now know how to cook them (RIP vegetarian nut roast) and appreciate their range of flavours and textures. Barley is no longer just for granny's Scotch broth, but is one of the coolest ingredients around. If you are keeping a tight hold on your purse strings and want to eat healthily there's no better food. You have to make a psychological leap, though. When you think 'starch', don't reach for the potato peeler; think about barley, bulgur and farro instead.

There's a grain for every mood. They can be comforting; there's nothing quite like eating cheesy risotto when you are upset. They can startle; I still remember the awe with which I tucked into a dish of *arroz negro*, Spanish rice coloured black with squid ink, in a Barcelona restaurant. They can be everyday – one of my favourite meals is the pilaf I make with Sunday roast leftovers – and they can be gorgeous, splattered with pomegranate seeds, nuts, dried fruit and herbs. Here's the know-how.

FARRO In a modest restaurant in northern Italy, a farro salad won me over. Dressed with olive oil and lemon, tossed with pomegranate seeds and chestnuts, farro was unexpected and delicious. Like barley, farro becomes slightly creamy when stirred in stock, but can also be cooked in water, drained and used as a salad base or side dish. In texture it is similar to barley, though remains nuttier and firmer.

PEARL BARLEY Barley has become so hip it is now used for risottos (stirred as it cooks) and pilafs. It has more texture and an earthier flavour than risotto or long-grain rice. When it is cooked in stock, so the liquid is absorbed, you are left with a gutsy, savoury panful. Chestnuts, leeks, bacon, pumpkin, parsley and sage are all good in barley pilafs and risottos.

LONG-GRAIN AND BROWN RICE Long-grain rice can be cooked simply in plain water. However, I almost always cook it by the absorption method. Rinse in a sieve until the water runs clear, then sauté chopped onion in butter until pale but soft. Stir in the rice to coat the grains, then add water or stock – I use 350ml (12fl oz) liquid for every 150g (5½oz) rice – and bring to the boil, uncovered. In 5 minutes you'll barely be able to see the liquid and the surface of the rice will look 'pitted' with holes. Now reduce the heat right down, cover and cook for 15–20 minutes (but check it). The last bit of liquid will be absorbed and the rice will steam. Don't stir. You should end up with separate, light grains. Fork through very gently before serving. Once you have mastered this, you can make perfect rice flavoured in a host of ways – cook spices with the buttery onion, use orange juice or coconut milk to replace some stock, or gently stir in flavoured butters or pastes at the end. Brown rice – also long-grained, but with only the husk removed – can be cooked in the same way but takes longer and never softens as much. It has a nutty flavour.

RISOTTO RICE A medium-grained rice; the variety you choose will have a distinct impact on your risotto. Arborio is most common and dependable, but Carnaroli is thought by many to be the king and makes the creamiest risotto. Vialone nano is my favourite (though it's not right for every risotto) as it delivers a more soupy, flowing dish, and seems lighter. It's worth cooking with each, to discover how they differ.

CALASPARRA AND LA BOMBA RICE Spanish calasparra is a short, round-grained rice that gives a moister, stickier consistency than long-grain varieties. It is used for paella and other Spanish rice dishes. La Bomba is more expensive and can absorb up to three times its weight in liquid while retaining a characteristic firmness. You need either Calasparra or La Bomba for Spanish rice dishes – no other rice will do. They're great for lazy cooks as, unlike risotto rice, they mustn't be stirred.

SHORT-GRAIN PUDDING RICE Used to make rice pudding, people either love it or loathe it (creamed rice is one of the great English puddings). Cooked in milk, it can be made on the stove top (the method I find easiest) or baked. Middle Eastern and Indian cooks use it for exotic puddings flavoured with flower waters or spices.

QUINOA A south American grain, this is perhaps the most usable of the 'new' grains coming into vogue. Its texture and grain size are somewhere between couscous and bulgur and it's lovely both hot and cold. Dress it while warm with vinaigrette, then add beans, chopped anchovies and olives, or slivers of persimmon and chunks of feta, or pomegranate seeds and masses of chopped herbs. There's one caveat: be wary of the packet instructions. You are usually exhorted to add too much liquid and end up with gruel. Use 675ml (1 pint 2½fl oz) liquid for every 300g (10½oz) quinoa to produce grains that are cooked but dry. Toasting the grains in a dry pan beforehand helps, too.

BULGUR WHEAT Quicker and easier than rice, with more body and flavour than couscous, and wonderfully nutty. Again you need to be careful how much liquid you use. I cook it by the absorption method (see long-grain rice, page 109) and use just under twice the volume of liquid to grain. You can use it in pilafs, sautéing an onion in butter or oil before adding the bulgur. Once it's cooked (it takes 15 minutes), fork it through, then cover and leave for another 5 minutes before serving. Cold bulgur can be made into salad by tossing with other ingredients and dressing, or be reheated by steaming, or frying in butter or oil.

COUSCOUS Not really a grain, but a product of a grain as it's made from pellets of rolled semolina. It's so easy you barely need a recipe. Just pour boiling water or stock over the grains (I like 175–200ml/6–7fl oz liquid to 200g/7oz couscous; this will serve four people as a side dish), cover and leave for 15 minutes. Finish with olive oil or melted butter and seasoning, and whatever other ingredients you want. Reheat in the same way as bulgur wheat.

Classic rice dishes

Pilafs, also known as plovs and pilaus, are found in the Middle East, Eastern Mediterranean, India, Pakistan and some former Soviet states. They are made with long-grain rice cooked by the absorption method (see long-grain rice, page 109). They can be a main course or side dish as they often contain meat or fish, dried fruit, pulses, vegetables, herbs and nuts. Pilafs are great for using up leftovers, so are very useful to have in your repertoire. The other ingredients can be cooked with the rice, or gently forked in afterwards. In Iran, where rice cookery is an art form, they use the absorption method in a very complex way, creating a crust – *tah dig* – at the bottom of the pan with butter and rice (and sometimes also egg, bread or yogurt too) and layering with different ingredients. Bulgur wheat can also be used for pilafs.

Spanish rice dishes are also made by the absorption method but the other ingredients are usually cooked along with the rice. The rice ends up stickier than long-grain rice but not as creamy as risotto. Leave the rice to cook in its liquid – never stir it – and serve in the cooking vessel.

Risottos aren't just soothing and cheap, they're brilliant for impromptu storecupboard meals too, using up leftovers and turning humble ingredients into something splendid. If you have risotto rice, stock, and a decent sausage, you can make risotto. It is a very satisfying and sensuous dish as it forms warm waves (as you pour it on to plates, a risotto almost unfolds itself). Don't be fooled by the mystery which surrounds it. Risottos are very easy to make as long as you know the score. Sauté chopped onion in butter or olive oil (or both), add the rice and turn in the fat until glossy. Now add a ladle of stock, which must be simmering, and stir constantly. The stirring helps the risotto develop its creaminess. Add the stock a ladle at a time and add more only when the previous amount has been absorbed. You must never drown the rice in liquid. You then have to judge when your risotto is perfectly cooked, thick and creamy – the Italians describe the texture as 'wavy' – with a *little* bite in the centre of each grain. Apart from the stirring, the important thing is the quality of your stock, so gather up those chicken bones and get them into a pot.

Leftover rice is perfect for making stir-fries and can be reheated, either by frying in butter or oil, heating in a microwave or by adding a little water, covering with a lid, putting over heat and steaming. But there is one very serious caveat – leftover rice can give you bad food poisoning if you don't handle it properly, so beware. Cool leftover rice quickly then keep it, covered, in the refrigerator and use within 24 hours of it being cooked. The longer cooked rice is left at room temperature, the more likely it is that bacteria, or the toxins they produce, could stop it being safe to eat. When using leftover rice, make sure to heat it through thoroughly, and reheat it only once.

Persian herb chilau

Rice cooked in the Iranian manner with a delicious crust on the bottom. The washing and rinsing of the rice is important, so don't miss out this step. And don't stint on the herbs: it's meant to be a very green, spring-like dish. You can add cooked broad beans to it as well when they're in season.

Serves 8 as a side dish

FOR THE RICE

425g (15oz) basmati rice
50g (1¾oz) butter
75ml (2½fl oz) olive oil
125g (4½oz) mixture of dill and flat leaf
  parsley or mint, chopped
salt and pepper

TO SERVE (optional)

25g (1oz) butter
a squeeze of lemon juice

1 Wash the rice well and rinse it in a sieve until the water runs clear. Cover it with water and leave it to soak for 2 hours. Wash and rinse again. Bring a saucepan of water to the boil, then tip in the rice. Cook for about 6 minutes, until it's just beginning to soften on the outside. Drain and rinse in lukewarm water.

2 Heat the butter and oil in a saucepan until foaming, then add half the drained rice. Cover with half the herbs, then the remaining rice and, finally, with the rest of the herbs, seasoning as you go along.

3 Reduce the heat to very low and make 3 steam holes in the rice with the handle of a wooden spoon. Wrap the lid of the pan in a tea towel and put the covered lid on to the saucepan (the tea towel will stop condensation from falling back into the rice and making it soggy). Leave to cook for a further 20 minutes or so. You can check how the rice is cooking (and make sure it isn't burning at the bottom) but try to do this without moving the grains around too much; leaving it alone produces light, fluffy rice with separate grains.

4 Empty the rice into a bowl, making sure you dislodge the lovely crispy bits at the bottom (break these up and add to the rest of the rice). You can serve the rice with extra melted butter on top, though you may feel that the dish is rich enough without it. Persian cooks actually put saffron in the butter before pouring it over. I like a squeeze of lemon as well.

Orange and pistachio pilaf

Beautiful, and not expensive.

Serves 6

300g (10½oz) basmati rice
1 orange
700ml (1¼ pints) chicken stock
40g (1½oz) butter
1 onion, finely chopped

2 garlic cloves, finely chopped
125g (4½oz) carrots, in matchsticks
½ tbsp caster sugar
25g (1oz) unsalted pistachios, chopped
3 tbsp chopped fresh coriander

1 Put the rice in a sieve and rinse until the water runs clear. Cut the zest from half the orange with a very sharp knife in broad strips, slicing away the white pith. Cut the zest into fine julienne. Squeeze the juice from the orange and add to the stock.

2 Heat 15g (½oz) of the butter in a heavy saucepan and sauté the onion until pale gold. Add the garlic and cook for 2 minutes. Now add the rice and stir until beginning to toast. Pour in the stock and bring to the boil; the rice will start to look pitted. Reduce the heat to the lowest possible setting and cover for 15 minutes. Do not stir or the rice will become sticky. Check to ensure it isn't burning at the bottom.

3 Melt the remaining butter in a saucepan and sauté the carrots until they lose their raw bite. Remove the carrots and put in the zest. Cook until softening – only 2 minutes – then add the sugar and stir until slightly caramelized. Gently fork this into the rice with the carrots, nuts and coriander. Serve immediately.

ALSO TRY...

Egyptian megadara Wash 70g (2½oz) brown lentils and 50g (1¾oz) long-grain rice and soak both for half an hour, then drain. Heat 4 tbsp olive oil and sauté 2 onions, finely sliced, until almost caramelized. Heat a further 2 tbsp olive oil in a heavy saucepan. Stir in the lentils and rice and add 1 tsp ground cumin and ½ tsp ground allspice. Cook for 1 minute, then add 200ml (7fl oz) chicken stock. Cook gently, uncovered, for 25 minutes (don't stir), then cover for 5 minutes so the bottom becomes browned. Stir, breaking the crispy bits from the bottom, and add most of the onions. Mix, check the seasoning and top with 2 tbsp Greek yogurt. Scatter the remaining onions on top and drizzle with olive oil. Tomato Sauce (see page 119), with 1 or 2 tsp harissa added, makes this a vegetarian main course. Serves 4.

LEFTOVERS...

There are more pilaf recipes in other chapters of this book (see Lamb Pilaf with Figs, Pomegranates, Feta and Pistachios, page 38 and Salmon and Dill Pilaf, page 150) but if you stick to the method in the main recipe here you can try salmon, leek and pea; lamb, date and aubergine; white fish, dill and feta; squid, chorizo and coriander...The permutations are endless.

Sausage, radicchio and red wine risotto

There are nights, I have to admit, when I don't feel much like stirring for the 25 or so minutes it takes to make a risotto… then I open a bottle of wine, get into the rhythm and am thoroughly mellow by the time I spoon it into my favourite flat soup plates. Arrive home from work feeling that slow death would be too good for your boss and – within half an hour – you find yourself purring.

Serves 4

175g (6oz) spicy sausage (preferably Italian)
2 tbsp olive oil
1 small onion, finely chopped
2 garlic cloves, finely chopped
250g (7oz) arborio rice
500ml (18fl oz) decent red wine
500ml (18fl oz) chicken stock

1 small head of radicchio (about 175g/6oz), halved, trimmed and sliced
salt and pepper
25g (1oz) butter
30g (1¼oz) Parmesan cheese, grated, plus more to serve

1 Cut the sausage into chunks, about the size of a walnut, then roll them slightly into little balls. Heat the olive oil in a heavy pan, add the sausage and sauté until well browned. Add the onion and cook until just softening. Tip in the garlic and cook for 1 minute, then add the rice and stir it round to get it coated in the juices.

2 Heat both the wine and the stock separately to simmering point and keep them simmering. Add the wine a little at a time, stirring continuously and adding more only once the previous lot has been absorbed. Now add the stock a ladleful at a time, stirring continuously. It will take about 25 minutes to add all the liquid. About 10 minutes before the end of cooking time, stir in the radicchio. It will wilt in the heat.

3 Taste for seasoning; both the wine and reduced stock are salty, so see how much salt you need to add. Season with pepper, too. Stir in the butter and the cheese and serve immediately, with extra Parmesan on the side.

ALSO TRY…

Cauliflower, leek and blue cheese risotto Break ½ head of cauliflower into florets and cook in lightly salted boiling water until just tender. Drain thoroughly. Melt 25g (1oz) butter in a saucepan and add 2 leeks, cut into rings and washed really well. Cook over a low heat until soft, about 10 minutes. Add 250g (9oz) risotto rice and cook as above, adding 1 litre (1¾ pints) hot chicken stock. About 3 minutes before the risotto is ready, carefully stir in the cauliflower (try not to break it up), 25g (1oz) Parmesan cheese, grated, and 100g (3½oz) creamy blue cheese, such as dolcelatte or Cashel blue, broken into small chunks. Serve more Parmesan on the side, if you like, though you shouldn't need it.

Pumpkin, bacon, chestnut and barley risotto Heat 2 tbsp olive oil in a large frying pan and cook 800g (1lb 12oz) squash or pumpkin (deseeded, peeled and cut into chunks) until slightly caramelized in patches (you don't need to cook it through). You'll probably have to do this in 2 batches. Lift the pumpkin out with a slotted spoon and set aside. Heat 15g (½oz) butter in a saucepan and add 1 small onion, chopped, 2 garlic cloves, chopped, 100g (3½oz) bacon lardons and 1 celery stick, very finely chopped. Cook over a medium heat until pale gold and the onions have softened. Add 300g (10½oz) pearl barley and proceed as for Sausage, Radicchio and Red Wine Risotto (see page 117), cooking the barley just like risotto rice. You'll need 1 litre (1¾ pints) chicken or vegetable stock. Don't forget to season. After about 40 minutes the barley will soften and become creamy. Stir in the pumpkin halfway through. Towards the end of the cooking time, quickly melt 15g (½oz) butter and sauté 75g (2½oz) cooked chestnuts (frozen are good) over a medium heat until warmed through. Stir into the risotto with the butter, then stir in 8 leaves of sage, chopped, or 1½ tbsp chopped parsley (both are nice but give different results). Serve with grated Parmesan cheese.

Mussel and fennel risotto Put 1.75kg (4lb) mussels into a sink and clean thoroughly, removing the beards and barnacles. Tap each on the sink and discard any that don't close. Put in a large saucepan over medium heat and add 250ml (9fl oz) dry white wine, a few parsley stalks and 6 black peppercorns. Cover and cook for 4–6 minutes; they should open. Shake the pan a couple of times during the cooking. Strain, reserving the liquor, and remove each mussel from its shell. Discard any that haven't opened. Strain the liquor through a muslin-lined sieve, then heat until gently simmering. Heat 5 tbsp olive oil in a heavy pan and sauté 1 onion, finely chopped, 3 garlic cloves, chopped, and ½ fennel bulb, trimmed and diced, over a medium heat until the onion is soft but not coloured. Stir in 300g (10½oz) risotto rice. Pour on 50ml (2fl oz) dry vermouth, then the mussels' cooking liquor a ladleful at a time, as for the method in the main recipe on page 117. If you run out of liquor, use water. When the rice is cooked – after about 20 minutes – stir in the mussels, 4 tbsp finely chopped parsley, and a good squeeze of lemon juice and check for seasoning – mussel stock is salty so you will probably only need pepper. Serve immediately. Fish risottos are not usually served with cheese.

THERE'S LITTLE THAT CAN'T BE MADE INTO A DELICIOUS RISOTTO…

Once you know the basics, you can transform the humblest ingredients into a steaming saucepan of bliss. It's the creaminess of the rice and the goodness of the stock which do all the magic. Try smoked haddock and leek; tomato and mozzarella (let the mozzarella melt into long strings); radicchio and goat's cheese; red onion, spicy sausage and chickpea; saffron and pea; dried wild mushroom; ham and Gruyère or fontina cheese…

Suppli al telefono with tomato sauce

Crisply encased balls of creamy risotto with mozzarella inside that melts into strings as you pull them apart – hence the name which is Italian for telephone wires.

Serves 4 as a starter

FOR THE TOMATO SAUCE

½ **onion, finely chopped**

1 **celery stick, diced**

2 **garlic cloves, chopped**

400g **can tomatoes (ideally cherry)**

2 tsp **tomato purée**

1 tbsp **olive oil**

1 tsp **caster sugar, or to taste**

1 tbsp **chopped herbs (parsley, oregano, thyme, or a mixture)**

salt and pepper

FOR THE SUPPLI AL TELEFONO

3 **large eggs**

500g (1lb 2oz) **leftover risotto**

50g (1¾oz) **Parmesan cheese, grated**

100g (3½oz) **plain flour**

100g (3½oz) **white breadcrumbs**

250g (9oz) **bag mozzarella cheese, drained and diced**

500ml (18fl oz) **oil, for deep-frying**

1 Put everything for the sauce into a saucepan with 150ml (¼ pint) water, bring to the boil, reduce the heat and simmer for 45 minutes until soft and thick. Taste for seasoning and purée in a food processor or blender.

2 Lightly beat 1 of the eggs and mix with the risotto and Parmesan. Beat the remaining eggs and put in a wide bowl. Place the flour and breadcrumbs on separate plates.

3 Take 2 tbsp risotto and form into a ball. Make a hole in it, place a nugget of mozzarella inside and reshape the ball. It will be about the size of a tangerine. Make all the other balls in the same way. Roll each in flour – tapping off the excess – then in egg, then breadcrumbs.

4 Heat the oil in a heavy saucepan until it's about 160–170°C/320–340°F. (If you don't have an oil thermometer, a cube of bread dropped in should turn golden in 60 seconds.) Deep-fry the balls – 3 at a time – for 6–8 minutes, turning halfway. Drain on kitchen paper and keep the cooked ones warm while you fry the rest. Serve with the sauce.

ALSO TRY…

Risotto cakes with mushroom sauce Mix 300g (10½oz) leftover risotto with 1 egg and 15g (½oz) Parmesan cheese, grated, and season. Pour boiling water over 10g (¼oz) dried wild mushrooms and leave for 15 minutes. Melt 15g (½oz) butter and sauté 75g (2½oz) fresh mushrooms, chopped, until well coloured. Drain the wild mushrooms (reserve the liquor), add to the pan and cook for 1 minute. Pour on 300ml (½ pint) chicken stock and the mushroom liquor and cook until reduced by two thirds. Add 100ml (3½fl oz) double cream and simmer until the sauce coats the back of a spoon. Take 3 tbsp risotto at a time, form into a ball, then flatten into a patty. Continue until you have used the mixture up. Dip in plain flour and shake off the excess. Fry in 1½ tbsp olive oil on both sides until golden. Serve with the sauce.

Coconut rice pudding with candied limes

Cheap, easy and incredibly more-ish.

Serves 6

FOR THE CANDIED LIMES
5 limes
450g (1lb) granulated sugar

FOR THE RICE PUDDING
250g (9oz) short-grain rice

100g (3½oz) caster sugar
800ml (1 pint 7fl oz) whole milk
400ml can coconut cream
4 tbsp double cream (optional)

1 Fill a large bowl with iced water then cut the limes into fine, fine slices, discarding any pips. Bring a saucepan of water to a rolling boil. Add the fruit, stir and cook until softened, about 1 minute. Drain, plunge into the iced water, then drain again.

2 Bring the granulated sugar and 500ml (18fl oz) water to the boil, stirring from time to time to help dissolve the sugar, then reduce heat to medium-low. Add the limes. Simmer gently until translucent and in thick syrup, about 45 minutes to 1 hour. Set aside.

3 Put the rice, caster sugar and milk in a heavy saucepan and heat gently until simmering. Simmer, stirring occasionally, until the grains are soft and the mixture thick and creamy, about 30 minutes. Take from the heat and stir in the coconut cream. The rice will seem wet but firms as it cools. Once it is cool, chill. Stir in the cream, if you want to use it. Serve in wide soup plates with the candied limes.

ALSO TRY...

Citrus and spice rice pudding Put 150g (5½oz) short-grain rice into a saucepan with 900ml (1½ pints) full-fat milk, 50g (1¾oz) caster sugar, the finely grated zest and juice of 2 lemons and finely grated zest of 1 orange and juice of ½. Add a pinch of ground cinnamon. Bring to the boil, stirring to dissolve the sugar, then reduce to a simmer. Add 30g (1¼oz) mixed dried fruit and candied peel, optional but delicious. Cook until the rice is soft, 20–30 minutes. Add more milk if it's absorbed before the rice is cooked. Cool a little. Stir in 100ml (3½fl oz) double cream and 3 tbsp Greek yogurt. Refrigerate. Sprinkle with chopped pistachios, toasted pine nuts or candied citrus zest before serving.

Creamy vanilla rice pudding with simple fruits Make as for Citrus and Spice Rice Pudding above, but add vanilla extract or cook the pudding with a split vanilla pod and its scraped-out seeds. Leave out the zests and juice, dried fruit and peel. Serve at room temperature with Strawberries in Beaujolais (see page 265), Wine-Poached Apples (see page 272), or fresh cherries.

Rose-and-cardamom-scented rice pudding Make as for Creamy Vanilla Rice Pudding above, but add the ground seeds of 8 cardamom pods instead of vanilla. Once the rice is cooked, add 2 tsp rosewater (don't overdo it) and a squeeze of lemon or lime juice. Serve with chopped pistachios and torn rose petals.

Spanish rice with pork and spinach

Layer upon layer of flavour for very little effort.

Serves 6 as a main course

350g (12oz) pork fillet
salt and pepper
7 tbsp olive oil
100g (3½oz) chorizo, skin removed, in chunks
300g (10½oz) bacon, in meaty chunks
2 large onions, roughly chopped
2 red peppers, deseeded and sliced
4 garlic cloves, finely chopped

2 tsp smoked paprika
¼ tsp dried chilli flakes
300g (10½oz) paella rice
1.2 litres (2 pints) hot chicken stock
  or water
650g (1lb 7oz) spinach
1 lemon

1 Cut the pork fillet in half lengthways, then slice. Season. Heat 3 tbsp of the oil in a big frying pan and quickly brown the pork on all sides until cooked through. Set aside.

2 Reduce the heat, add a further 3 tbsp of the oil and the chorizo and bacon. Sauté for 2 minutes, then add the onions and peppers and cook over a medium-low heat for 20 minutes until lovely and soft. Add the garlic, paprika and chilli and cook for 2 minutes, then add the rice. Stir it well into the juices, add the stock and season. Bring to the boil, then reduce to a simmer. Cook for 15 minutes until there's just a little moisture left. The rice should be almost tender.

3 Meanwhile, wilt the spinach in the remaining oil and season. Distribute over the rice and tuck the pork in, too. Check for seasoning, then reduce the heat to its lowest, cover and leave for 5 minutes. Squeeze lemon juice over the top and serve immediately.

ALSO TRY...

You must not stir Spanish paella rice, so it's great for the lazy cook. Using the proportions of rice to stock given above, you can create dishes at will: chicken, rabbit, fresh and cured sausage and pork, fish, beans, lentils and all sorts of vegetables can go in. Just make sure the meat is cooked through.

Spanish rice with chicken and chorizo Make as above with 6–8 bone-in chicken thighs instead of pork (omit the bacon). You need to cook the chicken for longer, so leave it in the pan while you sauté the onions and peppers, then add the rice and stock. Dissolve a good pinch of saffron threads in the stock to flavour the dish and, instead of spinach, add green beans or frozen peas towards the end to cook in the steam created by the covered rice.

Spanish rice with squid, beans and sausage Make as above, omitting the pork. Cook the rice with canned, drained beans or chickpeas and cooked spicy sausage. Briefly sauté the squid in hot olive oil and fork it through the rice when the dish is just about ready.

Quinoa with lime, chilli, coriander and rajas

Quinoa should be dry and nutty, not sloppy or wet. I toast it before cooking.

Serves 4

FOR THE QUINOA
300g (10½oz) quinoa
6 tbsp olive oil
1 small onion, finely chopped, plus
   1 large onion, finely sliced
2 red chillies, deseeded and very finely
   sliced
4 spring onions, chopped
3 garlic cloves, finely chopped
3 tsp ground cumin
salt and pepper
675ml (1 pint 2½fl oz) chicken or
   vegetable stock

6 red peppers or 12 poblano chillies
finely grated zest and juice of 2 limes
leaves from 1 bunch coriander,
   roughly chopped
3 tsp dried oregano
3 tbsp mild vinegar (such as champagne
   or rice)

TO SERVE
crumbled Lancashire, mild goat's or
   feta cheese
soured cream
lime wedges

1 Heat a frying pan and put in the quinoa. Toast for 2–3 minutes; it should turn a shade darker. Set aside.

2 Put 2 tbsp of the oil into the pan and add the chopped onion. Cook until soft and slightly golden. Add the chillies, spring onions, garlic and cumin and cook for 2 minutes, then add the quinoa and season. Pour in the stock, stir, then bring to the boil. Reduce the heat to the lowest possible and cook, covered, for 18 minutes.

3 Fry the sliced onion in another 2 tbsp of the oil in a frying pan until golden. Roast the peppers (or chillies) over a gas flame, or in your grill pan. They should be soft with blistered skin, charred in places. Peel off the skin, remove the seeds and slice the flesh.

4 Reheat the quinoa over a gentle heat and add the remaining oil, the lime juice and zest. Check for seasoning, then stir in the coriander. Add the peppers to the fried onion, season and reheat. Add the oregano and vinegar; it will splutter and reduce.

5 To serve, top the quinoa with the peppers and fried onion. Crumble cheese on top and serve with soured cream and lime wedges.

ALSO TRY...

Fruited quinoa Make as above, but omit the spring onions and use ground cinnamon instead of cumin. Toast the grain, then cook with the sautéed onion and spices. Thinly slice 3 plums and half an apple. Soak 75g (2½oz) each dried figs and cranberries in just-boiled water for 15 minutes and drain. Chop the figs. Melt 25g (1oz) butter in a pan, add the fresh fruit and cook until softening. Add 2 tsp soft light brown sugar and caramelize a little, then add the dried fruit. Gently mix with the hot quinoa and 2 tbsp finely chopped flat leaf parsley or coriander. Great with roast pork or chicken.

Spring couscous

There are few side dishes you can make with as little effort and have looking this sumptuous. Don't stint on the herbs, this is supposed to be a very green couscous.

Serves 4
200g (7oz) couscous
175ml (6fl oz) boiling chicken stock or water
salt and pepper
6 tbsp extra virgin olive oil
zest and juice of ½ lemon

25g (1oz) shelled, unsalted pistachio nuts, chopped
2 spring onions, finely chopped
2 tbsp each flat leaf parsley, mint and coriander

1 Sprinkle the couscous into a bowl and add the stock or water, seasoning and 2 tbsp olive oil. Cover with clingfilm. Let the couscous plump up for about 15 minutes, then fork it through to separate the grains and aerate it. It will still be hot.

2 Stir in the rest of the ingredients and taste for seasoning.

ALSO TRY...

Autumn couscous Soak the couscous as above. Meanwhile, heat 2 tbsp olive oil and sauté 1 onion, finely sliced, until golden brown. Add ½ tsp ground cinnamon and ½ tsp mixed spice and cook for 2 minutes. Now add 75–100g (2¾–3½oz) mixed dried fruit (raisins, sultanas, cranberries, apples), soaked in boiled water for half an hour then drained and chopped. Heat through. Add to the couscous along with 3 tbsp chopped parsley or coriander, the grated zest of ½ orange (plus a good squeeze of juice) and perhaps some chopped toasted nuts (hazelnuts and pecans are lovely). Season and taste. You may want to add want some melted butter or warm olive oil.

LEFTOVERS...

Tunisian red couscous This only works with a leftover dish of fairly plain couscous. Heat 2 tbsp olive oil in a frying pan and sauté 1 onion, finely chopped, until soft and golden. If you want a hot version, add 1 red chilli, finely chopped (or ½–1 tsp dried chilli flakes), then toss in your leftover couscous and stir in ½ tbsp tomato purée mixed with 2 tsp boiling water. Add chopped coriander or parsley. Squeeze over some lemon and serve.

Couscous, chickpea and feta salad Combine 400g (14oz) leftover couscous with 5 tbsp extra virgin olive oil, the juice of ½ lemon, 25g (1oz) chopped parsley, 1 small red onion, sliced wafer thin, 410g can of chickpeas (drained and rinsed) and a roasted red pepper, sliced. Check for seasoning. Crumble 100g (3½oz) feta cheese over and drizzle with more oil. Sprinkle with sumac if you have it. You can add cooked lamb or chicken to this, other vegetables (such as green beans) and shreds of preserved lemon.

Farro with greens, fennel and chilli

If you think healthy food is punishingly dull, try this. It's spicy, nutty, leafy and glossy with olive oil. Delicious.

Serves 4

4 tbsp olive oil

1 onion, finely chopped

1 celery stick, diced

250g (9oz) farro

about 700ml (1¼ pints) chicken or
 vegetable stock or water

1 red chilli, deseeded and chopped,
 (or to taste)

3 garlic cloves, very finely sliced

2 tsp fennel seeds

1 small Savoy cabbage, weighing about
 250g (9oz), leaves shredded

75g (2½oz) frisée lettuce leaves and rocket
 leaves

salt and pepper

extra virgin olive oil, to serve

1 Heat half the olive oil in a saucepan and add the onion and celery. Cook over a medium heat until soft but not coloured. Stir in the farro and add enough stock or water to come 4cm (1½in) above the level of the grain. Bring to the boil, then reduce to a simmer. Cook for about 35 minutes, until the farro is tender but with bite. Try not to stir; you don't want to release any starch. The liquid will be absorbed; if it gets too dry, add more water.

2 Heat the remaining oil in a large frying pan. Add the chilli, garlic and fennel seeds and cook for 2 minutes, or until the garlic is soft. Add the cabbage and a splash of water, cover and cook for 3 minutes over a medium-low heat, until the cabbage leaves wilt. Now uncover, add the other leaves and wilt for 1 minute. Add the cooked farro, season well, increase the heat and stir. Put into a heated serving dish and drizzle with extra virgin olive oil.

ALSO TRY...

Farro with pumpkin and feta Cook the farro as above. Preheat the oven to 200°C/ 400°F/gas mark 6 and roast 500g (1lb 2oz) pumpkin or squash (deseeded, peeled and cut into slim wedges), tossed with 2 tbsp olive oil and seasoning, for about 30 minutes, until tender and slightly caramelized. Gently combine the farro with the pumpkin, 200g (7oz) crumbled feta cheese, the juice of ½ lemon, salt and pepper, 3 tbsp extra virgin olive oil and 2–3 tbsp chopped flat leaf parsley, dill, coriander or basil.

Lots of farro salads Cook plain farro – you don't need to sauté onion and celery first – in water until tender but still with bite (about 35 minutes), then drain. Add seasoning, lemon juice and extra virgin olive oil. Now you have a base for all sorts of lovely nutty salads. Try the ingredients in my barley salads (see page 126); or cherry tomatoes, olives and basil with chopped anchovies; sautéed courgettes with herbs, crumbled ricotta and pecorino; apple, hazelnut, watercress and gorgonzola; smoked meat, blackberries or dried cranberries and walnuts; roast cauliflower, red pepper and feta...

Barley, parsley and pomegranate salad

Time was when barley turned up only in Scotch broth. Now it has chic, and there are endless ways in which to dress it. Soaked dried sour cherries or cranberries would be good here instead of pomegranates.

Serves 4

150g (5½oz) pearl barley
½ tbsp olive oil
salt and pepper
1 tbsp extra virgin olive oil

1½ tsp balsamic vinegar
seeds from ½ pomegranate
2 tbsp finely chopped flat leaf parsley

1 Put the barley in a saucepan and cover with water. Bring to the boil, reduce to a simmer and cook until just tender, about 30 minutes. It's good if the barley still has a little bite; it tastes nutty that way. It shouldn't cook so much that it goes 'creamy' and starchy.

2 Drain and add the plain olive oil, salt and pepper. This keeps the barley moist. I don't dress it further until it's cool, otherwise it just soaks up masses of vinaigrette. Once it has cooled, mix with the other ingredients, taste for seasoning and serve.

ALSO TRY...

Barley, spinach and mushroom salad Cook the barley as above. Fry 225g (8oz) mushrooms, sliced, in 15g (½oz) unsalted butter until well coloured and quite dry. Season and toss with the barley along with 75g (2½oz) baby spinach, shredded or torn, plus balsamic vinegar and extra virgin olive oil as above. Serves 6.

Warm barley, roast squash and chilli salad The other barley salads here are fine at room temperature but I prefer squash hot, so cook 750g (1lb 10oz) squash (deseeded, peeled and cut into chunks) with 2 tbsp olive oil and seasoning for about 30 minutes in an oven preheated to 200°C/400°F/gas mark 6. The squash should be completely tender and slightly caramelized. Meanwhile, cook the barley as in the main recipe but dress it immediately with the 1 tbsp extra virgin olive oil and 1½ tsp balsamic vinegar. Season and add 2 tbsp chopped fresh coriander and 2 red chillies, deseeded and finely sliced, and the squash. Serve immediately. Chunks of crumbled feta cheese don't go amiss here, either. Serves 6.

Lots more barley salads... Cook and dress barley (you can eat it hot or cold) and toss with cooked French beans and bacon; soaked dried fruits and hazelnuts; pitted cherries and mint or tarragon; preserved lemon, chorizo and mint; smoked fish, watercress and dill.

Fine fish

As a nation, we are rather frightened of fish. The rules about cooking meat are simple; after all, we mostly eat only three animals and a few birds. But fish? They're a whole different kettle. Cod, haddock, salmon – we just about know how to deal with these – but venture any further and we're a bit, well, at sea.

Guilt and anxiety now play their part too. It's impossible to ignore constant warnings about the depletion of fish stocks, and Charles Clover's book, *The End of the Line* (2008), in which he compares trawling to hunters stringing a mile of net between two huge vehicles and dragging it at speed across the plains of Africa, left me feeling morally obliged to get to grips with what and how we should fish.

I know the word 'sustainable' can sound uncomfortably worthy, but 'sustainable' fish are the only kind we can eat if we are to continue to eat fish at all. We are at a critical point. The UN's Food and Agriculture Organization states that, of the 600 fish stocks it monitors, a quarter have been overfished or exhausted, while a further half are being fished at maximum capacity (*Review of the State of World Marine Fisheries Resources*, 2002).

More 'efficient' fishing has meant landing more fish, but in fact we are taking too much and, too often, indiscriminately. Beam trawling, in which an iron beam with heavy chains is dragged along the seabed, dislodging fish into the net that follows behind, is perhaps the most destructive. It doesn't just catch fish, but all other sea life, which is then dumped back into the ocean…dead.

Campaigning has had a huge impact, so there is hope. Waitrose, for example, doesn't sell any beam-trawled fish and all the major supermarkets have made some effort both to source sustainable fish and consider fishing methods, but you need to shop armed with information. The Marine Conservation Society, a UK charity, cares for the conservation of the British sea and seashore and has an invaluable website (www.fishonline.org) with information on sustainable fish, fishing techniques, and a pocket *Good Fish Guide* which you can carry when you're shopping. The Marine Stewardship Council, an international charity, certifies sustainable fisheries and places its logo on products that have come from its top-rated fisheries. The only drawback is that some varieties are missing from the MSC list because the process of certifying fisheries is voluntary; gurnard, for example, is not mentioned because no gurnard fishery has come forward.

The good news is that the choice of fish we can eat is much larger than you might expect, though supermarkets could go a lot further in the variety they offer. The situation obviously changes from year to year, so you should keep yourself informed by checking the website mentioned above. But at the time of writing, the guide on page 130 is a useful tool. When you scan the list of fish we shouldn't eat (and I've limited the list to the best-known varieties), you'll probably think that doesn't leave much. Not so. There is a wealth of fish and seafood out there we can eat with a clear conscience. It's a good choice, especially if you can get excited about varieties you've never tried. Remember that monkfish was once derided as poor man's scampi.

Avoid

Atlantic cod

Atlantic salmon

bluefin tuna

haddock from the Faroes and the west of Scotland

hake

halibut

ling

plaice

rays

red or blackspot sea bream

skate

skipjack tuna

sole from the North or Irish Seas

swordfish

tiger prawns

turbot from the North Sea

Eat

black bream and sea bream

British red mullet

British squid

brown and spider crabs

clams

cold-water prawns

Cornish sardines

dab

diver-caught scallops

grey and red gurnard

grey mullet

haddock from the North East Arctic and the North Sea (preferably line-caught)

Icelandic cod and organically farmed cod

line-caught seabass

monkfish from the southwest

mussels

MSC-certified Cornish mackerel

MSC-certified Dover and lemon sole

Norwegian herring

organically farmed salmon, trout, turbot, seabass and bream

Pacific salmon

pollack

Fish farming

Managing wild stocks is not enough. There will have to be fish farming too, otherwise fish will become a treat only for the very rich. But fish farming has created as many problems as it has solved.

Farmed fish – and it's mostly salmon in this country – are often stocked at a high density, so they don't swim enough to develop flesh that will taste good. Worse than that, high stocking increases the risk of disease and parasites, which can be transmitted to wild stocks, and the strong chemicals used to treat sea-lice have a detrimental effect on the ecosystem surrounding fish farms. Farmed fish can also escape and mate with wild fish, creating hybrids which can't cope with the open sea.

But perhaps the worst thing is that farmed fish are fed on a diet of fish meal made from wild fish. Not only does this fish have to be hoovered up but also, if we are processing it, it's not there for other wild fish to eat. The World Wildlife Fund estimates that it takes about 3 tonnes of wild fish to produce 1 tonne of salmon. You don't need me to tell you that's a crazy use of resources.

But it is not all gloom. Jeremy Langley, Waitrose's fish buyer, hits the nail on the head when he says, 'Like all kinds of farming, there is good fish farming and bad fish farming. We just need to buy the good stuff.' For one thing, some types of fish take much better to being farmed. Shellfish, for example, present few problems. Mussels, scallops and oysters don't even require much 'farming', as they will eat whatever is in the water. All the fish farmer has to do is capture them while they are young and put them in a good site.

There are conscientious farmers of salmon and now cod, who practise good husbandry and are as concerned about ecology as they are about making a profit. The Soil Association has awarded organic status to some fish farms, based on their stocking densities and where they source their feed. Sustainable feed comes from the fish-processing industry, where the off-cuts and bones they don't need are made into fish meal.

If buying farmed fish, I always buy organic (apart from ecological considerations, it definitely tastes better) and even then I want to know where it is from – not just the area but the farm – and a good fishmonger (including one in a caring supermarket) should be able to tell you this. I buy farmed salmon, cod, seabass, trout, bream and shellfish. Farmed salmon is a naturally beige colour, but this was thought to be off-putting for consumers, so many farms add dye to their fishmeal. Instead of the natural pale pinky-orange of wild salmon, farmed stuff can be a startling orange colour. Also look at the texture. Farmed salmon gets less exercise than wild salmon, but it should still get some. Specimens that look over-fatty, or whose white stripes of fat look very broad, will taste fatty too.

The way forward

Shop armed with knowledge and always ask questions about where and how a fish was caught or farmed. Fish will rarely be a cheap option, though many varieties, such as mackerel, squid and gurnard, offer great value. They don't lend themselves to leftovers either, because the flesh spoils quickly (although there are lots of recipes in this chapter on what to do with leftover salmon, because that is something you can end up with in the summer months).

Fish has to be regarded as a treat, especially when we are talking about prized varieties such as wild seabass and salmon. I hate to think that there may be a time when it is impossible to sit at a seaside café, the smell of iodine in the air, squeezing lemon over a plate of succulent fish flesh, or to enjoy fish and chips on a beach at twilight. If we are responsible in our shopping and imaginative in our cooking, we should be able to eat fish both now and for a long time to come.

Spanish baked bream

Bream isn't rock-bottom cheap but it is less expensive than other fish of its type. Farmed bream has a good flavour and I often buy it. The Spanish have lots of bream recipes, none of them too complicated. If you don't like smoked paprika, just leave it out. Or sauté bacon lardons and scatter them over just before serving.

Serves 4

FOR THE BREAM
4 x 300g (10½oz) bream, gutted,
  trimmed and scaled
7 tbsp olive oil
juice of 1 lemon
salt and pepper
5 tsp smoked paprika

4 garlic cloves, crushed
35g (1¼oz) white breadcrumbs
small handful of flat leaf parsley,
  finely chopped

TO SERVE
extra virgin olive oil
wedges of lemon

1 Preheat the oven to 190°C/375°F/gas mark 5. Brush the fish inside and out with olive oil, squeeze on some lemon juice and season well. Lay the fish – in a single layer but close together – in an ovenproof dish. Mix the smoked paprika, garlic and breadcrumbs together and season. Sprinkle this all over the fish, then drizzle on the remaining oil and lemon juice.

2 Bake for 20 minutes. Throw on the parsley when the fish has cooked for 15 minutes. The bream is cooked when the flesh near the bone is white and opaque. Drizzle with extra virgin olive oil and serve with lemon wedges.

ALSO TRY...

Bake the bream drizzled with olive oil, seasoned and served with any of these sauces:

Anchovy and rosemary sauce In a mortar crush 2 tbsp rosemary leaves with 12 cured anchovies (rinsed, soaked in milk for 15 minutes, then drained) to a paste. Slowly pestle in the juice of 1 lemon and about 100ml (3½fl oz) olive oil. Taste to see if you want more lemon or oil. Stir in some black pepper. (You can also use a mini blender.)

Sherry vinegar and parsley sauce Put 90ml (3fl oz) each of sherry vinegar and chicken stock and 40g (1½oz) unsalted butter in a small pan and bring to the boil. Boil for about 2 minutes, until quite syrupy. Stir in 1 tbsp finely chopped flat leaf parsley, 1 shallot, very finely chopped, and ½ tsp Dijon mustard. Taste and season. Spoon this warm sauce over the fish.

Fennel, anchovy, caper and mint salsa Trim 1 large fennel bulb, quarter, remove the core and dice the flesh. Heat 2 tbsp olive oil in a frying pan and cook the fennel and 2 garlic cloves, chopped, over a medium heat, just until the fennel stops tasting raw but isn't yet soft. Tip into a bowl and add a 50g can anchovies, drained and chopped, 1½ tbsp finely chopped mint leaves, 2 tbsp capers, rinsed, 2 tsp balsamic vinegar, pepper and 6 tbsp extra virgin olive oil. Stir.

Fish pie with leek mash

Everyone needs a recipe for fish pie, and it doesn't have to be expensive. You can use cheap fish – such as pollack – and replace the prawns with more white fish (even hard-boiled eggs). Mustard and lemon help the flavour and I have my secret ingredient (don't be snobbish – try it!), but it isn't mandatory...

Serves 6

900g (2lb) skinless white fish fillets, in large chunks
425ml (15fl oz) full-fat milk
100g (3½oz) butter
50g (1¾oz) plain flour
salt and pepper
juice of ½ small lemon

3 tsp Dijon mustard
1½ tbsp Heinz salad cream (optional)
125ml (4fl oz) double cream
3 tbsp finely chopped dill or parsley
200g (7oz) cooked, peeled prawns
500g (1lb 2oz) leeks
800g (1lb 12oz) floury potatoes, in chunks

1 Put the fish into a sauté pan and pour on the milk. Bring to simmering point and poach for about 3 minutes. Remove the fish with a slotted spoon and set both it and the milk aside.

2 Melt 50g (1¾oz) of the butter in a saucepan and add the flour. Stir, then remove from the heat and gradually add the milk a little at a time, beating well after each addition to keep the mixture smooth. Return to the heat and bring to the boil, stirring. It should be very thick. Season, add the lemon juice, mustard and salad cream, if using. Reduce the heat and cook for 2 minutes. Add the cream and herbs and simmer for another minute. Taste; this needs to be well-flavoured.

3 Put the fish and prawns into a 2.4 litre (4 pint) pie dish. If there is any liquid under the fish, stir it into the sauce, or it will make watery patches in the pie. Pour the sauce over the fish and carefully mix. Taste and adjust the seasoning. Leave to cool, then refrigerate to make it easier to spread the mash on top. Preheat the oven to 200°C/400°F/gas mark 6.

4 Melt the remaining butter in a heavy saucepan and add the leeks. Turn to coat, season, add 2 tbsp water, cover and sweat over a low heat for about 15 minutes until really soft and sloppy. Add a splash of water every so often to ensure they don't burn.

5 Cook the potatoes in boiling, lightly salted water until tender, then drain. Return the potatoes to the saucepan, cover with a clean tea towel and a lid. Place over a very low heat for a couple of minutes to dry out a bit – this produces a better mash.

6 Mash the potatoes until smooth, add the leeks and their juices and season well. Spread the mash over the fish. Bake for 30 minutes, until golden and bubbling.

Gurnard on crushed potatoes with olives, parsley and lemon

Gurnard fillets are small and sweet-tasting. It is the chef's favourite to serve in place of cod or haddock, though its flakes are much smaller than those of cod, and I think it has a better flavour than haddock. It is still quite plentiful. If olives seem too strongly flavoured you can make a more subtle dish by crushing the potatoes with watercress (remove the coarse stalks). The leaves wilt slightly in the heat.

Serves 4

FOR THE POTATOES
800g (1lb 12oz) new potatoes
salt and pepper
175g (6oz) pitted black olives in olive oil
8 tbsp extra virgin olive oil, plus more
   to drizzle
juice of ½ lemon and finely grated zest of 1
2 tbsp coarsely chopped flat leaf parsley

FOR THE GURNARD
8 gurnard fillets, each weighing
   about 100g (3½oz)
4 tbsp olive oil
15g (½oz) unsalted butter
good squeeze of lemon juice

1 Boil the potatoes in salted water until tender. Drain the olives and chop coarsely. Drain the cooked potatoes and leave them in the pan in which they were cooked with a lid on, just to keep warm while you cook the fish.

2 Dry the gurnard fillets and season them all over. Heat the olive oil and butter in a nonstick frying pan and cook the fillets, flesh side down first, until pale gold and cooked through, about 2½ minutes each side. Squeeze over some lemon juice.

3 Crush the potatoes with a fork or potato masher – you just want to break them up, not mash them – and add all the other ingredients. Season and fork everything through. Serve on warm plates, with 2 fillets laid over the top of each portion of potatoes. Pour the pan juices from the fish over the fillets. Drizzle with a little more extra virgin olive oil.

Sushi any way you like it

Purists should look away now because I see no reason why you can't simply offer the elements and let your friends assemble their own sushi DIY-style. You can try to get to grips with making your sushi look beautiful with strips of nori or whatever (it's quite fun), but the main thing is you get to eat gorgeous (and cheap and healthy) food. Serve with green tea or beer.

Serves 4

FOR THE SUSHI
225g (8oz) sushi rice
55ml (2fl oz) mirin
200g (7oz) really fresh mackerel fillets
200g (7oz) really fresh wild Alaskan or
  organically farmed salmon fillet
6 nori sheets

TO SERVE
1 small cucumber, cut into batons
pickled ginger
wasabi paste
Japanese soy sauce
chopped spring onions

1 Wash the rice really well in a sieve. Put into a saucepan and pour over 600ml (1 pint) water. Bring to the boil, then reduce the heat and simmer for about 25 minutes. The water should have been absorbed. Remove from the heat, cover and leave to stand for 10 minutes.

2 Tip the rice on to a tray and spread it out so that it can cool down. Sprinkle on the mirin. The rice has to get completely cool before you can serve it.

3 Cut the mackerel and salmon into strips about the length of your little finger.

4 Serve the rice in a bowl and the fish on a platter with the nori and all the accompaniments in little bowls. Let everyone help themselves.

Moroccan fish cakes, minted cucumber salad and hot sauce

Fish cakes are good when you need to stretch fish. This recipe turns cheaper white fish into something exotic, not unlike Thai fish cakes in texture, but with different spices. The sauce does have one expensive ingredient – saffron – but you use only a pinch and can leave it out. The sauce is worth making for plain grilled or roast fish, too.

Serves 6

FOR THE HOT SAUCE
2 tbsp olive oil
2 red peppers, deseeded and sliced
1 carrot, chopped
2 shallots, chopped
1 red chilli, deseeded and sliced
¼ tsp saffron threads
50g (1¾oz) caster sugar
50ml (2fl oz) white wine vinegar

FOR THE FISH CAKES
700g (1lb 9oz) white fish, skinned and
    filleted (pollack, cod, haddock, gurnard,
    whatever is available)
3 tsp ground cumin
½ tsp dried chilli flakes

3 garlic cloves, chopped
½ preserved lemon, chopped
1 egg, lightly beaten
small handful of chopped coriander, or
    a mixture of coriander and parsley
salt and pepper
plain flour, to dust
flavourless oil (vegetable or groundnut),
    for frying

FOR THE CUCUMBER SALAD
1 large cucumber
4 tsp white wine vinegar
4 tsp caster sugar
2 tbsp olive oil
handful of chopped mint leaves

1 To make the hot sauce, heat the olive oil in a frying pan and cook the peppers, carrot, shallots and chilli until completely soft (after they get a good turn in the oil, reduce the heat, add a splash of water, cover and leave to sweat). Add the rest of the ingredients and 100ml (3½fl oz) water, cook on a low heat for 10–15 minutes, then leave to cool. Purée in a blender until you have a nice smooth mixture; set aside.

2 To make the fish cakes, put all the ingredients except the flour and oil in a food processor and pulse-blend very briefly; you just want everything to blend together, not to turn the fish into a paste. Put flour on your hands and make the mixture into little cakes. You should get 24 out of this mixture, or 4 for each serving.

3 Just before you cook the fish cakes, prepare the cucumber. Peel the cucumber, halve it lengthways and scoop out the seeds with a teaspoon. Discard the seeds. Finely slice the cucumber and mix with the vinegar, sugar, oil and mint. Season.

4 Put about 4cm (1½in) of oil in a sauté pan and heat. Cook the cakes for about 6 minutes, turning them over halfway through. (Test one by looking inside to see whether the fish in the middle has cooked.) Set on kitchen paper to soak up excess oil and sprinkle with sea salt. Serve with the sauce (either reheated or at room temperature) and the cucumber salad.

Mackerel with spiced rhubarb relish

Mackerel with rhubarb has been regarded for years as a winning combination, but I didn't know why until I made this. The relish is wonderful with all oily fish, and also with pork.

Serves 6

FOR THE RELISH
200ml (7fl oz) cider vinegar
300g (10½oz) caster sugar
2 star anise
1 globe crystallized ginger in syrup, shredded
1 small red chilli, deseeded and shredded
1 red onion, very finely sliced
350g (12oz) rhubarb, cut into short even lengths

FOR THE MACKEREL
salt and pepper
12 mackerel fillets
30g (1¼oz) unsalted butter
good squeeze of lemon juice

1 Put the vinegar and sugar in a pan and bring to the boil, stirring to help the sugar dissolve. Add the spices and simmer for 10 minutes. Add the onion and cook, simmering, for 10 minutes. The onion will soften and the mixture become thicker. Now add the rhubarb and simmer gently for 4 minutes, or until just tender. Don't overcook; you want the rhubarb pink and the pieces intact. Leave to cool. The mixture will thicken as it cools.

2 Season the mackerel on both sides and melt the butter in a nonstick frying pan. Fry the fillets, skin side down, until golden, then carefully turn and cook the other side for about 3 minutes. Squeeze over some lemon juice.

3 Serve the mackerel with the relish alongside.

ALSO TRY...

Salad of mackerel, anchovies and leeks with a soft-boiled egg Put 1 tbsp white wine vinegar, ½ tsp Dijon mustard, salt and pepper in a cup, then whisk in 8 tbsp extra virgin olive oil. Add a pinch of sugar and taste for seasoning. Cook 200g (7oz) waxy potatoes until tender. Drain and leave in the pan, covered, to keep warm. Plunge 200g (7oz) baby leeks into a large pan of boiling salted water and simmer for 5 minutes. Drain really well and season. Slice the potatoes into rounds slightly thinner than a £1 coin. Carefully toss with the leeks, 12 cured anchovies (drained), 1 tbsp finely chopped parsley and about two thirds of the dressing. Cook 4 eggs in boiling water for 4½ minutes, then plunge into cold water and leave until cool enough to shell. Score 4 large mackerel fillets (each 150g/5½oz) 4 times across their width. Season, lightly flour and shake off the excess. Heat 2 tbsp oil in a nonstick frying pan and fry the fish over medium heat for 2–3 minutes each side. Divide the salad between 4 plates and set a mackerel fillet on top. Carefully shell the eggs. Break an egg over the top of each serving so the yolk spills on to the mackerel and drizzle with the remaining dressing. Serve immediately. Serves 4.

Beetroot, celeriac and sweet smoked mackerel salad

Smoked mackerel is good for you and a little goes a long way, so it's a wise option if you are watching the pennies. I have suggested sweet smoked mackerel (you do sometimes see it), but if you can't get that, regular smoked mackerel will do.

Serves 6

FOR THE DRESSING
¾ tbsp white wine vinegar
½ tsp Dijon mustard
good pinch of caster sugar
salt and pepper
4 tbsp olive oil
2 tbsp finely chopped dill

FOR THE SALAD
500g (1lb 2oz) celeriac
juice of ½ lemon
500g (1lb 2oz) cooked beetroot
375g (13oz) sweet smoked mackerel
50g (1¾oz) watercress

1 To make the dressing, just mix everything together. Taste; it should be quite sweet, so make any adjustments necessary. Refrigerate until needed.

2 Peel the celeriac and cut the flesh into thick matchsticks. Put these immediately into a bowl of water mixed with lemon juice to prevent discolouration. Halve or quarter the beetroot, depending on size.

3 Break the fish into very large flakes, discarding the skin. Drain the celeriac and pat it dry. Toss it with the fish, watercress and most of the dressing. Add the beetroot (at the last minute, or it will stain the other ingredients) and drizzle on the remaining dressing. Serve immediately.

ALSO TRY...

Smoked mackerel with lentils, Jerusalem artichokes and mustard dressing
Make the same dressing as above but leave out the dill and use only a tiny pinch of sugar. Rinse 275g (9¾oz) green lentils (regular, Puy or Umbrian), then cover with cold water, bring to the boil and cook until tender, 20–30 minutes. Meanwhile, gently sauté ½ onion and 1 celery stick, both finely chopped, in ½ tbsp oil until soft but not coloured. Add the lentils, stir and add most of the dressing, and 1½ tbsp finely chopped flat leaf parsley then season to taste. Cook 350g (12oz) Jerusalem artichokes in boiling, salted water, to which you've added a good squeeze of lemon (to stop discolouration). Once they are tender, drain and slip off the skins. Slice into rounds, about 5mm (¼in) thick. Gently combine with the lentils. Put a mound of lentils and artichokes on each of 6 plates and top with a smoked mackerel fillet. Drizzle with the remaining dressing, add a good grind of black pepper and serve.

Roast mackerel on potatoes, lemon, garlic and thyme

Serve this in the dish in which it's been cooked.

Serves 4

900g (2lb) small waxy potatoes, halved

2 onions, cut into wedges

1 head of garlic, cloves separated

2 lemons, plus more wedges, to serve

8 thyme sprigs

salt and pepper

olive oil

4 whole mackerel, gutted

1 Preheat the oven to 200°C/400°F/gas mark 6. Put the potatoes and onions into a very broad, shallow ovenproof pan or roasting tin with the garlic. Cut 1 of the lemons into wedges and toss it in, then squeeze over the juice of the other. Add the thyme, season and pour on 8 tbsp olive oil. Turn with your hands to coat.

2 Roast for 30 minutes, then lay the mackerel on top. Drizzle with oil, season and cook for another 20 minutes. Check to see if they are cooked; if the fish are very big, they could take another 5 minutes.

ALSO TRY…

Roast mackerel with cumin and chermoula Make chermoula (see page 160). Mix ½ tbsp ground cumin with 2 tsp cayenne, salt and pepper and 4 tbsp olive oil. Rub this over 4 whole gutted mackerel, inside and outside. Put into a roasting tin or ovenproof dish and cook as above. Spoon the chermoula over and serve with couscous or Barley, Parsley and Pomegranate Salad (see page 126).

Indian-spiced mackerel with mango, coconut and chilli salad Put 75g (2½oz) desiccated coconut into a bowl and cover with boiling water. Leave for 30 minutes. Put the coconut, 1 tsp mustard seeds, 2 tsp caster sugar, salt and ½ tbsp dry sherry into a blender and whizz to a coarse paste. Layer up 2 ripe mangoes, sliced, with spoonfuls of the coconut paste, squeezing on lime juice and sprinkling with 2 red chillies, deseeded and shredded. Add a generous handful of mint leaves, torn (don't add the mint until ready to serve). Put 2 tsp coriander seeds, 2 tsp cumin seeds, 3 cloves and a 2cm (¾in) cinnamon stick into a small frying pan and toss for 2 minutes; the coriander will begin to 'pop'. Leave to cool, then grind with 4 garlic cloves, 1.5cm (¾in) fresh root ginger, peeled and finely grated, 2 tsp cayenne pepper, 2 tbsp sunflower oil and seasoning. You should have a lumpy paste. Take 4 whole gutted mackerel and make small slashes in the flesh on both sides, 2cm (¾in) apart. Rub the spice paste all over, outside and inside. Put the fish on oiled foil on a grill rack and cook for 5 minutes each side. Check they are cooked. (Roast them if you prefer, following the temperature and timings in the main recipe above.) Serve immediately with the salad.

Baked mackerel with Sicilian flavours

Mackerel, since they have an assertive taste, are good at standing up to other strong ingredients such as the classic sweet-savoury flavours so prevalent in Sicilian cooking. This is a simplified version of a Sicilian recipe which traditionally uses sardines. Coarsely chopped almonds and raisins will do just as well as pine nuts and currants.

Serves 4

1 large fennel bulb
about 6 tbsp olive oil
3 garlic cloves, finely chopped
85g (3oz) white breadcrumbs
75g (2½oz) currants
55g (2oz) pine nuts
1 tsp dried chilli flakes
small handful of flat leaf parsley,
    finely chopped

small handful of mint leaves, torn
salt and pepper
800g (1lb 12oz) mackerel fillets
juice of ½ lemon

TO SERVE
extra virgin olive oil
lemon wedges

1 Preheat the oven to 200°C/400°F/gas mark 6. Remove any tough or discoloured outer layers from the fennel. Quarter lengthways, cut the little hard core out of each piece, discard, and finely chop the rest. Heat 2 tbsp of the olive oil in a frying pan and gently sauté the fennel until just beginning to soften. Add the garlic and cook for another minute, then remove from the heat and add the breadcrumbs, currants, pine nuts, chilli, herbs and salt and pepper.

2 Layer up the mackerel in an ovenproof dish with the breadcrumb mixture, seasoning and drizzling on lemon juice and the remaining oil as you go. You should finish with a layer of breadcrumbs. Put into the oven and cook for 10 minutes.

3 Drizzle with extra virgin olive oil and serve with lemon wedges.

Baked salmon with Scandinavian cucumber

Baked salmon is the quintessential British summer dish. It is a beautiful sight –
grand and celebratory – but there are two problems. First, it can be overcooked,
so be careful with your timings. Second, as with Christmas turkey, there are always
leftovers, so I've given a raft of things to do with them on the following pages.
(I often enjoy those dishes more than the original.) I have suggested butter here as
the fat to use, but this is only if you are serving the dish warm. To serve cold, use
olive oil instead (butter will congeal).

Serves 6–8

FOR THE SALMON
1 x 2.25kg (5lb) organically farmed salmon,
   cleaned and gutted
75g (2½oz) butter, melted
salt and pepper
good fistful of parsley, chervil and
   tarragon, coarsely chopped
150ml (5fl oz) dry white wine or vermouth
juice of ½ lemon

FOR THE CUCUMBER
1 large cucumber
2 tbsp flaked sea salt
2 tbsp rice wine vinegar
3 tbsp caster sugar
2 tbsp chopped dill

1 Cut the ends from the cucumber and slice the rest into almost transparent slices.
Layer in a colander with the salt, place a plate on top and set over a bowl. Leave for
2 hours. Rinse the cucumber and pat dry. Mix with the remaining ingredients and keep
covered, in the refrigerator.

2 Preheat the oven to 220°C/425°F/gas mark 7. Wash the salmon inside and out and
pat dry. (Wash bloody bits well; they make the salmon bitter.) If you've taken it straight
from the refrigerator, leave for about 30 minutes so the chill goes off it. Melt the butter.

3 Put a large sheet of foil – big enough to enclose the salmon with room to spare – on
a baking sheet or in a large roasting tin. Brush with some butter. Season the fish inside
and out and put it on the buttered foil. Put the herbs inside, then drizzle the butter over
and inside. Pour on the wine and lemon juice. Tent the salmon with the foil (it needs
room to steam). Scrunch the edges together to make it airtight.

4 Bake for 45 minutes. It should be ready, but to check rub the skin with the tip of
a blunt knife: if it slips off easily, the salmon is done.

5 Remove the salmon from the parcel, being careful not to lose the juices. If you're
serving the fish hot, drain the juices into a pan and reheat them slightly, then pour into
a warmed sauce boat. Serve the salmon whole on a platter, or remove the skin and lift
pieces on to individual plates. Serve the cucumber alongside.

6 To serve it cold, leave the salmon to cool in the foil parcel and remove the skin
before serving.

Salmon, mango and wild rice salad with ginger and chilli

It's worth having cooked salmon around just to make this. You might not think it sounds like the perfect combination, but mango is a surprisingly good partner for salmon as long as there are Thai flavourings (chilli and ginger) in the mix. This also works with leftover chicken and pork.

Serves 6

FOR THE SALAD

100g (3½oz) wild rice
200g (7oz) brown rice
600ml (1 pint) chicken stock or water
200g (7oz) green beans, topped and halved
salt and pepper
2 smallish mangoes
400g (14oz) cooked salmon
75g (2½oz) unsalted pistachios, chopped
leaves from a small bunch of coriander,
   roughly chopped
squeeze of lemon juice

FOR THE DRESSING

1½ tbsp cider vinegar
¼ tsp Dijon mustard
1 garlic clove, crushed
1 tsp runny honey, or to taste
1 globe crystallized ginger, finely chopped,
   plus syrup from the jar
2 red chillies, deseeded and shredded
salt and pepper
3 tbsp groundnut oil
4 tbsp olive oil

1 Put the wild and brown rice into a saucepan with the stock or water. Bring to the boil, cover and cook for about 30 minutes. Wild rice never goes completely soft, but retains a nutty bite. It should absorb the stock as it cooks, but keep an eye on it to make sure the rice doesn't go dry and add a little water if you need to.

2 Cook the beans in boiling salted water until *al dente*. Drain and rinse under cold water to set the green colour. Peel the mangoes and cut off the 'cheeks' – the fleshy parts on either side of the stone. Slice these to about the thickness of a 50 pence piece. (Use the rest of the mango flesh for something else.)

3 Make the dressing by whisking all the ingredients together and stir it into the warm rice with the beans. Break the salmon into chunks and add it to the rice along with the mango, pistachios, coriander, salt and pepper and a squeeze of lemon juice (the dish can take quite a lot of salt, though it depends on whether you've used stock or water for cooking the rice). Taste everything for seasoning and adjust if you need to.

Salmon and dill pilaf

Pilafs are great vehicles for leftovers (read more about them in the chapters on grains (page 114) and roasts (page 38)). You can stir cooked buttery leeks or chopped wilted spinach into this as well and, if you have it, pour a slug of dry vermouth into the rice before adding the stock.

Serves 6

300g (10½oz) long-grain rice	salt and pepper
1 onion, finely chopped	500g (1lb 2oz) cooked salmon
25g (1oz) butter	15g (½oz) dill or parsley, finely chopped
700ml (1¼ pints) fish or chicken stock	lemon juice, to taste

1 Rinse the rice in a sieve until the water runs clear, then sauté the onion in the butter until soft but not coloured. Stir in the rice to coat the grains. When it is really glossy add the stock, season and bring to the boil with the lid off. In 4–7 minutes you will barely be able to see the liquid and the surface will seem 'pitted' with holes. Now reduce the heat, cover and leave to cook (about another 15–20 minutes, but keep checking). The last little bit of liquid will be absorbed during this time and the rice will steam. Don't stir or it will spoil the texture.

2 When the rice has about 4 minutes of cooking time left, gently put the salmon on top and replace the lid. The salmon will warm through in the steam.

3 Gently fork the rice and salmon together with your chosen herb. Add a good squeeze of lemon juice and taste for seasoning. You should end up with separate, light grains and warm salmon.

ALSO TRY...

Making this with smoked haddock or smoked cod.

Simple kedgeree Proceed as above but use 50g (1¾oz) butter to sauté the chopped onion and fry some spices (½ tsp ground cinnamon, ground seeds from 5 cardamom pods, ½ tsp ground turmeric and 1 tsp curry powder) for 2 minutes along with the onion once it has softened. Use cooked salmon or cooked undyed smoked haddock (or a mixture). Add quartered hard-boiled eggs, fried onion slices (cut finely and fry until golden brown in groundnut or sunflower oil) and chopped coriander (omit the dill or parsley). Stir in 1–2 tbsp cream if you have it just before serving and make sure the dish is well seasoned.

Salmon hash

There are lots of variations on the hash theme, all using leftovers, and, in my opinion, quite often you end up with something better than the original dish. They are all basically fry-ups, and this is rather more healthy than most. You don't need to use any smoked salmon – you can use all fresh cooked salmon – but it is lovely, and I always think those little packs of inexpensive smoked salmon trimmings are crying out to be used.

Serves 4

25g (1oz) unsalted butter
½ tbsp oil
1 onion, finely chopped
400g (14oz) cooked potatoes, in chunks
350g (12oz) cooked salmon and smoked salmon trimmings (in a 2:1 ratio)

250g (9oz) spinach leaves, coarse stalks discarded and shredded
salt and pepper
squeeze of lemon juice
small bunch flat leaf parsley or dill, finely chopped

1 Heat the butter and oil in a large frying pan and add the onion and potatoes. Fry over a medium heat until the onion is soft and both potatoes and onion are golden. The potatoes will be brown in places.

2 Flake the cooked salmon into large chunks, discarding the skin (and look out for the bones too) and stir this in along with the smoked salmon and spinach. Stir everything around gently and allow the spinach to wilt a little and the salmon to heat through.

3 Season to taste, add the lemon juice and your chosen herb. If you want to smarten this dish up, serve with creamy mustard sauce (see page 155).

ALSO TRY...

Making the above with undyed smoked haddock or a mixture of haddock (or pollack) and smoked haddock.

Salmon on lentils with herb relish

Salmon fillets – like chops – are one of the things we turn to most often for an easy meal. Farmed organic fillets are reasonably inexpensive, healthy, and there's never any waste. This recipe is also lovely made with gurnard (cook as on page 135).

Serves 4

FOR THE LENTILS

2 tbsp olive oil
½ small onion, finely chopped
1 celery stick, diced
1 small carrot, diced
150g (5½oz) Puy lentils
2 thyme sprigs
275ml (9½fl oz) chicken stock or water
salt and pepper
squeeze of lemon juice
extra virgin olive oil

FOR THE HERB RELISH

50g (1¾oz) herb leaves (flat leaf parsley,
    basil, mint and chives)
1½ tbsp capers, rinsed
2 garlic cloves, very finely chopped
juice of 1 lemon
7½ tbsp extra virgin olive oil

FOR THE SALMON

30g (1¼oz) unsalted butter
1 tbsp groundnut oil
4 x 175g (6oz) salmon fillets

1 To make the lentils, heat the oil in a saucepan and gently cook the onion, celery and carrot until softening. Stir in the lentils, thyme and stock. Season with pepper. Bring to the boil, reduce to a simmer and cook for 15–20 minutes. Watch carefully; the lentils can collapse very quickly.

2 Meanwhile, chop the herbs very finely and mix with the other relish ingredients.

3 Heat the butter and oil for the salmon in a large frying pan. Season the fish on both sides and cook over a medium heat, flesh down, for 1½–2 minutes, until golden. Turn and cook for 1½–2 minutes. Reduce the heat, cover and cook until done but still moist.

4 When the lentils are cooked, add the lemon juice and a good slug of extra virgin olive oil and taste for seasoning. Put some lentils on each plate and top with salmon and a good spoonful of relish.

ALSO TRY...

Crispy-skinned salmon with Vietnamese caramel sauce Heat ½ tbsp groundnut oil and sauté 2.5cm (1in) fresh root ginger, peeled and finely chopped, and 2 garlic cloves, chopped, until soft. Add 3 tbsp light soy sauce and 100g (3½oz) light brown sugar. Stir to melt and cook over a high heat until you smell caramel. Immediately add 1½ tbsp fish sauce and 2 tbsp water. It will splutter, so take care. Add 2 tsp tamarind paste and the juice of ½ lime and stir. Taste; it should be syrupy and intense. You may want another splash of water. Season 4 salmon fillets and heat 2 tbsp groundnut oil until hot. Put the salmon in skin side down, and cook for 3 minutes until crispy. Turn and cook for 2–3 minutes, until golden. Check for doneness on the flesh side with a fine, sharp knife. Serve with the warm sauce, boiled rice and stir-fried greens.

Fillet of salmon with sweet-sour beetroot and dill crème fraîche

Scandinavia is the perfect place to look for salmon recipes as so much of it is eaten there. Beetroot is an excellent partner and, after years in the wilderness, seems to be making a comeback and rightly so, as it's both inexpensive and gorgeous.

Serves 6

FOR THE DILL CRÈME FRAÎCHE
200g (7oz) crème fraîche
2 tbsp grain mustard
1½ tbsp chopped dill

FOR THE BEETROOT
500g (1lb 2oz) cooked beetroot
50g (1¾oz) unsalted butter
½ tbsp groundnut oil
2 red onions, very finely sliced

2 tbsp caster sugar
1½ tbsp red wine vinegar
salt and pepper

FOR THE SALMON
30g (1¼oz) unsalted butter
1 tbsp oil (sunflower, groundnut or olive)
6 x 175g (6oz) salmon fillets
good squeeze of lemon juice

1 To make the dill crème fraîche, simply mix the crème fraîche, mustard and dill together. Refrigerate until you need it.

2 If you have vacuum-packed cooked beetroot, take it out of the packet and pat dry with kitchen paper. Cut each globe into quarters or, if they are small, halves. Set aside.

3 Heat the butter and oil in a frying pan and cook the onions over a medium heat until completely soft. Add the beetroot and increase the heat. Cook for 2 minutes, then add the sugar and stir until the mixture is beginning to caramelize. Add the vinegar and let it bubble. Season and taste for sweet-sour balance; you may want more sugar or vinegar. Set aside; you can reheat the beetroot before serving or serve at room temperature.

4 Heat the butter and oil in a large frying pan. Season the salmon on both sides and cook over medium heat, flesh side down, for 1½–2 minutes or until golden. Turn over and cook for 1½–2 minutes. Reduce the heat, cover and cook until done but still moist. (How long this takes depends on the fillets' thickness.) Squeeze on some lemon juice.

5 Serve the salmon with beetroot and dill crème fraîche. Boiled new potatoes are the obvious accompaniment, but I also love it with a warm barley salad (see page 126).

ALSO TRY...

Salmon with mushrooms, melted butter and fresh horseradish Cook the salmon as above. Meanwhile, melt 50g (1¾oz) butter and briskly cook 250g (9oz) mushrooms (mixed wild and cultivated), sliced, until well coloured. Season, add a squeeze of lemon juice and ½ tbsp finely chopped parsley. Melt 50g (1¾oz) butter. Put a salmon fillet on each of 4 plates, spoon the mushrooms around, drizzle with butter, sprinkle with 75g (2½oz) fresh horseradish, grated, and serve.

Smoked haddock stovie with fried eggs and mustard sauce

A combination of fish cakes and bubble and squeak and just the kind of dish I always want for Saturday night supper: British, substantial, soothing. Perfect for tucking into in front of the telly. You only need a fork.

Serves 4

FOR THE SAUCE
275ml (9½fl oz) double cream
1½ tbsp grain mustard
generous squeeze of lemon juice
salt and pepper

FOR THE STOVIES AND EGGS
2 large baking potatoes
250g (9oz) undyed smoked haddock
200ml (7fl oz) milk

2 large leeks, cut into chunks and washed really well
3 tsp grated horseradish (or horseradish cream)
2 tbsp finely chopped flat leaf parsley
groundnut or sunflower oil, for frying
25g (1oz) butter
4 eggs

1 Make the sauce first so you just have to reheat it before serving. Heat the cream until boiling, then boil for about 4 minutes to reduce. Add the mustard, lemon juice and salt and pepper. The sauce will thicken because of the lemon. Taste for seasoning.

2 Preheat the oven to 200°C/400°F/gas mark 6. Bake the potatoes for about 50 minutes, or until just tender (not falling apart; they'll be cooked further).

3 Put the haddock into a saucepan or sauté pan and cover with the milk. Bring to the boil, then immediately reduce the heat to very low. Cover and poach for 4–5 minutes. Once the fish is cool enough to handle, remove from the pan, break into large flakes, discarding the skin and any little bones. (You could use the poaching milk to make a parsley sauce, see page 196).

4 Cook the leeks in boiling salted water for 5–6 minutes, until tender. Drain really well, then transfer to a bowl. Remove and discard the skin from the potato, then coarsely chop the flesh and add to the leeks with the haddock, horseradish and parsley. Season really well and mix everything together.

5 Heat 1 tbsp oil and all the butter in a large nonstick frying pan. Add the mixture and flatten into a large pancake. Cook for about 6 minutes over a medium heat, then turn it over by inverting it on to a plate and then sliding it back into the pan. Cook for another 4–5 minutes, until the bottom is golden and has a good crust. While the stovie is in the last stages of cooking, fry the eggs in more oil.

6 Reheat the sauce. Cut the stovie into 4 wedges and serve each topped with a fried egg and a generous drizzle of sauce.

Smoked haddock brandade with spinach and poached egg

This is a British version of the French classic made with salt cod. It makes a little bit of smoked fish go a long way. If you aren't a great egg poacher, serve with a soft-boiled egg instead. Take a look at Salad of Mackerel, Anchovies and Leeks with a Soft-boiled Egg (see page 140) for how to do that.

Serves 4

FOR THE BRANDADE
1 baking potato, about 200g (7oz)
200g (7oz) undyed smoked haddock
300ml (½ pint) milk
2 garlic cloves, roughly chopped
1 large bay leaf
4 tbsp double cream
2 tbsp extra virgin olive oil
juice of ½ lemon
25g (1oz) Parmesan cheese, grated
4 large eggs

salt and pepper
200g (7oz) young spinach leaves

FOR THE VINAIGRETTE
½ tsp Dijon mustard
pinch of caster sugar
1 tbsp white wine vinegar
3½ tbsp extra virgin olive oil

TO SERVE
extra virgin olive oil
couple of pinches of cayenne pepper

1 Bake or boil the potato (in its skin) until tender. Meanwhile, make the vinaigrette by mixing the mustard, sugar and vinegar with salt and pepper in a cup and whisking in the olive oil. When the potato is ready, halve it and scoop the flesh into a large bowl. Mash with a fork and season.

2 Put the haddock in a pan and cover with the milk. Add the garlic and bay leaf. Bring to the boil, then immediately reduce the heat and poach – covered – for about 4 minutes, or until just firm. Strain off the milk (discard the flavourings) and reserve. Break the fish into fine flakes, discarding the skin and checking for bones as you go.

3 Mash the fish with the potato until well blended, then beat in about 5 tbsp of the reserved milk, the cream and extra virgin oil using a wooden spoon. Add the lemon juice and Parmesan. Check the seasoning. Keep the brandade mixture warm while you poach the 4 eggs.

4 Dress the spinach with the vinaigrette and divide between 4 plates. Top with the brandade and a poached egg. Sprinkle with a little extra virgin olive oil and cayenne and serve.

Genoese squid with potatoes

If you're a squid enthusiast you are in luck, as it's cheap and plentiful. The smell of it frying reminds me so much of the sea and sand that cooking it always makes me feel as though I'm on holiday. Portugal, Spain, Greece…it reeks of hot sun and blue skies, which makes it very cheering to eat. Squid must be cooked with care, though, to avoid a plateful of rubber. The rule of thumb is to cook it quickly at a very high heat, or slowly over a gentle one. Both approaches produce flesh which is quite melting. Your fishmonger can clean and prepare squid for you.

Serves 4

750g (1lb 10oz) squid, cleaned
550g (1lb 4oz) waxy potatoes
5 tbsp olive oil
4 garlic cloves, chopped
350ml (12fl oz) dry white wine

leaves from 2 oregano or marjoram sprigs
2½ tbsp chopped flat leaf parsley
400g can tomatoes (ideally cherry) in thick juice
salt and pepper
extra virgin olive oil, to serve

1 Wash the squid and check whether there's any gunge inside the bodies. If there is, pull it out and discard. Cut the bodies into 2.5cm (1in) thick rings. Cut the knobbly bit off the bottom of each tentacle and slice the wings into 2 or 3, depending on size. Cut the tentacles in half if they're large. Rinse in a sieve and dry well with kitchen paper.

2 If the potatoes have thin skins you don't need to peel them; just wash well and cut into 4cm (1½in) thick slices.

3 Heat the olive oil in a saucepan or sauté pan. When it's really hot, add the squid and garlic. Turn these over in the hot oil, frying briskly for about a minute. Add the wine, oregano, 1½ tbsp of the parsley and the tomatoes. Season, cover, reduce the heat and simmer for 30 minutes.

4 Add the potatoes, season again and cover. Cook on low heat for about 30 minutes, until the potatoes are tender. Taste for seasoning, scatter with the remaining parsley and serve. A little extra virgin olive oil drizzled over just finishes it off.

ALSO TRY…

Braised squid with fennel Make as above but, before you fry the squid, heat half the olive oil and fry 1 small onion, finely chopped, for a few minutes. Add 1 large fennel bulb, trimmed, cored and finely sliced lengthways, and sauté until the fennel is golden and the onion soft. Add 3 cloves garlic, finely chopped, and cook for another couple of minutes. Put the remaining oil in another pan and sauté the squid very fast over high heat. Add the squid to the onion and fennel, then add the wine and tomatoes as above. Add 2 tbsp chopped parsley. Cook as above, adding only 400g (14oz) potatoes. Stir in another 2 tbsp chopped parsley before serving. You could also add a small handful of black olives in the last 5 minutes.

Squid, chorizo and bean stew with chilli and coriander

This started off one night as a stir-fry, and sheer hunger (that's never going to be enough, I thought as I looked at the pan) caused it to grow. It features the irresistible Iberian combination of pork and seafood.

Serves 6

250g (9oz) chorizo
900g (2lb) squid, cleaned
olive oil
1 large onion, in crescent moon-shaped slices
500g (1lb 2oz) waxy potatoes, cubed
2 red chillies, deseeded and chopped
4 garlic cloves, crushed
8 large plum tomatoes, cut into wedges

salt and pepper
250g (9oz) cooked cannellini or haricot beans, rinsed
500ml (18fl oz) light chicken, fish or vegetable stock
juice of ½ lemon
generous bunch of fresh coriander, roughly chopped

1 Pull the skin from the chorizo and cut into chunks. Wash and prepare the squid as for Genoese Squid, opposite.

2 Heat 2 tbsp olive oil in a large saucepan and sauté the onion and potatoes until the latter are golden and the onion is soft. Add the chilli and garlic and sauté for another minute. Add the tomatoes, season and sauté for 3 minutes.

3 Heat 2 tbsp olive oil in another frying pan and sauté the chorizo until coloured. Add to the stew with the beans, then the stock. Bring to the boil, reduce the heat and simmer for 5 minutes. Remove from the heat.

4 Meanwhile, heat 2 tbsp olive oil in a frying pan and sauté the squid in batches, over a high heat, for 1 minute. Season, squeeze over a little lemon juice and add to the stew.

5 Stir the stew, heat it through, add the remaining lemon juice, check the seasoning and stir in the coriander. Serve in flat soup plates with good coarse country bread.

ALSO TRY...

Hot stir-fried squid It's amazing that something this delicious – and with multi-dimensional flavours – is this quick to make. Heat 1 tbsp groundnut oil in a wok and add 2 garlic cloves, finely sliced, 1cm (½in) fresh root ginger, peeled and finely chopped, 2 lemon grass stalks (optional), chopped, and 1 red chilli, deseeded and shredded. Cook for 1 minute. Add 900g (2lb) cleaned squid, prepared as on page 158. It's very important that it is dry or it won't fry properly. Cook over a very high heat for 1 minute. Reduce the heat, add 4 spring onions, diagonally sliced, 1–2 tsp caster sugar and 1 tbsp dry sherry. Cook for another minute, then serve on warmed plates with rice and stir-fried greens. Serves 4.

Griddled squid with chickpeas, peppers and chermoula

Despite relatively cheap ingredients – squid and chickpeas – this dish has a certain magnificence. The sight of griddled squid, in all its tentacled loveliness, and the green of chermoula (a Moroccan herb and spice blend) against the red of roast peppers laid out on a big platter is very impressive. And then there's the aroma… Be sure to provide plenty of lime wedges on the side.

Serves 8

FOR THE SQUID

5 red peppers, halved and deseeded
olive oil
salt and pepper
2 x 400g cans chickpeas,
   drained and rinsed
1kg (2lb 4oz) squid, cleaned
½ lime

FOR THE CHERMOULA

juice of ½ lime
1 red chilli, deseeded and very
   finely sliced
8 tbsp extra virgin olive oil
½ tsp ground cumin
½ tsp hot smoked paprika
20g (¾oz) coriander, chopped
10g (¼oz) flat leaf parsley, chopped

1 Preheat the oven to 180°C/350°F/gas mark 4. Brush the peppers with olive oil, season and put into a roasting tin. Cook for about 35 minutes, depending on size. They should be completely tender and slightly blistered. I don't skin them as I like the slightly charred skin. Slice in broad strips once cool enough to handle.

2 To make the chermoula, just mix everything together. Mix the peppers and the chickpeas with the chermoula in a broad, shallow bowl.

3 Cut the little wings from the squid and put them aside with the tentacles. Cut the bodies down one side so they open out. If your squid are very big, halve the main body lengthways. Clean the inside (there's always a little bit of gunk). Score the flesh on the inside and dry well on kitchen paper. Put in a bowl with enough oil just to moisten the outside and heat a griddle pan until very, very hot.

4 Season the squid and cook it on both sides on the griddle pan in batches. It needs only about 20 seconds on each side. The squid will turn opaque and should have lovely griddle marks and a really good golden colour. I like to squeeze lime over it as soon as it is ready. Toss the cooked squid with the other ingredients in the bowl. Taste everything for seasoning. You can serve this either now while the squid is hot, or at room temperature.

Thai mussels with coconut, chilli and lime

Serving mussels to friends creates a kind of holiday feeling. It's the fact that you eat them with your hands, actively digging out the food, and you get messy. Before long the table is littered with shells (what beautiful debris – the bluish wash inside looks as if it were applied by the most careful watercolourist), squeezed lemon wedges and crumpled napkins. Another bottle of wine is opened and people decide to stay 'just a bit longer'. Food that has this profound an effect is definitely worth cooking. Mussels are also good for you, cheap and sustainable. What more could you want? This dish is utterly addictive.

Serves 4

FOR THE MUSSELS
2kg (4lb 8oz) mussels
1½ tbsp groundnut oil
1 onion, finely chopped
2 garlic cloves, finely chopped
2cm (¾in) square fresh root ginger, peeled and finely chopped
2 red chillies, deseeded and shredded
2 x 400ml cans coconut milk

juice of 1 lime
½ tbsp soft light brown sugar
2 kaffir lime leaves, cut into strips (or grated zest of 1 lime)

TO SERVE
2 kaffir lime leaves, cut into strips (or grated zest of 1 lime)
4 tbsp roughly chopped coriander
½ red chilli, deseeded and shredded

1 Wash the mussels really well, scrubbing off barnacles and removing any 'beards'. Tap each on the side of the sink. If it doesn't close, chuck it away. Rinse the mussels well.

2 Heat the oil in a large saucepan. Add the onion, garlic, ginger and chillies. Cook over a medium heat until the onion is soft and very pale gold. Add the coconut milk, lime juice, sugar and lime leaves. Bring to just under the boil, then add the mussels.

3 Cover and cook for 4 minutes or until the mussels have opened, shaking the pan a couple of times. Throw away any which haven't opened (and remind your diners to do the same).

4 To serve, stir, then throw the lime leaves, coriander and chilli on top.

ALSO TRY...

Spanish mussels with cider and chorizo Prepare 2kg (4lb 8oz) mussels as above. Heat 3 tbsp olive oil in a large pan and sauté 200g (7oz) chorizo (skinned and cut into chunks) and 2 onions, finely chopped, until slightly coloured and the onions have softened. Add 2 garlic cloves, finely chopped, and cook for 2 minutes to soften. Throw in the mussels, 500ml (18fl oz) dry cider and pepper and cover. Bring to the boil, reduce the heat to medium and leave the mussels to steam open, about 4 minutes. Throw away any that haven't opened (or tell your diners to do so), stir in 3 tbsp finely chopped parsley and serve immediately in soup plates.

Choice cuts

When I was growing up – and certainly when my parents were – we cooked cuts of meat that children (and most adults) now would barely recognize. Those joints – shin of beef, pork cheeks, brisket – have lots of connective tissue which dissolves during slow cooking. They require time and care to cook to tenderness, but your reward is meat that practically falls apart as you stick your fork in it. They provide the sweetest, most melt-in-the-mouth kind of eating.

It seems crazy that many of these bargain cuts are now routinely used in inferior, commercially made pies, sausages and pet food. These days we're all for grilling, searing and flash-frying; many people don't know how to cook any other way. We want food instantly and this requires leaner, more expensive meat. Trying old-fashioned cuts – I call them 'choice' because they often provide better eating – means slower cooking, making a bit more effort and acquiring some new knowledge.

I have always been careful with the food budget. Fillet or sirloin of beef, for example, is rarely on the menu in my house and I have routinely cooked less expensive cuts, but over the last few years I've cooked them even more. A workshop I attended on old-fashioned cuts not only convinced me that I would eat more enjoyably if I explored them, but also showed me that it's the only sane way to eat, as you use the whole beast. What kind of society takes the leanest meat from an animal and – because the rest of the carcass is too much trouble to cook or, on the part of the retailer, make money from – turns it into substandard sausages and pet food?

Since I have gone back to the cuts of my childhood I have saved money – but it has also changed the feel of my house. Beef shin has simmered away on the cooker, we've had pot after pot of sticky oxtail, and scrag end of lamb has once again been on my shopping list. The kitchen smells very like my mother's and my grandmother's. There is proper cooking going on and I have had to use more imagination.

I am not saying you shouldn't buy expensive cuts – in fact there's a whole chapter on them at the beginning of this book – but cooking them sometimes means turning to cheaper cuts at other times. It's a balance. And it does make for more satisfying eating.

You may well feel daunted by my exhortations to try old-fashioned cuts. It's scary to ask a butcher for something with which you're unfamiliar. But persist. Get to know your butcher and ask him questions. There is real pleasure in turning cheaper cuts into great food. You get a kick out of knowing you haven't simply cooked 'the best' of what's available, but that you have made the best of what's available. You know that saying, 'You can't make a silk purse out of a sow's ear'? It ain't true.

Buying unusual cuts

The majority of large supermarkets don't buy whole animals (only the parts we most use), so for more unusual cuts you need to find a good butcher.

In the past, your mum or granny cultivated a butcher, visited regularly, and relied on him to supply good meat, track down special orders and issue sound advice. For cooking old-fashioned cuts, a relationship with a good butcher is vital. At first you may find he doesn't have what you are looking for (of course, he stocks what he can sell), but I bet he'll be pleased you are interested and will be glad to source cuts for you.

The alternative is to buy directly from good meat producers and farm shops. Many sell online. And there's something very rewarding about connecting with the people who produce the food you eat.

Beef choice cuts

SHIN The smell of a beefy pot of shin simmering on the hob takes me back to when I was nine years old. Shin comes from the top of the foreleg and is great value. It can be cooked on the bone in a soup or stew, cut in cross sections and cooked like osso bucco with wine, onions and tomatoes, or cut off the bone and braised. My mum would simmer it for a few hours with onions, carrots and celery and use the stock as the basis for a soup or stew, leaving the meat to cool before removing it from the bone.

BRISKET Quite fatty as it comes from the belly, but full of flavour and very good for salting, so you can use it for the salt beef in this chapter.

MINCED BEEF Ready-minced beef is pretty finely ground (especially supermarket stuff). Ask your butcher to grind it more coarsely. Use minced skirt, topside or silverside for burgers and minced stewing cuts for pies or sauces.

SILVERSIDE From the back of the thigh, silverside is a pair of overlapping muscles and can be tough. Some people roast it (it's often wrapped in fat, tied and sold as a roasting joint), but it doesn't work well. It takes reasonably well to slow pot roasting. I rarely cook it except minced or slowly braised.

TOPSIDE Looks similar to silverside, but is much more successful as a cheap roast (well, cheaper than sirloin) and good for pot roasting, too. It is the long, inner muscle of the thigh.

BRAISING BEEF What is called 'braising steak' usually comes from the leg top. You can buy it in slices (my granny braised them with carrots and onions), but it's more often cut into chunks for braising and stewing. 'Chuck steak' is also sold for this purpose. It comes from the blade bone around the shoulder. Shin (see above) can also be taken off the bone and braised or stewed.

SKIRT A strange-looking cut: a big steak with long fibres which look pleated, hence the name. The biggest piece comes from inside the flank, another from the inner

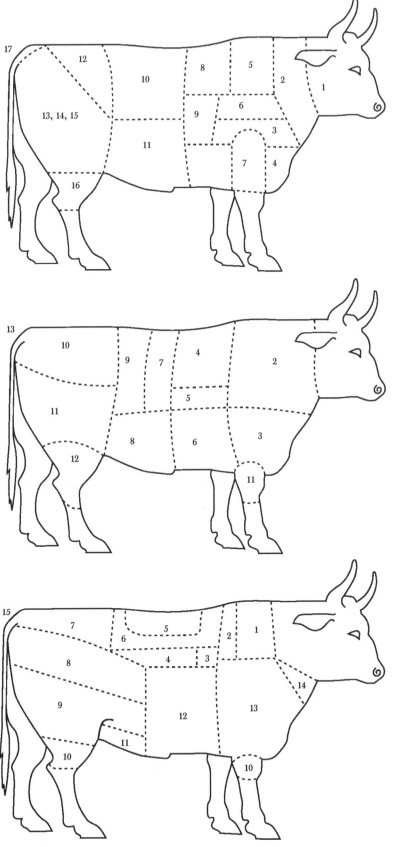

UK BEEF CUTS

1 Cheek
2 Neck/Clod/Stewing steak
3 Leg top (braising steak)
4 Brisket
5 Rolled backrib
6 Chuck steak
7 Shin
8 Rib
9 Forequarter flank, short ribs
10 Sirloin: fillet and fillet steak, T-bone steak, wing rib, sirloin roast, sirloin steak
11 Skirt
12 Rump steak
13 Top rump
14 Silverside
15 Topside
16 Leg
17 Oxtail

US BEEF CUTS

1 Cheek
2 Chuck
3 Brisket
4 Rib
5 Short rib
6 Plate/Skirt
7 Short loin
8 Flank
9 Sirloin
10 Rump
11 Round
12 Shank
13 Oxtail

FRENCH BEEF CUTS

1 Côte couvert (rolled rib)
2 Entrecôte (steak)
3 Châteaubriand (thick end)
4 Filet (includes Châteaubriand)
5 Aloyau (loin)
6 Contrefilet or faux filet (sirloin)
7 Aiguillette (rump)
8 Semelle (topside)
9 Tranche (silverside)
10 Jarret (shin)
11 Onglet and hampe (skirt)
12 Plat de côte (plate)
13 Boule de macreuse (shoulder)
14 Paleron (neck)
15 Queue de boeuf (oxtail)

thigh. It is lean but very tasty when cooked long and slow. It can also be beaten and marinated to break down the fibres and tenderize, then cooked more quickly.

OXTAIL No cut of beef makes your mouth as sticky with melting meat as oxtail. There's no mistaking the cut – it looks like a tail – and it is usually cut into short lengths to make it easier to deal with. It needs to be cooked gently and slowly (at least 3 hours), but you're rewarded with the tenderest meat that is beautifully rich.

BEEF CHEEKS Cheeks of beef are dark in colour, and require even longer gentle cooking than pigs' cheeks. Braise them with beer, shallots and carrots, with pickled walnuts, or with Chinese flavourings. Other beef stews will seem pale in comparison.

Pork choice cuts

SHOULDER A whole pork shoulder is massive – too big for most gatherings as it feeds about 20 – but you can buy part of one. It makes a most delicious meal (I actually prefer it to belly) as it becomes so soft you can almost spoon it. Despite its being cheap there is something very feast-like and celebratory about a shoulder. It can take strong flavours such as mustard and spices. Roast it either on or off the bone. Cut into cubes, shoulder is what is usually sold for braising.

BELLY The sound says it all. 'Belly' is soft and yielding, fatty and succulent. But pork belly has come into vogue only recently, the result of chefs turning to more old-fashioned cuts. Formerly, in Britain at least, it was the kind of cut you bought only if you were going to make your own pâté or terrines. Commercially, it was mostly used for streaky bacon and pancetta. Now it is almost a cliché of gastropub menus and at last, thankfully, it has made its way into our home kitchens. The bit at the head end, called the thick end, is the best bit for roasting and produces the crispiest crackling, but there is much more to it than roasting, something the Chinese know well. You barely need teeth to eat pork belly when it has been cut into chunks and braised slowly – it simply dissolves in your mouth. In composite dishes with beans, like French cassoulet or American Boston baked beans, chunks of pork belly don't just provide the meat element but flavour the cooking liquid and the beans too, and exude fat which creates an unctuous texture. And soft but crispy chunks are even good in salads.

PORK LEG Sold either on the bone or boned and rolled, leg of pork can be roasted, though it's a lean cut so needs a good layer of fat on it if it isn't to dry out. (I certainly prefer shoulder or belly.) It's best suited to slow roasting, but whack up the heat at the end for good crackling. The leg can also be cubed and used for braised dishes.

HOCK I usually cook this only in its cured form, when it is called ham hock or knuckle of bacon. It looks a bit like a small lamb's shank and is unappealing in appearance when cooked – it is covered in gelatinous skin and fat – but the flesh is soft and moist with a rich, hammy flavour. You just have to take the meat off the bone and discard the fat. It's a great plateful to have with parsley or mustard sauce, piccalilli or beetroot and horseradish. It's also a good cut to use for making terrines, the best, most chunky ham sandwiches, and for tossing into warm salads (with bitter

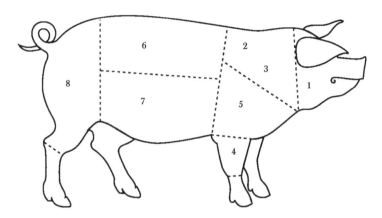

UK PORK CUTS

1 Cheek
2 Spare rib
3 Shoulder
4 Hock
5 Hand and Hock
6 Loin: rack of pork, loin chop, tenderloin (pork fillet), escalope, chump chop
7 Belly, rack of spare ribs
8 Leg

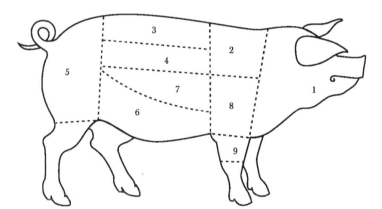

US PORK CUTS

1 Cheek
2 Shoulder
3 Loin
4 Tenderloin
5 Leg
6 Belly
7 Sparerib
8 Picnic shoulder
9 Hock

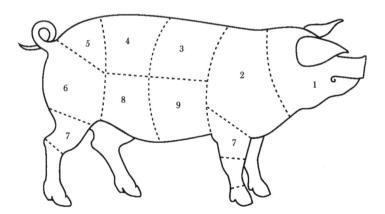

FRENCH PORK CUTS

1 Cheek
2 Echine (shoulder)
3 Carré (spare rib)
4 Filet (loin)
5 Pointe (tenderloin)
6 Jambon (leg)
7 Jambonneau (hock)
8 Poitrine (belly)
9 Plat de côte (forequarter flank)

leaves or lentils and a punchy mustardy vinaigrette), and provides great stock for soup (it makes particularly good lentil and bean soups). If you are using it for stock make sure it isn't too salty; sometimes it can be unusable, or needs watering down.

SPARE RIBS Great to get your teeth round; I always forget just how satisfying spare ribs are. I have tended to keep them for barbecue weather or Halloween, but don't leave them just for special times of the year – pork ribs are uniquely suited to both cold and warm weather eating and are terrific value for money. The cut is made up of the trimmed ribs from inside the belly and they usually come as a rack of five or six. Marinate spare ribs in Eastern flavours (a sweet-and-sour glaze) and bake in the oven, protecting your roasting tin with foil. They're always a huge hit with children.

CHEEKS Pig cheeks: that's exactly what they are and they come in the most beautiful little medallions about the size of the fleshy bit of your palm. Braise them with Chinese spices (they're great with star anise, orange and ginger) or with wild mushrooms and onions. They can be hard to track down. Butchers often say they can buy them only in large quantities and, since not many people know about them let alone cook them, they are reluctant to buy large bags which they can't sell. Waitrose, though, has been selling them in their Forgotten Cuts range (sadly available only in certain stores).

Lamb choice cuts

SHANK The vogue for 'peasant food' has driven up the price of lamb shanks, which used to be relatively cheap. A smallish shank serves one person and, braised, they make a warming, succulent dish. Because they are sweet, shanks take well to strong flavours such as eastern ingredients (see Vietnamese Lamb Shanks, page 180).

SHOULDER Many people prefer this fantastic cut to a leg of lamb. It has sweet, melting flesh and is particularly good with sharp, salty ingredients (anchovies and mustard, or Middle Eastern preserved lemons, are all wonderful). I usually cook it boned and stuffed, when you can either roll and tie it – the fat is then within the joint and lubricates the meat as it cooks – or cook it '*en ballon*', where the meat is pulled up round the stuffing to make a ball-shaped parcel (so you can use more stuffing).

MIDDLE NECK AND SCRAG END Scrag end was the only meat I cooked at university. I used it to make navarin of lamb, braising it slowly with tomatoes, carrot and swede before adding peas or beans, and for Irish stew. The only laborious thing is removing the meat from the bones after cooking before returning it to the pot.

MINCED LAMB As with minced beef, ask your butcher to grind this coarsely. It doesn't have to be lean; the fat gives flavour and keeps dishes such as kofta (meatballs) moist and tender. There's a wealth of great Middle Eastern dishes (some in this chapter) to be made with minced lamb.

BREAST Some cooks think this an underrated cut, but I find it so fatty that I rarely cook it. It can be stuffed and slowly pot roasted, but I prefer to roast it flat, cut it up and use it in slow-cooked bean dishes, such as Cassoulet (see page 172).

UK LAMB CUTS

1 Scrag end
2 Neck fillet/Middle neck
3 Shoulder
4 Rack of lamb (best end of neck)
5 Loin, loin chop
4 & 5 Saddle
6 Breast
7 Chump, chump chop
8 Leg
9 Shank

US LAMB CUTS

1 Neck
2 Shoulder
3 Rib
4 Saddle
5 Loin
6 Leg
7 Hind shank
8 Breast
9 Fore shank

FRENCH LAMB CUTS

1 Collet (scrag end)
2 Epaule (shoulder)
3 Carré (rack and best end of neck)
4 Careé de côtes premières (cutlets)
5 Filet (loin)
6 Selle (saddle)
7 Gigot (leg)
8 Gigot d'agneau (shank)
9 Poitrine (breast)

Cassoulet

I often make this particularly inexpensive version of cassoulet without duck confit, but always include breast of lamb. It is a cheap cut I find difficult to use – it's so fatty – except in dishes where that fat melts to flavour and season other cheap ingredients (such as beans). Then it's perfect.

Serves 10

900g (2lb) dried haricot beans
250g (9oz) bacon, in one piece
1 onion, studded with 6 cloves
1 bouquet garni
8 garlic cloves, crushed
800g (1lb 12oz) boned breast of lamb
350g (12oz) pork blade
225g (8oz) good-quality sausages,
   preferably Toulouse or Cumberland

10 large tomatoes, very roughly chopped
leaves from 8 thyme sprigs
10g (¼oz) flat leaf parsley, roughly chopped
salt and pepper
1 tbsp tomato purée
about 8 tbsp white breadcrumbs (you may
   need more)

1 Soak the beans overnight in cold water. Drain, rinse well and put in a pan with fresh water to cover completely. Cut the rind off the bacon and add, together with the onion with its cloves, bouquet garni and half the garlic. Bring to the boil, skim, then reduce the heat and simmer for 1¾ hours, or until the beans are tender (it partly depends on how old they are).

2 Preheat the oven to 190°C/375°F/gas mark 5. Put the lamb, pork, bacon and sausages into a roasting tin and cook in the oven for 30 minutes. Tip out and reserve the fat. Cut the pork, bacon and lamb into chunks about 2.5–4cm (1–1½in) square and slice the sausages into thick rounds.

3 When the beans are tender, drain off and reserve the liquid. Discard the rind, onion and bouquet garni. Reduce the oven temperature to 170°C/340°F/gas mark 3½. Layer the meat, sausages, tomatoes, remaining garlic and the herbs in a large casserole, starting and finishing with a layer of beans. Season really well as you go. Measure 600ml (1 pint) of the bean liquor and mix it with the reserved meat fat and the tomato purée. Pour this over the dish. Sprinkle some breadcrumbs on top (reserve some for later). Cover and put in the oven for 1½ hours. After 45 minutes, uncover and stir, put more breadcrumbs on top and return to the oven.

4 You now have to work on the cassoulet's thickness while it finishes cooking. If it isn't thick enough, add more breadcrumbs to the surface, let them go golden, then stir them in. If, on the other hand, it is a bit dry, add more bean liquor. It is hard to be prescriptive about quantities as it depends how much liquid your beans absorb. When the cooking time is up there should be a layer of golden crumbs on top. Watch the seasoning: this dish needs a lot because of the quantity of beans. Be prepared to add more herbs if you think it necessary.

Spanish lamb with beans and chorizo

Dead easy, as long as you remember to soak your beans the day before. It's best served with plain boiled rice or rice pilaf and greens on the side (kale is good).

Serves 6

300g (10½oz) dried haricot or butter beans (or other white beans)
1 piece of bacon rind, if available (ask your butcher)
2 onions
3 bay leaves
3 tbsp olive oil
750g (1lb 10oz) braising lamb, in large chunks

250g (9oz) chorizo, in chunks
4 garlic cloves, finely chopped
½ tbsp ground cumin
½ tbsp smoked paprika
2 x 400g cans tomatoes (ideally cherry) in thick juice
a few thyme or rosemary sprigs
pinch of sugar
salt and pepper
3 tbsp roughly chopped flat leaf parsley

1 Cover the beans with cold water and soak overnight. Drain and rinse. Put into a saucepan with the bacon rind, 1 of the onions, quartered, and 2 of the bay leaves. Cover with cold water and bring to the boil. Skim the surface and reduce the heat to low. Cover and cook until the beans are almost tender. It could take 45 minutes, it could take 1½ hours, depending on their age.

2 Heat the olive oil in a large saucepan or flameproof casserole and brown the lamb on all sides, in batches so that it doesn't sweat but browns properly. Set the meat aside. Add the chorizo to the pan and briskly colour that, too. Set aside.

3 Roughly chop the remaining onion and fry it in the pan in which you browned the lamb. When it's soft and golden, add the garlic and spices and cook for a couple of minutes, then add the tomatoes. Return the lamb and chorizo with the remaining bay leaf, the herbs, sugar and seasoning. Add the beans and their cooking water (discard the onion and bacon rind). Stir everything and bring to the boil, then reduce the heat and cook, uncovered, for 1½ hours. Check the seasoning. The beans should be soft and some should have collapsed (to thicken the stew). Stir in the parsley and serve.

Lamb with olives and preserved lemons

Not authentically Moroccan, because Moroccan cooks wouldn't brown the meat, but I think it produces a better flavour. A company called Belazu makes preserved lemons but the lemons are very small (a Moroccan variety we don't get here), so if you're using homemade preserved lemons you'll need just one of them.

Serves 6

6 tbsp olive oil

25g (1oz) butter

1.5kg (3lb 5oz) lamb shoulder, in 5cm (2in) chunks

2 large onions, finely chopped

4 garlic cloves, finely chopped

3 tsp ground ginger

2 tsp cayenne

¾ tbsp ground cumin

good pinch of saffron threads

salt and pepper

700ml (1¼ pints) lamb or chicken stock or water

1 large or 2 small preserved lemons

225g (8oz) green olives in brine, rinsed

2 tbsp each roughly chopped flat leaf parsley and coriander

1 Heat the olive oil and the butter in a heavy-bottomed pan and brown the lamb on all sides. Add the onions, stir them round in the juices and cook for a minute, then add the garlic, spices and seasoning (easy on the salt as the preserved lemons make the dish salty later on) and cook for another minute.

2 Add the stock or water, bring to the boil, then reduce to a simmer. Put the lid on the pan and reduce the heat to very low. Cook for 1 hour, stirring from time to time.

3 Discard the preserved lemon flesh and cut the rind into shreds. Take the lid off the pan and add the olives and most of the lemon. Cook for another 15 minutes, during which time the juices will reduce. Check the lamb: it should be tender. Stir in most of the herbs, sprinkle with the remaining lemon and herbs and serve.

ALSO TRY...

Tajine of lamb with apricots, saffron and honey Heat olive oil and butter and brown the lamb as above. Add the onions as above, then add 4 garlic cloves, finely chopped, 3 tsp ground ginger, 2 tsp ground cinnamon and seasoning and cook for another minute. Throw in 225g (8oz) dried apricots and 50g (1¾oz) dried sour berries (barberries, cranberries or sour cherries). Add 700ml (1¼ pints) lamb or chicken stock or water and a good pinch of saffron, if you have it. Cook as above for 1 hour, then remove the lid and cook for 15 minutes. The lamb should be tender. Stir in 2 tbsp honey, a good squeeze of lemon juice and 2 tsp orange flower water, if you have it. Add 2 tbsp roughly chopped flat leaf parsley, mint or coriander and check for seasoning and flavour; you may want more honey. Sprinkle with 2 tbsp chopped pistachios or almonds before serving.

Roast lamb shoulder with butter beans, spinach and apple allioli

Lamb shoulder is one of the cheapest roasting cuts you can buy, so it's brilliant for a crowd, and it has a sweeter flavour than leg. This is earthy country food with a Catalan twist. Apple and garlic 'allioli', or mayonnaise, works brilliantly and is made without egg yolks. It's good with rabbit, pork and chicken as well.

Serves 6

1.8kg (4lb) boned lamb shoulder

FOR THE STUFFING

½ onion, finely chopped
100g (3½oz) pancetta or streaky bacon, chopped
1 tbsp olive oil
25g (1oz) pine nuts or almonds, toasted
100g (3½oz) white breadcrumbs
1 small egg, beaten
leaves from 4 thyme sprigs
3 tbsp chopped flat leaf parsley
salt and pepper

FOR THE ALLIOLI

2 Granny Smith apples, peeled, cored and cut into chunks

2 garlic cloves
½ tsp rock salt
70ml (2½fl oz) fruity extra virgin olive oil
1 tsp white wine vinegar
1½ tbsp runny honey

FOR THE BEANS

250g (9oz) spinach, washed
4 tbsp olive oil
leaves from 1 thyme sprig
800g (1lb 12oz) cooked butter beans, drained
good squeeze of lemon juice

1 Preheat the oven to 220°C/425°F/gas mark 7. For the stuffing, sauté the onion and pancetta or bacon in the oil until golden. Put in a bowl with all the other stuffing ingredients and mix. Open the lamb out and trim any excess fat. Season well inside, then stuff. Roll up and tie up using thin kitchen string. Season the outside, put in a roasting tin and cook for 20 minutes. Reduce the heat to 160°C/325°F/gas mark 3 and cook for another 50 minutes (reckoning on 15 minutes per 500g/1lb 2oz).

2 To make the allioli, put the apples in a small saucepan and cover with water. Cook until very tender. Drain. Chop the garlic cloves and crush with the rock salt in a mortar, then add the apple and crush to a purée. When it is quite smooth, slowly add the extra virgin olive oil, a drop at a time, beating as you go (as if making mayonnaise), until you have a thick sauce. Add the vinegar and honey and refrigerate until needed.

3 When the lamb is cooked, cover with foil, insulate with towels or tea towels and allow to rest for 25 minutes or so.

4 Wilt the spinach in the water that clings to it after washing. It should take 4 minutes. Drain, squeeze out the water and chop. Heat the oil in a wide pan. Add the spinach, salt, pepper and thyme. Cook for a minute, stirring, then add the beans, being careful not to break them up. Cook until hot, then add the lemon juice and more seasoning (beans need quite a lot). Serve with the lamb and allioli.

ALSO TRY...

Stuffed Samos lamb This Greek dish is to die for; you'll relish the gasps as you take it to the table. It's very simple to put together and the ingredients won't break the bank, but it looks like the centrepiece of a wonderful feast. Preheat the oven to 220°C/425°F/gas mark 7. Saute ½ red onion, finely chopped, in 2 tbsp olive oil. Add 1 small fennel bulb, trimmed and chopped (reserve any little feathery fronds). Once the onion is soft, add 3 garlic cloves, finely chopped, and cook for 2 minutes, then add 200g (7oz) basmati rice which you've rinsed until the water runs clear. Pour on enough water just to cover. Season. Bring to the boil and boil hard until the water has disappeared and the surface looks 'pitted', then reduce the heat, cover and cook gently for about 12 minutes. The rice should still be a bit *al dente*. Fork it gently and mix with the finely grated zest of 1 lemon and 3 tbsp each finely chopped dill and parsley (this is a very herby stuffing). Check for seasoning. Prepare and stuff the lamb as on page 177, using a 2.3kg (5lb) boned shoulder. Season the outside, squeeze over the juice of ½ lemon and drizzle with olive oil. Roast for 20 minutes, then reduce the heat to 160°C/325°F/gas mark 3 and cook for another 1¼ hours. Rest and insulate the lamb as on page 177 and serve on a heated platter. Serves 8.

Lamb shawarma Way better than anything you ever got in the kebab shop! (And I'm very partial to takeaway kebabs.) Mix together 450g (1lb) lamb shoulder, thinly sliced, with 1 onion, finely sliced, 2 garlic cloves, roughly chopped, the juice of 1 lemon, 50ml (2fl oz) olive oil, 1 tsp each ground cinnamon and ground allspice, the leaves from 3 thyme sprigs and salt and pepper. Cover and put in the fridge to marinate for 3 hours, turning occasionally. If you have a griddle pan, warm it until it is very hot. Lift the meat from the marinade and griddle briefly (it needs only a couple of minutes on each side, it is so tender), adding more seasoning. Lift the onion out of the marinade and fry on the same griddle – but on a lower heat – until golden brown. Spoon on the marinade and let it bubble away to almost nothing. If you don't have a griddle pan, you can use a frying pan instead (you just won't get the marks). Serve hot with warm pitta bread and Greek yogurt (you can add chopped cucumber and mint) or tahini dressing (see page 82). The contrast of temperatures is fantastic.

Lamb, black pudding and mustard hot pot

Since I'm not from Lancashire I don't mind mucking about with hot pot, but if you prefer to be traditional, leave out the black pudding and mustard.

Serves 4

3 tbsp groundnut or sunflower oil
  or dripping
2 large onions, finely sliced
350g (12oz) black pudding, sliced
8 lamb chops (middle neck cutlets)
900g (2lb) potatoes, very thinly sliced

2 tbsp grain mustard
salt and pepper
5 tbsp finely chopped parsley
leaves from 6 thyme sprigs
750ml (1¼ pints) lamb or beef stock,
  or stock and water
15g (½oz) butter

1 Heat half the oil in a frying pan and cook the onions until soft and turning golden. Set aside. Add the remaining oil to the pan and fry the black pudding for a minute each side. Set aside. Briefly cook the chops over high heat to get a good colour. Set them aside, too. Preheat the oven to 180°C/350°F/gas mark 4.

2 Starting with the potatoes, layer them with the onions and meat in a casserole in which everything fits snugly. Dot the mustard over the black pudding, season well and sprinkle with herbs as you go. You should have two layers of chops and end with a layer of potatoes.

3 Arrange the top layer of potatoes in neat overlapping slices. Heat the stock and pour it on, then melt the butter and brush the top. Cover and bake for 1½ hours, then uncover and continue to cook and bake for a further 30 minutes.

ALSO TRY...

My Irish stew People have remarked that my Irish stew is not 'traditional', but I grew up with this and I am Irish! It's a great way to use a cheap cut. Put 1.5kg (3lb 5oz) middle neck or scrag end of lamb into a large saucepan with a handful of parsley stalks, 1 onion, halved, 1 large carrot, halved, and 6 black peppercorns. Cover with water, bring to the boil and skim. Reduce to a simmer, cover and cook until tender. It should take 1–1½ hours. Strain and reserve the stock. Cut another 3 large carrots into rounds and 4 large, peeled, floury potatoes into chunks. Roughly chop 2 large onions. Put the vegetables into a clean saucepan, and add the stock, 3 thyme sprigs and seasoning. Bring to the boil, reduce the heat and cook, uncovered, until the vegetables are tender and the potatoes partly fallen apart (they thicken the stew). Remove the lamb from the bones and cut into large chunks. (Be careful not to include little bits of bone if you're using scrag end.) Add the meat to the stew. Heat through and check the seasoning. Scatter with finely chopped parsley before serving. Serves 4–6.

Braised lamb shanks with gremolata

Lamb shanks aren't as cheap as they were but are still good value and great reheated, so can be eaten over a couple of meals. You'll have to take whatever size shanks the butcher has, which makes cooking times difficult to specify. Just cook them gently until the meat is parting from the bone. The timings here are for the weight of shanks given; if yours are smaller, check to see when they're ready.

Serves 8

FOR THE SHANKS
8 lamb shanks, about 400g (14oz) each
salt and pepper
5 tbsp olive oil
2 onions, chopped
8 carrots, chopped
4 celery sticks, chopped
3 x 400g cans tomatoes in thick juice
600ml (1 pint) dry white wine

several rosemary sprigs
2 bay leaves
3 strips orange zest

FOR THE GREMOLATA
finely grated zest of 1 unwaxed orange
4 garlic cloves, very finely chopped
about 4 tbsp finely chopped flat
  leaf parsley

1 Preheat the oven to 150°C/300°F/gas mark 2. Remove the fat covering the lamb with a sharp knife. Season the meat. Heat the oil in a large flameproof casserole and brown the lamb, in two batches, on all sides. Set aside. Add the vegetables to the casserole and cook until the onions are soft but not coloured. Add the tomatoes, wine and flavourings and bring to the boil. Return the shanks and put in the oven with the lid on for 3–3½ hours, or until the meat is coming away from the bone.

2 Remove the lamb and reduce the liquid by boiling until quite thick. Meanwhile, make the gremolata by mixing the ingredients together. Sprinkle over the shanks and serve.

ALSO TRY...

Vietnamese lamb shanks with sweet potatoes Gorgeously fragrant and quite 'brothy', so serve in broad, flat soup plates. Preheat the oven to 160°C/325°F/gas mark 3. Heat 2 tbsp groundnut oil in a heavy flameproof casserole, season 4 lamb shanks (about 350g/12oz each) and brown well. Remove from the casserole. Briskly fry 2 onions, in crescent moon-shaped slices, until golden, then add 2.5cm (1in) fresh root ginger, peeled and finely chopped, 2 red chillies, deseeded and finely sliced, and 3 garlic cloves, finely sliced. Reduce the heat and cook for a minute. Stir in 1 tbsp soft dark brown sugar, 3 star anise, 2 bruised lemon grass stalks, 1.2 litres (2 pints) lamb stock, 1½ tbsp tomato purée and seasoning. Add 4 sweet potatoes, peeled and cut into chunks, and return the lamb. Bring to the boil, reduce the heat and cook in the oven with the lid on for 2½ hours, or until the meat is almost falling off the bones. Stir in 2 tbsp fish sauce, the juice of 2 limes and another tsp of brown sugar. Taste for seasoning, scatter with torn basil and mint and serve with boiled rice. Serves 4.

Turkish lamb kofta with cherries and yogurt

Minced meat, though much maligned, can be made into dishes that aren't just good, but have magic. Kofta are little meatballs eaten in the Middle East, India, Pakistan, all over the eastern Mediterranean, in Russia and many other parts of the former Soviet Union. They are so easy to make; just spiced, pummelled mince formed into little balls and fried. This, dark red with cherries and splattered with yogurt, is a lovely-looking dish. It's obviously best made when cherries are slightly less expensive (though they're never cheap). Increase the quantity of dried cherries to replace some of the fresh if you want, or make with a mixture of fresh and dried apricots instead.

Serves 6

1kg (2lb 4oz) minced lamb
3 tsp ground cinnamon
2 tsp ground cumin
1 tsp ground cloves
1 tsp cayenne pepper
salt and pepper
3 tbsp olive oil
15g (½oz) butter
1 onion, finely chopped
350g (12oz) fresh cherries, pitted

100g (3½oz) sour dried cherries, soaked
   in just-boiled water for 15 minutes
   and drained
1–2 tbsp soft light brown sugar
juice of ½ lemon
100ml (3½fl oz) lamb or chicken stock

TO SERVE
Greek yogurt
a little milk or buttermilk
chopped mint, parsley or coriander

1 Put the lamb in a bowl and add all the spices except 1 tsp of the cinnamon. Season. Pummel the meat until really soft and everything is well blended. If you don't mind raw lamb (it won't do you any harm), eat a tiny bit to check the seasoning and spicing (otherwise fry a little chunk, then taste; the seasoning and spicing are paramount). With wet hands, form into walnut-sized balls.

2 Heat the oil in a large sauté pan and fry the kofta in batches, making sure they are well browned. Scoop them out on to kitchen paper as you cook them.

3 Pour the oil out of the pan, return it to the heat and add the butter. Heat until foaming, then add the onion and sauté until soft and golden. Add 250g (9oz) of the fresh cherries and all the dried ones with the remaining cinnamon and cook for a minute until softening, then add the sugar and lemon juice.

4 Return the kofta and add the stock. Bring to the boil, then reduce to a simmer and cook for 20 minutes, uncovered, until cooked through and the mixture is thick. Press some of the cherries so they disintegrate. If your mixture isn't thick enough, remove the meatballs and boil the liquid to reduce, then return the kofta. Put the remaining fresh cherries in towards the end of cooking to soften slightly and heat through. Serve drizzled with Greek yogurt (let down with a little with milk or buttermilk) and scattered with chopped parsley, mint or coriander.

ALSO TRY...

Tajine of kofta and dates with preserved lemons Heat 2 tbsp olive oil in a frying pan and gently sauté 1 small onion, grated (squeeze out excess liquid first), until soft. Add 3 garlic cloves, crushed, 1 tsp each ground ginger, mixed spice and cayenne and 1 tbsp ground cumin. Cook for another minute. Mix into 900g (2lb) minced lamb (use your hands) and season really well. Using wet hands, form into golf-ball-sized rounds. Heat another 2 tbsp oil in a flameproof casserole and brown the kofta on all sides in batches. Remove with a slotted spoon as you go and set aside. Add 1 onion cut into slim wedges, and fry in the remaining oil until golden. Add 3 tsp each ground cumin and ground ginger and cook for another minute. Return the kofta to the casserole and add 200g (7oz) dates, pitted, and 800ml (1½ pints) lamb or chicken stock. Stir in a good pinch of saffron threads and 1 tbsp honey. Season. Bring to the boil then immediately reduce to a simmer and cook for 15–20 minutes. The kofta should be cooked but tender and the cooking liquid should have reduced. Remove and discard the flesh from 1 preserved lemon. Cut the rind into slivers and add to the casserole with 4 tbsp torn mint leaves. Taste for seasoning. Serve with Arab flatbread, couscous or rice. Serves 6.

Kofta don't always have to be served in a stew or sauce. Use different spices to flavour them (see page 183) or put them on to skewers, grill and serve them with the following accompaniments:

Tahini sauce (see page 82)

Greek yogurt, mixed with chopped garlic and mint

Orange and Pistachio Pilaf (see page 114)

Split Pea Purée (see page 103)

Tarator (see page 58)

You can also brown kofta then add them to Kaye Korma Curry (see page 74), Turkish Potatoes with Tomatoes and Black Olives (see page 85), or Creamy Lentils and Pumpkin with Ginger and Cumin (see page 101). They need to cook in these dishes for 15–20 minutes.

Pork rillettes with sweet-and-sour plums

Rillettes are very cheap to make and a good thing to stash in the refrigerator if you have a crowd of friends coming. With some dressed lentils, a few cornichons and decent bread you have a perfect lunch. They also make wonderful picnic food.

Serves 8–10, makes about 1kg (2lb 4oz)

FOR THE RILLETTES

500g (1lb 2oz) pork shoulder
500g (1lb 2oz) pork belly (bones and rind removed)
300g (10½oz) rendered pork fat or lard
4 thyme sprigs
3 bay leaves
4 cloves
¼ tsp ground mixed spice
very generous grating of nutmeg
salt and pepper

FOR THE PLUMS

100ml (3½fl oz) red wine vinegar
100ml (3½fl oz) sherry vinegar
250g (12oz) granulated sugar
5cm (2in) cinnamon stick
350g (12oz) fresh ripe plums

1 Cut the pork shoulder into strips 2cm (¾in) across, slicing along the grain. Cut the pork belly into slices 1cm (½in) thick. Put the fat and 100ml (3½fl oz) water into a broad, heavy-bottomed pan and set over a very low heat. Add the meat. Tie the thyme, bay and cloves in a square of muslin (or bit of new J Cloth) and put this in, too.

2 Cook over a very low heat so the liquid is shivering, not bubbling, for about 4 hours, on top of the cooker where you can keep an eye on it. The meat shouldn't brown; just poach. Make sure it doesn't stick and turn it occasionally. It's ready when you can pull it gently apart.

3 Leave to cool, remove the spices and herbs and shred the meat with two forks into soft strands. Add the mixed spice and nutmeg and season well with salt and pepper. Put into a couple of bowls and cover with greaseproof paper that you've greased with more pork fat.

4 The rillettes taste better after a couple of days in the refrigerator, but I find them too much of a temptation. If you pack the rillettes into jars with no air pockets and cover with a good 5mm (¼in) pork fat, they should last for about 4 months.

5 To make the plums, put the vinegars into a saucepan and add the sugar and cinnamon. Dissolve the sugar over a low heat, stirring from time to time, then bring to the boil. Reduce the heat immediately and simmer for 7 minutes, until slightly syrupy. Halve and stone the plums, add them and simmer for 4 minutes, depending on ripeness; they should be just tender. Leave to cool. The fruit will develop a good flavour in the syrup and the liquid will thicken as it cools.

6 Serve the rillettes with the plums, lightly dressed salad and good baguette or sourdough bread. Rillettes are also wonderful in the summer with pickled cherries.

Succulent pork belly with soy and star anise

A pot of eastern deliciousness that is irresistibly more-ish. It also takes very little effort. Mushrooms make a good addition if you want to extend the dish with vegetables. You can obviously tailor this to suit your palate; not everyone is a big fan of star anise, for example, but stick to eastern flavours.

Serves 6–8

1.5kg (3lb 5oz) pork belly, bones removed, rind left on

120ml (4fl oz) dark soy sauce

75ml (2½fl oz) Chinese rice wine or dry sherry

25ml (spare 1fl oz) rice vinegar

2½ tbsp soft light brown sugar

5cm (2in) square of fresh root ginger, peeled and finely sliced

3 star anise

3 garlic cloves, finely sliced

1 red chilli, deseeded and finely sliced

12 spring onions, sliced on the diagonal

1 Cut the pork belly into chunks (or ask your butcher to do it for you) about 5cm (2in) square. Put these in a saucepan and add enough water to cover. Bring to the boil, reduce the heat so that the water is simmering and cook the pork for 5 minutes. Skim the surface of any scum that rises.

2 Strain the pork (discard the cooking water), rinse the pan and return the pork. Add about 1.4 litres (2½ pints) water (or light chicken stock if you have it), plus all the other ingredients (using only half the spring onions). Bring this up to the boil, then immediately reduce to a gentle simmer, cover tightly with a lid and leave to cook very gently for about 2 hours, or until the pork is completely tender. Make sure it doesn't boil dry and add more water if needed.

3 Scoop the pork out of the cooking liquor with a slotted spoon and set aside. Reduce the cooking liquor by boiling it until you have a good, intensified flavour (but don't take it so far that it is unpalatably salty). Return the pork to the liquid and heat through. Serve in bowls over noodles, or with boiled rice, with the rest of the spring onions sprinkled over the top. Some kind of stir-fried greens – cabbage or bok choi – are good served on the side, too.

Crispy pork belly with potatoes, eggs and gribiche dressing

It may seem unusual to put chunks of pork belly in a salad, but this French dish works beautifully. Cooked this way chunks of pork belly can also be used for salads made with lentils dressed in a good mustardy vinaigrette, or in oriental-style salads with noodles, bean sprouts, mushrooms and strongly flavoured greens tossed in a spicy dressing.

Serves 6

FOR THE SALAD
6 thick slices of pork belly
500g (1lb 2oz) small waxy potatoes
6 eggs
175g (6oz) salad leaves (watercress or
   spinach are both good)

FOR THE DRESSING
smidgen of Dijon mustard
salt and pepper

½ tbsp white wine vinegar
4 tbsp extra virgin olive oil
1 small shallot, very finely chopped
2 large gherkins, finely chopped
1 tbsp capers, rinsed and chopped
leaves from 2 tarragon sprigs, chopped
2 tbsp chopped flat leaf parsley

1 Preheat the oven to 180°C/350°F/gas mark 4. Pierce the skin side of the pork belly pieces with a fork and plunge them into boiling water (this helps them crisp up more). Remove, place the pieces on a rack set over a roasting tin and cook in the oven for 1 hour. The pork should be tender and crisp. Cut into bite-sized chunks.

2 Half an hour before you are ready to eat, make the dressing and boil the potatoes. To make the dressing, put the mustard, salt, pepper and vinegar into a small bowl and whisk in the olive oil. Add all the other dressing ingredients and check for seasoning. Cook the potatoes in boiling salted water until just tender. Drain and carefully halve the potatoes lengthways. Toss them straight away in a little of the dressing and keep them warm.

3 Cook the eggs in boiling water for 5–6 minutes. They should be just between boiled and hard-boiled. Take their shells off once they are cool enough to handle, and halve lengthways.

4 Gently toss the leaves, warm potatoes and pork with most of the dressing. Divide between six plates. Add the warm halved eggs and drizzle more dressing over the top. Serve immediately.

Thyme-roasted belly of pork with baked apples

Pork belly has everything going for it. It can be roasted with a crispy crackling or braised to produce tender, melting mouthfuls. And it's cheap.

Serves 8

1.8kg (4lb) thick end of pork belly, rind
    scored (ask your butcher for the last 6 ribs)
leaves from 1 small bunch of thyme
fine flaked sea salt
freshly ground black pepper
8 smallish eating apples, preferably
    with tawny or russet skin

200ml (7fl oz) dry cider, white wine or
    apple juice
50g (1¾oz) soft light brown sugar
juice of ½ lemon

1 Preheat the oven to 220°C/425°F/gas mark 7. Lay the joint, skin side up, in a roasting tin. Rub the thyme leaves and salt and pepper into the skin. Be generous with the salt as this gives crisp crackling. Roast for 30 minutes.

2 Run a knife horizonally round the middle of each apple and put in a baking dish. Heat the cider and sugar gently until the sugar dissolves. Bring just to the boil, add the lemon juice and pour over the apples. Reduce the oven temperature to 180°C/350°F/ gas mark 4. Put the apples in the oven and roast them alongside the pork for a further hour (but do check before then: they should be tender yet not collapsing).

3 Test the pork: the juices should run clear when the meat is pierced. If the crackling isn't crispy enough, increase the oven temperature to 220°C/425°F/gas mark 7 and check again after 5 minutes. Serve each person some meat and crackling, a baked apple and its juices.

ALSO TRY...

Spiced pork belly with fennel, chilli and lentils Crush together 1½ tbsp fennel seeds, 1½ tsp dried chilli flakes, ¾ tbsp thyme leaves and ¾ tbsp flaked sea salt. Mix in 3 tbsp olive oil and rub over 1.5kg (3lb 5oz) pork belly (rind scored). Refrigerate, covered, for an hour. Preheat the oven to 220°C/425°F/gas mark 7. Roast the pork, skin side up, for 30 minutes. Reduce the heat to 170°C/340°F/gas mark 3½ and pour in 300ml (½ pint) white wine or cider. Cook for 1½ hours, pouring in another 300ml (½ pint) liquid (wine, cider or water) after 1 hour. Heat 2 tbsp olive oil and gently sauté 1 small onion, chopped, 1 carrot, diced, and 1 celery stick, diced, for 10 minutes. Add 300g (10½oz) green lentils, 450ml (16fl oz) chicken stock or water and 1 bay leaf and bring to the boil. Reduce to a simmer, season and cook, covered, for 25 minutes. Take the pork from the oven and insulate to rest. Skim the fat from the juices. Stir 3 tsp red wine vinegar, 2 tbsp extra virgin olive oil and 2 tbsp chopped parsley into the lentils. Serve the pork with the lentils and cooking juices. Serves 6.

Slow-roast shoulder of pork with stuffed squash

Sunday lunch can seem dauntingly expensive if you're trying to feed a crowd. But slow-cooked pork shoulder is one of the most satisfying joints (so tender) and, relatively, very cheap. It also looks magnificent. You can vary the stuffing by using dried fruit instead of mushrooms, or add grated Parmesan or wilted spinach.

Serves 8

FOR THE PORK
sea salt and pepper
2.8kg (6lb) boned shoulder of pork, rind scored
4 tbsp olive oil
800ml (1½ pints) dry cider or white wine

FOR THE SQUASH
2 small squash or pumpkins
60g (2oz) butter

1 onion, finely chopped
75g (2½oz) pancetta, chopped
200g (7oz) mushrooms, quartered
200g (7oz) brown basmati, wild and Camargue red rice (or just brown and wild)
500ml (18fl oz) chicken stock or water

1 Preheat the oven to 200°C/400°F/gas mark 6. Season the inside of the pork. Roll up and tie at intervals with kitchen string. Rub with oil and season well. Put in a roasting tin and cook in the oven for 25 minutes. Reduce the heat to 160°C/325°F/gas mark 3 and pour in half the alcohol. Cook for another 25 minutes per 500g (1lb 2oz) – about 2½ hours in total – basting and adding more cider or wine as you go.

2 Meanwhile, halve the squash and scoop out the fibres and seeds. Score a lattice on the flesh. Put in a roasting tin and smear with 15g (½oz) of the butter. Season and roast for 20 minutes. Remove from the oven.

3 Melt another 15g (½oz) of the butter in a saucepan and sauté the onion until quite soft. Add the pancetta, mushrooms and remaining butter and sauté until coloured. Stir in the rice to coat, season and add the stock or water. Cover, bring to the boil, reduce the heat to low and cook for 15 minutes.

4 When the pork is cooked (the juices should run clear, with no trace of pink, when you pierce the meat), take it from the oven and put on a heated platter. Cover with foil, insulate well and rest for 30 minutes. Increase the oven temperature to 190°C/375°F/ gas mark 5.

5 Spoon the rice stuffing into the squash cavities, mixing it with the butter that has collected there. Return to the oven for 30 minutes. The flesh should become completely tender and the tops golden.

6 Meanwhile, pour the cooking juices from the pork into a jug and remove the fat. Deglaze the roasting tin with more cider, white wine or water (only about 100ml/ 3½fl oz), add the pork juices and bubble away until you have a thin, tasty gravy. Serve the pork with the gravy and squash.

ALSO TRY...

Porc au four A brilliant celebration or big Sunday lunch dish. The pork is practically melting. Serve with roast potatoes or lentils, watercress salad and baked red onions (see page 32). Put 7 garlic cloves, chopped, ¾ tbsp sea salt flakes, a generous grinding of black pepper and the leaves from 5 thyme sprigs into a mortar and pound to a rough paste. Add 3 tbsp Dijon mustard and 5 tbsp olive oil. Make small incisions all over the flesh of a 2.3kg (5lb) shoulder of pork on the bone. Paint the mustard mixture all over the flesh (not the rind), pushing it into the slits. Cover loosely and refrigerate for a few hours, or ideally overnight. Bring to room temperature and preheat the oven to 220°C/425°F/gas mark 7. Season the rind with sea salt. Roast the pork for 30 minutes, then reduce the heat to 160°C/325°F/gas mark 3 and cook for 25 minutes per 500g (1lb 2oz) – just over 2 hours. Cover with foil about two-thirds of the way through. Once the pork is cooked, remove from the oven, cover and insulate for 30 minutes to rest. Make a light gravy (see page 190). Serves 10.

Lechon asado Cuban roast pork. The last time I made this I couldn't get people to sit down to eat it; they stood at the kitchen counter and pulled it from the bones. Serve with rice and – preferably – black beans, or an avocado, spinach and orange salad. The marinade (*mojo*) is also great with roast chicken or lamb. Dry-fry 1½ tbsp cumin seeds and ½ tbsp black peppercorns until fragrant, then grind with 6 fat garlic cloves, sea salt flakes and 1 tbsp dried oregano until you have a paste. Stir in the juice of 1 orange and 2 limes plus 25ml (1fl oz) rum and 2 tbsp olive oil. Pierce a 1.8kg (4lb) shoulder of pork all over with a sharp knife. Put into a large bowl and pour the marinade over. Cover loosely and refrigerate for 12–24 hours, turning regularly. Preheat the oven to 220°C/425°F/gas mark 7. Lift the pork from the marinade and put into a roasting pan. Roast for 30 minutes, then reduce the heat to 160°C/325°F/ gas mark 3 and roast for 1 hour 40 minutes, or until cooked through, regularly basting with pan juices and the marinade. Transfer to a carving board, cover loosely with foil, insulate and rest for 30 minutes. Pour the juices into a saucepan and skim the fat. Bring to the boil. Carve the pork and serve with the juices. Serves 6–8.

Pigs' cheeks with mustard lentils

The first time I ate pigs' cheeks was in Paris (braised, with wild mushrooms) and I just couldn't wait to get my hands on them. There's nothing squeamish about them – we are not talking piggy tails or ears, they are little medallions about the size of the fleshy bit of your palm and cook into the most tender chunks of meat. You'll have to make a special order with your butcher though. Waitrose started stocking cheeks in some stores a couple of years back.

Serves 4

FOR THE PIGS' CHEEKS
8 pigs' cheeks
salt and pepper
plain flour, to dust
1 tbsp sunflower or groundnut oil
100ml (3½fl oz) dry cider
250ml (8fl oz) chicken stock

FOR THE LENTILS
10g (¼oz) butter
1 small onion, finely chopped

1 celery stick, diced
1 carrot, diced
225g (8oz) Puy lentils
1 thyme sprig
450ml (16fl oz) chicken stock
100ml (3½fl oz) double cream
8 tsp Dijon mustard
chopped flat leaf parsley, to serve

1 Trim the cheeks and remove any excess fat. Drop them in seasoned flour – shaking off the excess – and heat the oil in a casserole. Brown the cheeks on both sides, then add the cider and let that bubble away. Pour on the stock and bring to the boil.

2 Immediately reduce the heat to very low, cover and simmer gently for 2 hours. Make sure the cheeks don't boil dry: add a little more water but don't drown them – you just need enough to keep the cooking ticking over. The cheeks will eventually be soft and falling apart.

3 You need to start cooking the lentils about half an hour before the pork is ready. Melt the butter and gently cook the onion, celery and carrot until just softening but not coloured. Add the lentils and stir them in the fat and cooking juices, then add the thyme and stock. Season with pepper. Bring the stock to the boil, then reduce to a simmer and leave to cook. The lentils should take 20 minutes but keep an eye on them: they should be tender but not collapsing and can go soft very quickly. The stock should all be absorbed (for this reason, there isn't too much liquid here, but make sure that the lentils don't boil dry).

4 When the lentils are cooked, add the cream and mustard, stir and heat through. The cream will reduce as it heats. You don't want a 'soupy' mixture. Adjust the seasoning. Lift the cheeks out of their cooking liquid and boil to reduce until quite syrupy. Return the cheeks to heat through. Serve with their cooking juices and the lentils, scattering everything with parsley.

Mexican tinga poblana

At least one up on regular chilli, this uses pork shoulder and is adapted from a recipe by Mexican expert Rick Bayless. If you can't find chorizo, use another spicy sausage but add 2 tsp smoked paprika with the cumin. Chipotle chillies are smoked as well as dried, and can be bought from Seasoned Pioneers (www.seasonedpioneers.co.uk).

Serves 6–8

FOR THE TINGA POBLANA
4 dried chipotle chillies
1.3kg (3lb) plum tomatoes, halved
olive oil
salt and pepper
1½ tsp sugar
225g (8oz) chorizo or other spicy sausage
1.3kg (3lb) pork shoulder, cut into
   4cm (1½in) cubes
2 onions, roughly chopped
3 garlic cloves, crushed
1 tsp ground cumin

3 thyme sprigs
1 tsp dried oregano
about 225ml (8fl oz) chicken stock or water
brown sugar, to taste (optional)

TO SERVE
2 ripe avocados
juice of 1 lime
200g (7oz) soured cream
150g (5½oz) mild soft goat's cheese or feta
   cheese, crumbled
about 2 tbsp roughly chopped coriander

1 Preheat the oven to 190°C/375°F/gas mark 5. Cover the chipotles with just-boiled water and leave to soak. Put the tomatoes, cut side up, in a roasting tin where they fit in a single layer. Drizzle with oil, season and sprinkle with sugar. Roast for 50 minutes, until soft, slightly scorched and shrunken.

2 Remove the sausage from its casing and break into pieces. Heat 1 tbsp olive oil in a large frying pan and sauté the sausage pieces until well coloured. Put into a flameproof casserole, retaining the fat in the pan. Brown the pork well in this fat to a really good colour (cook the pork in batches so the temperature stays high and you are frying, not steaming, the meat).

3 Remove the meat and put it in the casserole, leaving behind any fat. Add a little more oil to the frying pan if needed and fry the onions to a good deep gold. Add the garlic and cumin and cook for 2 minutes more, then add to the casserole with the thyme, oregano, seasoning and enough stock or water to cover. Simmer, partially covered, over a low heat until just tender (about 50 minutes).

4 Fifteen minutes before the cooking time is up, tip the tomatoes and juices into the casserole. Remove the chillies from their liquid, take off the stalks and deseed. Roughly chop the flesh and add this, with the soaking liquid, to the casserole. Gently cook for 15 minutes. Check the seasoning; you may want to add a little brown sugar.

5 To serve, slice the avocados and squeeze lime juice all over them. Season. Put the meat into a large broad bowl (or leave it in the casserole) and spoon over the soured cream, add the avocado slices, then scatter with the cheese and coriander. Serve with boiled rice.

Silesian heaven

Braised pork, eastern European style. I sometimes add leeks as well (cut a couple into chunks and sauté along with the onions). Be careful to get the sweet-savoury balance right: taste and alter with a little more cider vinegar or brown sugar.

Serves 4

250g (9oz) dried fruit (apples, pears, sour cherries, prunes)
about 250ml (9fl oz) cold tea
1 tbsp sunflower oil
25g (1oz) butter
1kg (2lb 4oz) pork shoulder, cut into large cubes
1 large onion, cut into crescent moon-shaped slices
1 celery stick, diced
3 tsp ground mixed spice
3 tbsp plain flour
salt and pepper
about 100ml (3½fl oz) dry cider (optional)
1 tbsp soft dark brown sugar
1 tbsp cider vinegar
3 thyme sprigs
1 bay leaf
chopped parsley, to serve

1 Soak the dried fruit overnight in just enough cold tea to cover. Heat the oil and butter in a large flameproof casserole and brown the pork on all sides. It's best to do this in batches so it browns properly instead of sweating. Remove the pork and, in the same pan, sauté the onion and celery until soft and lightly coloured. Add the mixed spice and cook for another minute. Return the pork and stir in the flour and seasoning. Cook for another minute.

2 Drain the fruit. Measure the fruit soaking liquid and make it up to 350ml (12fl oz) with the cider, if using, or water. Add to the pork with the fruits, sugar, vinegar, thyme and bay leaf. Season. Bring to the boil, then reduce the heat to very low. Stir well and cover. Cook gently for 1½ hours, uncovering after 1 hour so that some of the liquid can evaporate, but keep an eye on it as you don't want the mixture to become too dry. Replace the lid or add more liquid as necessary. The meat should be completely tender and melting.

3 Adjust the seasoning and scatter with chopped parsley. I love this with brown rice or bulgur wheat, with Greek yogurt on the side.

Ham hock with parsley sauce and cabbage

One of my mum's dishes this shows how worthwhile it is to try less-common cuts. It's a wonderful supper and provides great leftovers for lots of dishes.

Serves 6

FOR THE HAM

2 x 1.2kg (2lb 12oz) ham hocks
8 peppercorns
1 large carrot, cut into chunks
1 onion, quartered
2 celery sticks, chopped
1 bay leaf
handful of parsley stalks, bruised

FOR THE PARSLEY SAUCE

600ml (1 pint) full-fat milk
½ onion, sliced
small bunch of flat leaf parsley, stalks
  separated and leaves finely chopped

8 peppercorns
1 bay leaf
50g (1¾oz) butter
50g (1¾oz) plain flour
salt and pepper
6 tbsp double cream
really generous squeeze of lemon juice
dollop of Dijon mustard (optional)

FOR THE CABBAGE

675g (1½lb) Savoy cabbage
35g (1¼oz) butter

1 Soak the hocks for 24 hours, changing the water twice.

2 Put the hocks in a large pan and cover with water. Add the other ingredients and bring to the boil. Skim and cook gently until the meat is coming from the bone. It usually takes 2–3 hours. (You can also cook this in advance and gently reheat in the stock.)

3 To make the sauce, heat the milk with the onion, parsley stalks, peppercorns and bay. Bring to the boil, remove from the heat and infuse for 15 minutes. Strain.

4 Melt the butter in a heavy saucepan and add the flour. Stir over low heat for a minute. Slowly add the infused milk, stirring to incorporate before you add more. Return to the heat. Bring to the boil, stirring, then simmer for 4 minutes. Season, add the cream, finely chopped parsley leaves and lemon juice. Taste; you may want mustard, more lemon juice or extra seasoning. Cover to keep warm.

5 Core and shred the cabbage. Melt the butter in a heavy saucepan, add the cabbage, season and add 2 tbsp water. Reduce the heat to low, cover and cook for 4 minutes, shaking. Stir, so the butter coats the cabbage. Cover, but don't let it sit for too long.

6 Remove and discard the fat from the hocks and break the meat into large pieces. Serve the ham with the parsley sauce, and the cabbage. It's also great served with boiled potatoes.

LEFTOVERS...

Break the ham into large flakes and toss with watercress, warm waxy potatoes and mustardy dressing. Make a hash (see page 151) or a stovie (see page 155) with ham instead of fish. Or add to bubble and squeak (see page 89).

Ham hock and grain mustard terrine

This, served at The Potting Shed pub (attached to the Rectory Hotel in Malmesbury in Wiltshire), is one of the best terrines I have ever eaten and really moist. If you've never made one before it can seem a bit daunting…but just look how simple this is!

Serves 6

1 carrot

½ onion

1 celery stick

1 large ham hock, soaked in water
   for 24 hours (see page 196)

3–4 thyme sprigs

1 bay leaf

1 garlic clove

1 star anise (optional)

3 tsp grain mustard

3 tbsp finely chopped flat leaf parsley

salt and pepper

1 Roughly chop all the vegetables and put them in a large pan with the ham hock, thyme, bay, garlic and star anise. Cover with water. Bring to the boil then turn the heat down low and simmer until the meat begins to fall off the bone (2–3 hours). Check the hock during this time to make sure the water is still covering it; top up as required.

2 Once it is cooked, remove the hock and leave to cool. Shred the meat with your fingers, picking through it and discarding any fat or sinew. Add the mustard and parsley.

3 Reduce the ham cooking liquor by boiling until only 75ml (2½ fl oz) remains. Add it to the meat and season to taste. Press the mixture into a terrine or small loaf tin lined with clingfilm and chill. Or, if you don't have a terrine dish, the mixture can be put into ramekins and served as 'potted ham'. It's best to leave it for a couple of days before eating. Serve with pickles, chutney or Piccalilli (see page 209) and good toast.

Asian pork balls with chilli dipping sauce

Another spin on the meatball theme, these aren't remotely authentic but are what I make when I want to serve a selection of Asian-inspired main courses or starters. They're as good tossed with noodles and hoisin sauce as eaten with the chilli sauce below and a bowl of plain rice. This recipe makes more chilli sauce than you need, but I can never see the point of making enough for just 6 people. It keeps in the refrigerator for months.

Serves 6

FOR THE CHILLI SAUCE

6 large red chillies, 3 deseeded
  and roughly chopped
5cm (2in) fresh root ginger, peeled and
  roughly chopped
grated zest of 3 and juice of 2 limes
12 garlic cloves
1 large bunch of coriander, leaves only
300g (10½oz) caster sugar
50ml (2fl oz) Thai fish sauce
120ml (4fl oz) white wine vinegar

FOR THE PORK BALLS

1kg (2lb 4oz) minced pork
200g (7oz) bacon, very finely chopped
4 garlic cloves, crushed
2cm (¾in) fresh root ginger, peeled
  and grated
1 red chilli, deseeded and chopped
grated zest of 1 and juice of ½ lime
3 spring onions, finely chopped
10g (¼oz) coriander, finely chopped
salt and pepper
groundnut oil, for frying

1 First make the chilli sauce. Put the chillies, ginger, lime zest and juice, garlic and coriander leaves into a food processor and purée into a coarse paste. Put the sugar into a thick-bottomed pan with 6 tbsp water and place on medium heat until the sugar dissolves. Increase the heat slowly and gradually boil until the syrup becomes a caramel colour. Stir in the paste, fish sauce and vinegar and simmer for 2 minutes. Leave to cool.

2 Mix everything for the pork balls (not the oil) together in a large bowl, combining all the ingredients with your hands to make sure they get well mixed. Season well. Pull off chunks and form into balls about the size of a walnut. It is better to chill these before cooking them, otherwise they tend to fall apart, so lay them on a baking sheet, cover with clingfilm and refrigerate for an hour or so.

3 Heat about 1cm (½in) oil in a frying pan and cook the pork balls in batches, colouring them all over. It takes about 4 minutes, but do check you are frying them long enough for the pork in the middle to be cooked.

4 Serve with the chilli sauce (or indeed a bought dipping sauce, such as Thai chilli or plum) and eat with plain boiled rice and stir-fried vegetables.

Beef and carrots in stout with parsley and horseradish dumplings

The stout mellows in the oven to a lovely deep, chocolatey flavour. You don't need potatoes, making this dish very cook-friendly. Buttered cabbage is delicious with it.

Serves 4–6

FOR THE BEEF

3 tbsp groundnut or sunflower oil
1kg (2lb 4oz) braising beef, in large chunks
350g (12oz) carrots, sliced
300g (10½oz) leeks, sliced
50g (1¾oz) pearl barley
1 x 330ml bottle stout
salt and pepper

FOR THE DUMPLINGS

½ onion, very finely chopped
15g (½oz) butter
4 tbsp finely chopped parsley
80g (2¾oz) breadcrumbs
1 large egg
3 generous tbsp creamed horseradish

1 Preheat the oven to 160°C/325°F/gas mark 3. Heat 2 tbsp of the oil in a heavy flameproof casserole and brown the meat in batches. Remove and set aside. Add the remaining oil to the pan and fry the vegetables until lightly coloured, then tip in the barley.

2 Add the stout and stir to deglaze the pan. Pour in 750ml (1¼ pints) water, return the meat and season. Bring to the boil, reduce the heat, cover and put in the oven for 2 hours. Check to make sure the casserole hasn't become dry; add more water if needed.

3 Make the dumplings: sauté the onion in the butter, put into a bowl and add the remaining ingredients. Bring the mixture together and form into 12 little golf-ball-sized dumplings. The mixture will be rather loose, but persevere. Dot the dumplings on top of the beef. Cook, covered, for 20 minutes, then uncover and cook for another 10 minutes.

ALSO TRY...

Braised beef with anchovies and olives Preheat the oven to 170°C/340°F/gas mark 3½. Heat 3 tbsp olive oil in a heavy flameproof casserole and brown 2kg (4lb 8oz) braising beef, in chunks, in batches. Set aside. Add 1 tbsp more oil and fry 1 large onion, roughly chopped, 8 garlic cloves, chopped, and 2 fennel bulbs, trimmed and diced, until dark gold. Add 12 cured anchovies, drained, cook until they disintegrate, then add 1 tsp ground cinnamon. Cook for another minute. Add a bottle of red wine and stir to deglaze the pan. Return the meat and add 1 tbsp tomato purée, 2 broad strips of orange zest and the juice of 1 orange, 2 rosemary sprigs and pepper. Bring to the boil, reduce the heat and cover. Cook in the oven for 2 hours. Uncover, mix in 200g (7oz) small wrinkly black olives and cook for 20–30 minutes. Chop together a small handful of flat leaf parsley, 2 garlic cloves and the finely grated zest of 1 unwaxed lemon to make a gremolata. Stir some into the beef and sprinkle the rest on top. Serves 6.

Granny Miller's beef, potato and parsley stew

Along with Irish stew, this was a core dish of my childhood. Funnily enough, I used to think everybody cooked it…but in fact it's a dish that only my grandmother made. It would be hard to think of a cheaper meal: you take a cheap cut of beef and add potato, celery, leek and parsley. It's a great lunch dish on a cold Saturday.

Serves 6

1kg (2lb 4oz) shin of beef on the bone
900g (2lb) Maris Piper potatoes, halved or quartered, depending on size
2 celery sticks (and any celery leaves you have), roughly chopped
2 leeks, diced
salt and pepper
40g (1½oz) parsley, roughly chopped

1 Put the beef into a big saucepan (big enough to hold all the vegetables later) and add enough cold water to cover. Bring to the boil, then reduce the heat and simmer steadily for 1½ hours, or until the beef is falling off the bone. Skim from time to time. Lift the meat from its cooking liquid and leave to cool.

2 Add the potatoes to the beef stock and cook for about 30 minutes, until they start to break up (you should have a mixture of potato chunks and a soupy potato purée). Now add the celery and leeks and season really well. (There is so much potato in this it needs it.) Simmer for a further 15 minutes.

3 When the beef is cool enough to handle, remove it from the bones, discarding any fatty bits and sinew. I find using my hands is the easiest way. The meat should be in bite-sized chunks, but it doesn't have to be exact. Stir the beef into the stew with the parsley and heat it through. Check the seasoning and serve the stew in flat soup plates.

Marinated skirt steak with horseradish butter

A very interesting cut, so called for its wide, open-grained fibres that look 'pleated'. Ask the butcher for 'outside' skirt. Properly trimmed, skirt makes a terrific steak. It benefits greatly from marinating, and this marinade is based on a recipe by the great American chef Thomas Keller. Serve medium-rare.

Serves 6

FOR THE STEAKS
½ **head of garlic**
6 **thyme sprigs**
2 **rosemary sprigs**
1 **tbsp black peppercorns**
150ml (5fl oz) **olive oil**

6 x 175g (6oz) **thin-cut skirt steaks**
salt and pepper

FOR THE BUTTER
100g (3½oz) **butter, softened**
freshly grated horseradish

1 Bash the unpeeled garlic cloves with a rolling pin. Put the herbs, pepper and garlic in a pan with the oil and bring to a simmer. Leave to cool. Remove excess fat and any silverskin from the meat. Put in a dish, pour the marinade over, cover and refrigerate overnight.

2 Mash the butter with the horseradish and season. Refrigerate until firm, then work into a sausage shape and roll in baking parchment. Chill until completely firm.

3 Bring the steaks to room temperature. Lift them from the marinade and pat dry with kitchen paper, then lightly rub with oil. Heat a griddle or nonstick frying pan and, when it is very hot, sear the steaks on both sides for a couple of minutes, then reduce the heat and cook until done to your liking. Slice across the grain.

4 Serve the steaks with melting rounds of horseradish butter and watercress salad. Roasted regular or sweet potato wedges are great alongside.

ALSO TRY...

With soy sauce and wasabi Prepare and cook the steaks as above. Serve with bowls of soy sauce and wasabi, boiled rice and cucumber batons.

With chimichurri Put a generous bunch of flat leaf parsley (leaves only), 3 garlic cloves, chopped, 2 tbsp red wine vinegar, juice of ½ lime, 1 tsp each ground cumin and smoked paprika, 2 tbsp oregano leaves and 120ml (4fl oz) extra virgin olive oil into a blender and whizz. Season to taste. Serve with the steaks, cooked as above.

Sandwich with horseradish cream Mix 1 heaped tbsp grated fresh horseradish with 200ml (7fl oz) crème fraîche, 1½ tsp Dijon mustard and seasoning. Thinly slice 1 onion and cook over a medium heat in 2 tbsp oil. Increase the heat and cook the onion until almost crisp. Prepare and cook the steaks as above and make into baguette or sourdough sandwiches with the onion and horseradish.

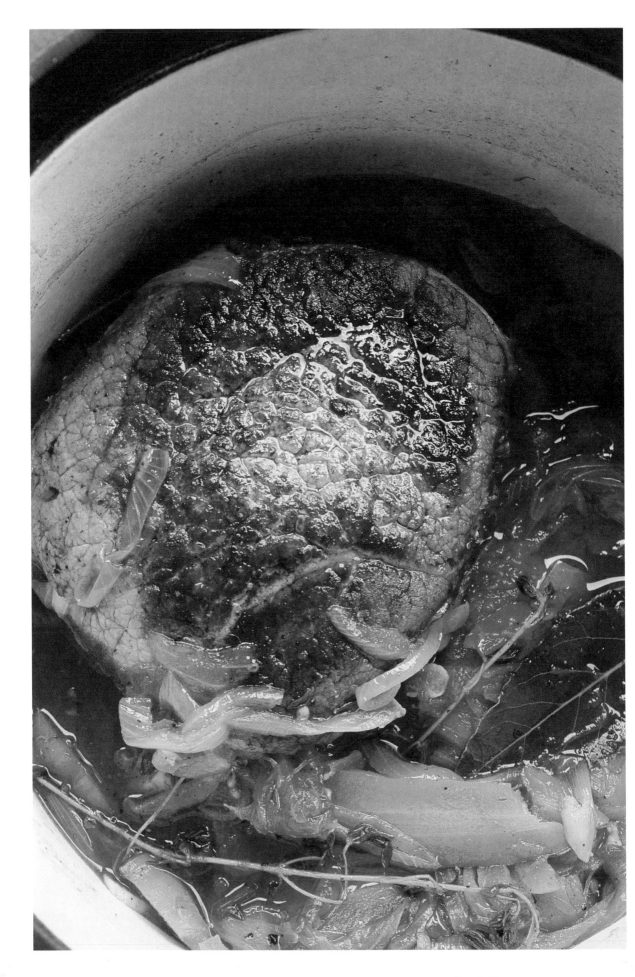

Clothilde's beef with wine, bay and thyme

I had never eaten a pot roast until I went on an exchange to France where my opposite number, Clothilde (only 15 and a very accomplished cook) made this. A slow-cooked silverside turns into lovely savoury slices with copious amounts of juice and completely soft vegetables. Everything tastes so much of itself; it's a pure dish. My French family didn't eat this with potatoes, but with bread or a delicious gratin of macaroni. The macaroni was either moistened with juice from the pot roast or with cream, then topped with Parmesan or Gruyère cheese and baked or grilled. It makes an excellent side dish for braised beef.

Serves 4

salt and pepper
1kg (2lb 4oz) silverside of beef
1 tbsp groundnut oil
2 onions, halved and cut into crescent moons
3 garlic cloves, chopped
150ml (5fl oz) dry white or red wine

4 carrots, halved lengthways
2 plum tomatoes, quartered
3 thyme sprigs
3 bay leaves
150ml (5fl oz) chicken or beef stock

1 Preheat the oven to 140°C/275°F/gas mark 1. Season the beef and heat the oil in a frying pan. Brown the joint well all over. Remove and put into a casserole. Add the onions to the frying pan (use the same oil and don't wash out the pan) and cook until golden. Add the garlic for another couple of minutes, then add the wine and bring to the boil, scraping the pan to make sure all the flavour goes into the liquid. Put this into the casserole with the beef and add the other vegetables and the herbs.

2 Heat the stock in the frying pan and pour that over too. Season well, cover and put into the oven for 2½ hours. The meat and vegetables should be tender. Serve from the casserole, cutting the meat into thick slices.

LEFTOVERS...

Remove the meat and vegetables from the cooking juices and chop them. Reduce the cooking juices, then toss the meat, veg and reduced juices with pasta and grated Parmesan. Chopped finely, the meat can also provide the base for a cottage pie.

ALSO TRY...

Rare roast topside Preheat the oven to 220°C/425°F/gas mark 7. Rub a 1.3kg (3lb) topside of beef (at room temperature) with olive oil and sprinkle with seasoning. Put in a roasting tin and roast for 30 minutes. Reduce the heat to 150°C/300°F/gas mark 2 and cook for a further 25 minutes. This will give lovely rare beef; don't be tempted to cook it for longer. Take the beef from the oven, insulate and leave to rest. Serve hot, with the usual accompaniments, or leave to cool, then refrigerate. It makes great sandwiches. Serves 8.

Oxtail with prunes and orange

Sweet, sticky, unctuous, there is no mistaking a pot of braised oxtail. I don't know why people don't cook it more, since it is the tenderest and most wonderfully flavoured cut. A dish for the depths of winter.

Serves 4–6

2 oxtails, cut into 2.5cm (1in) lengths
salt and pepper
plain flour
2½ tbsp oil
1 large onion, roughly chopped
2 celery sticks, finely chopped
2 garlic cloves, finely chopped
300ml (½ pint) red wine
500ml (18fl oz) chicken or beef stock

juice of 1 orange and 2 broad strips of zest
½ cinnamon stick
8 juniper berries, crushed
1 bouquet garni
16 shallots or baby onions
knob of unsalted butter
2 tsp caster sugar
16 moist prunes
2 tbsp finely chopped flat leaf parsley

1 Preheat the oven to 150°C/300°F/gas mark 2. Wash and dry the oxtail pieces. Cut off any excess fat and toss the pieces in seasoned flour. Heat most of the oil in a heavy flameproof casserole and colour the oxtail all over: you need a good brown colour. Remove the oxtail from the pan, add another drizzle of oil and sauté the onion and celery until soft and golden. Add the garlic and cook for another couple of minutes, then pour on the wine and scrape up all the bits of juice that have stuck to the bottom of the pan.

2 Return the meat and add the stock, orange juice and zest, cinnamon, juniper and bouquet garni. Season. Bring to the boil, then immediately reduce to a simmer, cover and put in the oven for about 3 hours, or until the meat is falling off the bone. Check every so often to make sure the liquid is still just about covering the meat.

3 I like to add the baby onions and prunes 1½ hours before the end of the cooking time, otherwise they completely fall apart. To prepare the onions, fry them in the butter until golden all over, then add the sugar to caramelize the outside a little. Add these to the stew with the prunes.

4 Lift the bouquet garni and cinnamon out before serving. If you happen to see it and it hasn't disintegrated, take the peel out too. If the juices seem a little runny, lift out the meat, small onions and prunes and reduce the juices by boiling. Return the meat, onions and prunes and heat through. Serve the oxtail with the parsley scattered over the top. Mashed potato seems an obvious accompaniment and is glorious but rich. I prefer to serve this stew with farro or even bulgur wheat.

Indian beef with peas

Based on a recipe called Kheema Matar in Madhur Jaffrey's *Indian Cookery* from 1982, I've been cooking it ever since. Her family ate it lukewarm on picnics with parathas, but I serve it hot.

Serves 6

2 tbsp oil

750g (1lb 10oz) minced beef

2 onions, finely chopped

6 garlic cloves, finely chopped

2.5cm (1in) fresh root ginger, peeled and very finely chopped

2 green chillies, deseeded and finely chopped

1 tsp ground coriander

2 tsp ground cumin

¼ tsp cayenne

275ml (9½fl oz) beef or chicken stock or water

1 tbsp tomato purée

pinch of soft dark brown sugar (optional)

salt and pepper

200g (7oz) podded or frozen peas

6 tbsp chopped fresh coriander

juice of 1 lime

1 tsp garam masala

1 Heat the oil in a casserole or sauté pan. Cook the beef over a high heat to a good brown colour (in batches if your pan isn't big enough for all of it at once). A good colour gives a dark, deep-tasting dish, rather than a pile of grey mince. Remove to a bowl.

2 Add the onions to the pan, reduce the heat and cook until soft and pale gold. Add the garlic, ginger, chillies, ground coriander, cumin and cayenne and cook for another couple of minutes. Return the beef, add two-thirds of the stock or water, the tomato purée, sugar (if using) and seasoning and bring to the boil. Reduce the heat and cook, covered, for 30 minutes.

3 Add the peas and remaining stock or water and cook for 10 minutes more. You should have a thick mixture. If not, whack up the heat to boil off some liquid. Stir in the chopped coriander, lime juice and garam masala and taste. Serve with rice or warm Indian bread. Try chutney and chopped cucumber with yogurt and mint on the side.

ALSO TRY...

Picadillo Sauté 750g (1lb 10oz) minced beef as above. Set aside. Add 1 onion, 1 red pepper and 1 green pepper (all chopped) to the pan and cook until soft and the onion is golden. Add 4 garlic cloves, chopped, 2 red chillies, deseeded and chopped, and ½ tbsp ground cumin. Cook for another minute, then add a handful of fat raisins, a can of tomatoes (ideally cherry) in thick juice, 1 tbsp tomato purée, 1 tsp soft dark brown sugar and 200ml (7fl oz) stock or water. Cook, uncovered, for 40 minutes, stirring occasionally. The result should be thick, like chilli con carne. Add the juice of a lime, with 50g (1¾oz) green olives, pitted and chopped, and seasoning. Stir in a handful of chopped coriander and sprinkle with toasted almonds. Serve with rice or warm tortillas, avocado slices, soured cream and grated Caerphilly or Wensleydale cheese.

Spiced meatballs in tomato sauce

The word 'meatball' doesn't generally inspire British eaters, yet there are wonderful versions from all over the world (quite a few appear in this book). It was a plateful of chilli-hot meatballs in Tuscany which alerted me to their potential. I made this shortly after and have tweaked the spicing over time. Add the chilli according to taste but don't stint on the cinnamon – it gives a lovely sweet warmth.

Serves 6

FOR THE SAUCE

2 x 400 cans tomatoes (ideally cherry) in thick juice
1 onion, finely chopped
2 garlic cloves, crushed
leaves from 4 oregano sprigs
½ tbsp tomato purée
3 tbsp olive oil
1 tbsp soft light brown sugar
salt and pepper

FOR THE MEATBALLS

3 tbsp olive oil
1 onion, finely chopped
4 garlic cloves, crushed
1 red chilli, deseeded and chopped
900g (2lb) minced beef
1 tbsp ground cinnamon
1 tsp freshly grated nutmeg
2 tsp ground mixed spice
3 tbsp finely chopped parsley

1 First make the sauce. Put all the ingredients into a saucepan (no need to brown anything) and bring to the boil. Reduce to a simmer and leave to cook for 30 minutes; the sauce will thicken and the tomatoes collapse. Stir from time to time, adding a little water if needed. Taste and adjust the seasoning.

2 For the meatballs, put 1 tbsp of the oil into a pan and cook the onion until soft and pale gold. Add the garlic and chilli and cook for another minute and a half. Put this into a bowl with the beef, spices and parsley. Season really well. Pull off a little chunk and fry in some oil. Eat. This helps you decide whether you need more seasoning or spices. Form the beef into meatballs using wet hands.

3 Heat the remaining oil in a frying pan and brown the meatballs in batches. You don't need to cook them through; just colour the outside. Once they are done, tip in the tomato sauce and stir gently. Cook for 10–15 minutes.

4 Serve with pasta (penne or spaghetti are both good; you'll need 100g/3½oz per person). Stir it with the sauce and meatballs in a large heated shallow bowl and serve.

ALSO TRY...

Baked meatballs with penne Preheat the oven to 180°C/350°F/gas mark 4. Increase the tomato sauce quantities in the main recipe by half. Make the sauce and meatballs as above, then cook 350g (12oz) penne and drain. Season the pasta and add a knob of butter. Layer in a deep gratin dish with the meatballs and sauce and 2 x 225g packets mozzarella cheese, sliced (reserve some). Lay the reserved slices on top and sprinkle on 150g (5½oz) grated Parmesan. Bake for 20 minutes or until golden and bubbling.

Salt beef

I love salt beef but it seemed a faff to make until I tried it. It was simple. You'll get a feast from a cheap cut. Wonderful for Sunday lunch (with plenty left for sarnies).

Serves 10, with leftovers

FOR THE BRINE

500g (1lb 2oz) light brown sugar
1.5kg (3lb 5oz) coarse sea salt
2 tsp black peppercorns
2 tsp juniper berries
4 cloves
4 bay leaves
2 thyme sprigs
50g (1¾oz) saltpetre (optional)

FOR THE BEEF

3kg (6lb 8oz) piece of beef brisket
1 bouquet garni
1 large carrot, roughly chopped
1 onion, roughly chopped
1 celery stick, roughly chopped
1 leek, cut into chunks
½ head of garlic

1 Put all the brine ingredients, with 5 litres (9 pints) water, into a very large saucepan and bring to the boil, stirring. Bubble for 2 minutes. Cool completely. Put the beef in a large, non-metallic container and cover with brine. (Weigh it down if necessary.) Leave in a cool place for 7 days.

2 Take the beef from the brine and soak in fresh water for 24 hours, changing the water a couple of times. Put in a pan with the other ingredients and cover with water. Poach gently for 2½–3 hours until tender. Serve with Piccalilli (see below), and boiled potatoes.

Piccalilli

Makes 3 x 340g (12oz) jars

1kg (2lb 4oz) vegetables, including
    marrow, cucumber, green beans, baby
    onions, cauliflower and carrot
50g (1¾oz) fine salt
30g (1¼oz) cornflour
½ tbsp English mustard powder

1 tbsp ground turmeric
½ tbsp yellow mustard seeds
1½ tsp ground ginger
1 tsp crushed coriander seeds
600ml (1 pint) cider vinegar
165g (5¾oz) soft light brown sugar

1 Halve the marrow and cucumber, scoop out the seeds and cube. Trim and halve the beans. Halve the onions, break the cauliflower into florets and cube the carrots. Layer in a large bowl, sprinkling with salt. Cover and leave for 24 hours. Rinse and drain.

2 Mix the cornflour and spices with a little vinegar to make a paste. Put the rest of the vinegar in a saucepan with the sugar and bring to the boil, stirring to dissolve the sugar. Pour some of the liquid (about 50ml/2fl oz) over the paste, stir, and add back to the pan.

3 Bring gently to the boil so the sauce can thicken. Boil for 4 minutes. Add the vegetables, stir, and simmer for 2 minutes. Ladle into warm sterilized jars (see page 242) and cover with non-reactive lids. Leave for 4 weeks before eating, or up to a year.

Soup, beautiful soup

Soup is just about the most sensible dish you can make. For a start it is based on stock that you can use cooked, leftover bones to produce. Food writers are forever exhorting us to use only what is spanking fresh, but I often make soup from carrots that are getting soft, or wilted salad (vinaigrette and all, see page 216). And leftover braises are a perfect base for a warming bowlful. But soup is not dull. A pot of soup is something you hug to yourself like a secret. Hurrying home on a cold day, you can feel miserable until you remember that there is soup in the house. The prospect is as cheering as being greeted by someone you love.

In our house, soup is often made on a Sunday night and eaten over the next three days. The carcass from the Sunday-lunch chicken is thrown into a pot with onion, carrot, celery, parsley and peppercorns, covered with water and simmered for a few hours. (Never add salt, skim the surface when it needs it, and don't boil as it makes the stock murky.) The stock you use is paramount – your soup will only be as good as your stock – and judicious seasoning is also important, but a cookery course opened my eyes to another important element. We made a creamy vegetable soup (just leeks, potatoes and carrots) the prospect of which didn't particularly wow me, but it was one of the loveliest I have ever tasted. Why? The slow, careful sweating of the vegetables to bring out their sweetness. Of course the butter you use adds greatly to the flavour but – in case your health alarm bells are ringing – you don't need much. Just melt enough to get the vegetables to exude their juices, cover the pan, and regularly add splashes of water to keep everything moist and stop the vegetables from catching. In soups which are Mediterranean in tone, olive oil does the same job.

A bit of thought given to garnishes opens up new worlds, too. There is nothing wrong with a humble bowl of spiced lentil soup, but top it with yogurt and chilli-fried onions and you have a wonderful interplay of hot and cold, a trip for your tastebuds. Flavoured creams – such as chilli for a pea and coriander soup, for example – can take your bowl to new heights, and more gutsy embellishments, like chunks of ricotta or shavings of cheese, transform a plain dish into a special one.

With careful sweating of the vegetables, good stock and judicious seasoning (with soup you have to taste, taste, taste, and a good squeeze of lemon juice will often heighten and bring the flavours together more than another scattering of salt) you can make a dish which hasn't broken the bank and somehow becomes more than the sum of its parts. Soup is a perfect example of sane and feel-good cooking.

Chilled roast tomato soup with anchovy and Parmesan toasts

Long, slow cooking brings out the flavour of tomatoes. You can also serve this hot.

Serves 8

FOR THE SOUP
2.5kg (5lb 8oz) plum tomatoes, halved
125ml (4fl oz) olive oil
salt and pepper
1½ tbsp sugar, plus more if needed
1 large onion, finely chopped
2 garlic cloves, finely chopped

FOR THE TOASTS
16 slices baguette, about 8mm (⅓ in) thick
50g (1¾oz) butter, melted
30g (1oz) Parmesan cheese, grated
8 canned anchovies, halved

1 Preheat the oven to 180°C/350°F/gas mark 4. Put the tomatoes in a roasting tin (or tins) where they can lie in a single layer. Add 6 tbsp of the oil, season and turn to coat. Sprinkle with the sugar. Roast until soft and slightly caramelized (about 40 minutes).

2 Heat the remaining oil in a heavy pan and sauté the onion until soft but not coloured. Add the garlic and sauté without browning. Add the tomatoes, their juices and about 750ml (1¼ pints) water. Bring to the boil and simmer for 10 minutes.

3 Purée in a food processor (not a blender, which crushes the seeds and makes the soup bitter), then push through a sieve. Adjust the seasoning – you may need more sugar – and add water until you have the consistency you want (it thickens considerably once cool). Refrigerate until serving.

4 To make the toasts, preheat the oven to 180°C/350°F/gas mark 4. Brush both sides of the bread with butter and set on a baking sheet. Sprinkle with cheese and top each with a halved anchovy. Bake for 12 minutes. Serve the toasts with the chilled soup.

ALSO TRY…

With basil cream Put 25g (1oz) basil leaves in a blender with 150ml (5fl oz) whipping cream, a little salt and white pepper and 1 small garlic clove, chopped. Whizz and taste. You might want to add a good squeeze of lemon juice.

Roast pepper soup with saffron cream Put 8 large red peppers in a roasting tin and drizzle with 5 tbsp olive oil. Roast in a preheated oven at 190°C/375°F/gas mark 5 for 50 minutes, or until completely soft and slightly scorched, then discard the stems and seeds and chop. Heat 3 tbsp olive oil in a saucepan and add 2 onions, chopped. Sweat, over a low heat, until soft but not coloured. Add the peppers, 2 tsp chilli sauce, 1 litre (1¾ pints) chicken or vegetable stock and seasoning. Simmer for 5 minutes, then cool. Blend, adding 2 tbsp balsamic vinegar and the juice of 1 small lemon. Taste for seasoning and refrigerate. Meanwhile, put a generous pinch of saffron threads in a cup with 2 tbsp just-boiled water and leave to infuse. Add 150ml (5fl oz) double cream and mix. Serve the soup cold with a swirl of saffron cream.

Ribollita

I never liked the idea of ribollita – it is, after all, cabbage soup, and I've spent too much of my life on the cabbage soup diet – but this is a wonderful, rich, multi-dimensional dish. I learned how to make it (and how important the stock and olive oil are to the final flavour) on a cookery course in Florence. Don't rush it; make it with care and good ingredients and you will be rewarded. Made well, this is one of the world's great soups.

Serves 4

250g (9oz) **Savoy cabbage or kale**
30g (1¼oz) **butter**
100g (3½oz) **leeks, chopped**
1 **celery stick, finely chopped**
75g (2½oz) **carrots, diced**
100g (3½oz) **waxy potatoes, diced**
1 litre (1¾ pints) **chicken or beef stock**
50ml (2fl oz) **extra virgin olive oil, plus more to serve**

2 **rosemary sprigs**
3 **garlic cloves**
6 **slices coarse white country bread, weighing about 20g (¾oz) each**
125g (4½oz) **cooked cannellini beans**
2 **large plum tomatoes**

1 Cut the coarse central core from the cabbage and slice the leaves. Melt the butter in a large, heavy pan and sauté the leeks and celery until pale gold, about 5 minutes. Add the carrots, cabbage or kale and potatoes and cook for another 12 minutes, turning the vegetables over in the butter every so often. Add the stock, bring to the boil, reduce to a simmer and cook for 45 minutes.

2 Meanwhile, heat the olive oil in a pan with the rosemary and 2 of the garlic cloves (leave them whole and unpeeled). When the oil starts to shimmer and the ingredients turn light brown, remove from the heat and leave to infuse.

3 Toast the bread and rub each piece with the remaining garlic clove (peeled, this time). Add the beans to the soup and cook for another 10 minutes.

4 Drop the tomatoes into a bowl of boiling water and leave for 10 seconds. Lift them out and rinse in cold water, then slip off the skins. Halve the tomatoes, scoop out the seeds (discard them) and cube the flesh. Add the tomatoes and flavoured oil to the soup and taste for seasoning.

5 In another large saucepan, layer up the soup with the bread (break it up to help spread it out) and leave to cool. Put the soup in the refrigerator overnight. The next day, bring it to room temperature, then bring to the boil again. Serve, drizzled lavishly with more extra virgin olive oil.

Pea and coriander soup

Frozen peas are a great ingredient to have on hand. This is easy, has a real kick, and you can serve it hot or cold.

Serves 6–8

FOR THE SOUP

2 tbsp olive oil

30g (1¼ oz) butter

1 onion, roughly chopped

1 potato, chopped

1½ tsp ground cumin

large bunch of coriander

900g (2lb) frozen peas

1 litre (1¾ pints) chicken stock

lemon juice, to taste

FOR THE CREAM

½ tbsp olive oil

2 red chillies, deseeded and sliced

125ml (4fl oz) whipping cream

juice of ½ lemon

salt and pepper

pinch of caster sugar (optional)

1 Heat the oil and butter in a heavy-bottomed pan. Add the onion and potato and stir. Add the cumin and stir for a minute to release the aroma. Chop the coriander stems (reserve the leaves) and add them as well, stir, add a splash of water and cover. Sweat for about 20 minutes, adding a splash of water every so often to prevent it catching on the bottom of the pan.

2 Add the peas, stock, coriander leaves and seasoning and bring to the boil. Simmer for 3 minutes, then leave to cool. When at room temperature, purée in a blender and add lemon juice to taste.

3 To make the cream, heat the olive oil and sauté the chillies until soft. Put into a blender and add the cream, lemon juice and a bit of salt. Blend briefly until broken down. Add a little water to thin it out (it should be able to float on the soup but not be in thick blobs). Check the seasoning. You might think it needs the tiniest pinch of sugar. Reheat the soup before serving (or serve cold) and garnish with the cream.

ALSO TRY...

Pea and ham soup Cook the soup as above but use stock made from a ham bone (ensure the stock isn't too salty – dilute with water if it is). Serve with a swirl of cream and flakes of cooked ham on top.

Pea soup with mint oil Make the soup as above but omit the cumin and the coriander; this must have a pure pea flavour. To make the oil, put 125ml (4fl oz) mild olive oil, the leaves from 4 large mint sprigs, ¼ tsp caster sugar and a good squeeze of lemon juice in a blender and whizz. Cover and refrigerate to let the flavours infuse. Strain through a sieve and taste. Serve spoonfuls on top of the soup. Mint oil is also delicious drizzled over seared salmon fillets, or with griddled squid and chorizo. It must be eaten on the day it's made, or it loses its fresh colour and flavour.

Cool lettuce and herb soup

Probably, like me, you hate throwing out leftover dressed salad. This is what to do with it.

Serves 4

50g (1¾oz) butter

8 spring onions, chopped

about 4 small butterhead lettuces, or baby Gem lettuces, plus leftover dressed salad (including cucumber and tomato)

small bunch of soft herbs (mint, basil or chervil)

800ml (1 pint 7fl oz) warm chicken stock

salt and pepper

good squeeze of lemon juice

2 tbsp double cream or crème fraîche (optional)

1 Melt the butter in a heavy-bottomed pan and sweat the spring onions for 5 minutes, until completely soft. Trim the base of each lettuce, then slice it and add to the onions with the leftover salad (including vinaigrette). Heat until the lettuce wilts.

2 Add the herbs and stock. Season, then blend. Taste, add lemon juice, seasoning and the cream or crème fraîche, if you want. Chill. This is lovely with a spoonful of vinaigrette on top and a scattering of the herb you have used.

ALSO TRY...

With tomato, mint and basil relish Make the lettuce soup as above and chill. Halve 100g (3½oz) cherry tomatoes and deseed half (I like some seeds but it shouldn't be too watery). Chop into small chunks. Put in a bowl and add 2 tbsp torn basil, 2 tbsp chopped mint, 3 tbsp extra virgin olive oil, 1 tsp white wine vinegar, a pinch of sugar, a squeeze of lemon juice and seasoning. Serve spooned on the lettuce soup.

Hungarian iced cucumber and dill soup Melt 45g (1½oz) butter in a heavy saucepan and add 1 onion, chopped. Cook gently for 4 minutes, add a splash of water and sweat over a low heat, covered, for 15 minutes, until soft but not coloured. You will need another splash of water. Add 2 cucumbers, peeled and diced, and 50g (1¾oz) potato, diced, and cook for a couple of minutes, then stir in 1½ tbsp flour. Cook for 2½ minutes, stirring, then add 300ml (½ pint) chicken stock and season. Bring to the boil, reduce to a simmer and cook for 15 minutes. Cool, then purée with 25g (1oz) dill, a squeeze of lemon juice and 200ml (7fl oz) milk. Taste. You may want more lemon or seasoning. Add 4 tbsp crème fraîche or soured cream and taste again. Chill. Serve garnished with sprigs of dill.

Cucumber, dill and prawn soup Make as for Hungarian Iced Cucumber and Dill Soup (see above), but purée some cooked prawns in the soup and serve more on top, with soured cream and dill.

Cucumber, dill and smoked trout soup As above, but purée smoked trout, not prawns, in the soup and top with more flakes, the soured cream and dill toserve.

Soup Savoyarde

There are many versions of this vegetable soup enriched with cheese, which melts into long strings. A great soup for keeping out the cold.

Serves 6–8

50–75g (1¾-2½oz) butter

1 large or 2 medium leeks, cut into
 rounds

350g (12oz) carrots, chopped

200g (7oz) parsnips, chopped

75g (2½oz) potato, cut into chunks

salt and pepper

1 litre (1¾ pints) chicken stock

250ml (9fl oz) full-fat milk

6–8 slices country bread

120–160g (4–5¾oz) Beaufort or Gruyère
 cheese, grated

1 Melt the butter in a large, heavy-bottomed saucepan and add the vegetables, salt and pepper. Turn everything round in the butter to coat. Add a good splash of water, cover the pan and set over a low heat. Sweat the vegetables for 35 minutes to bring out their sweetness, adding a splash of water every so often.

2 Add the stock, season and bring to the boil. Simmer for about 15 minutes; the vegetables should be completely soft. Leave to cool before purèeing (blending hot soup is very dangerous), then pour into a clean pan. Heat and add milk to taste (you may want to add more, or a little water). Adjust the seasoning.

3 To serve, lightly toast the bread and put a slice in the bottom of each bowl. Put the cheese on top then add the hot soup. Serve immediately.

ALSO TRY…

Soups made with roots and pulses are just about the cheapest you can make and are deeply comforting. Using the recipe above as a blueprint, you can make a soup based only on leeks and potatoes; or on parsnips (good with a little curry powder, which you cook for a minute with the vegetables once they are soft); or with carrot and potato (classically called *potage Crécy*); or Jerusalem artichokes (no need to peel). They are simple soups but, if you sweat the vegetables to bring out their optimum flavour and taste and season well, they can be some of the most satisfying things to eat.

Moroccan lentil soup with yogurt and chilli-fried onions

If you don't want to make the chilli onions, add 2 chopped, deseeded chillies to the soup, or some harissa to taste, instead.

Serves 8

FOR THE SOUP
3 tbsp olive oil
1 onion, finely chopped
2 sticks celery, finely chopped
3 garlic cloves, finely chopped
1 tbsp ground cumin
½ tbsp ground coriander
2 tsp ras al hanout
280g (10oz) red lentils
400g can chopped tomatoes
1.2 litres (2 pints) chicken stock or water
salt and pepper

6 tbsp roughly chopped coriander, plus
  extra to garnish

FOR THE CHILLI-FRIED ONIONS
2 onions, very finely sliced
2 tbsp olive oil
½ tsp ground cinnamon
2 tsp soft brown sugar
1 red chilli, deseeded and finely chopped
juice of ½ small lemon

TO SERVE
Greek yogurt

1 Heat the oil in a heavy pan and sauté the onion and celery until soft but not coloured. Add the garlic and spices and cook for 1 minute, then add the remaining soup ingredients apart from the coriander. Bring to the boil, reduce to a simmer and cook for 30 minutes, or until the lentils become a purée. Season and stir in the chopped coriander.

2 To make the chilli-fried onions, quickly fry the sliced onions in very hot olive oil until golden brown with crispy bits. Add the cinnamon, sugar and chilli. Stir and, once the sugar has melted, add the lemon juice and season. Serve the soup in hot bowls with a dollop of yogurt and the chilli-fried onions. Garnish with coriander leaves.

ALSO TRY...

Ham and lentil soup with caraway Make following the method above but omit the spices, celery, garlic, tomatoes and chilli-fried onions. Cook 2 onions, 1 potato, 2 carrots (all chopped) and 170g (6oz) lentils in oil. Replace the chicken stock with 1.5 litres (generous 2½ pints) stock made from a ham bone (make sure it isn't too salty; dilute with water if it is). Sauté flakes of ham or chunks of bacon in butter, adding 2 tsp caraway seeds. Scatter on top of the soup, with a swirl of cream, if you like.

Lentil and spinach soup Heat 3 tbsp olive oil in a heavy pan and gently cook 1 onion, chopped, and 1 celery stick, diced, for 8 minutes. Add 2 garlic cloves, chopped, and ½ tsp dried chilli flakes and cook for 1 minute. Add 250g (9oz) brown lentils, 3 tomatoes, chopped, 2 thyme sprigs and 1 litre (1¾ pints) water or chicken stock. Bring to the boil, reduce the heat, cover and cook until tender – about 45 minutes – topping up if it's too thick. Season well. Shred 250g (9oz) spinach and add to the soup to wilt. Add the juice of ½ lemon and stir in 4 tbsp extra virgin olive oil. Serves 4.

Ethiopian spiced pumpkin soup (*d'ba zigni*)

This, based on a recipe by food writer Celia Brooks Brown, is a cracking soup: sweet, warming and great for clearing the sinuses. You will have more spice blend than you need here, but keep it in a screw-top jar and use when you want a bit of heat.

Serves 4

FOR THE BERBERE (Ethiopian hot spice powder)

2 tsp cumin seeds
8 cloves
1 tsp cardamom seeds
½ tsp black peppercorns
1 tsp fenugreek seeds
1 tsp coriander seeds
8 small dried red chillies
½ tsp ground ginger
¼ tsp ground allspice
¼ tsp ground turmeric
1 tsp salt
¼ tsp ground cinnamon
3 tbsp paprika

FOR THE SOUP

2 tbsp sunflower oil
1 large onion, finely chopped
5cm (2in) fresh root ginger, peeled and
  finely chopped
750g (1lb 10oz) pumpkin or squash, peeled
  and cut into chunks
3 tbsp tomato purée
1 tsp salt

TO SERVE

Greek yogurt
small bunch of coriander

1 To make the berbere, toast the cumin, cloves, cardamom, peppercorns, fenugreek, coriander and chillies in a dry frying pan over a medium heat for about 2 minutes to release the aroma. Shake the pan often. Cool, then grind to a fine powder in a pestle and mortar with the ginger, allspice, turmeric, salt, cinnamon and paprika.

2 Heat a saucepan over a medium heat and add the oil. Cook the onion until quite soft and pale gold, then stir in the fresh ginger and 2 tsp of the berbere and cook for 2 minutes. Add the pumpkin and coat with the spices. Add the tomato purée, salt and 500ml (18fl oz) water. Stir, cover and bring to the boil.

3 Simmer for 15–20 minutes, or until the pumpkin is soft. If you prefer the soup thicker remove a few pieces of pumpkin and mash them, then return to the pot. Check for seasoning and serve with Greek yogurt (not authentic but good) and torn coriander.

ALSO TRY...

Pumpkin, bean and spinach soup Make as above but omit the berbere and fresh ginger and use 1 litre (1¾ pints) well-flavoured chicken stock instead of water. When the pumpkin is soft add 225g (8oz) cooked and rinsed cannellini or borlotti beans or chickpeas. Heat through and add 250g (9oz) shredded spinach to wilt. Check the seasoning. If you have used beans, serve with grated Parmesan cheese or Parsley and walnut Pesto (see page 228). Fried chunks of pancetta are good, too. If you have used chickpeas mix 2 tbsp harissa with boiling water, spoon yogurt on top of the soup and drizzle with the harissa.

Black bean soup with pico de gallo

You can make this warming Mexican soup more of a main course by serving with slices of avocado, soured cream or grated Cheshire cheese, torn coriander leaves and a squeeze of lime.

Serves 6

FOR THE SOUP

250g (9oz) dried black beans
3 tbsp olive oil
100g (3½oz) smoked streaky bacon, chopped
1 onion, finely chopped
1 small carrot, chopped
1 celery stick, plus leaves, finely chopped
stalks from 15g (½oz) bunch coriander
½ small red chilli, deseeded and chopped
2 tsp cumin seeds
3 garlic cloves, chopped
1 litre (1¾ pints) chicken stock
salt and pepper
juice of ½ lime

FOR THE PICO DE GALLO

2 tbsp finely diced red onion
400g (14oz) tomatoes, chopped
1 red chilli, halved, deseeded and finely
  chopped
2 tsp caster sugar
2 tbsp finely chopped coriander
juice of 1 lime
2 tbsp lager
salt, to taste

TO SERVE

soured cream
crumbled Cheshire cheese (optional)

1 Cover the beans with water and leave to soak overnight. Drain and rinse. Heat the oil in a heavy pan and cook the bacon for about 5 minutes. Reduce the heat and add the onion, carrot, celery, coriander stalks and chilli. Stir. Add 3 tbsp water and cover the pan. Leave to sweat for about 10 minutes. The vegetables should be quite soft.

2 Toast the cumin in a dry pan, then grind with a pestle and mortar and add to the pan with the garlic. Cook for 2 minutes, then add the beans and stock. Bring to the boil, reduce the heat and simmer for 1½ hours. The beans should be tender. Season, then cool. Purèe in a blender or food processor. Add the lime juice and check the seasoning.

3 To make the pico de gallo, mix everything together. Cover and refrigerate for 30 minutes before serving. Serve the soup hot, with a swirl of soured cream and a spoon of pico de gallo. Add cheese if you like. Serve the remaining pico de gallo on the side.

ALSO TRY...

Black bean soup with avocado salsa Make the soup as above, but without the pico de gallo. Mix the following ingredients together not more than an hour before serving: 200g (7oz) tomatoes and 2 avocados, both diced, 1 tsp ground cumin, 2 garlic cloves and 2 spring onions, both finely chopped, 2 red chillies, deseeded and finely sliced, the juice of ½ lime, 2 handfuls of chopped coriander, 4 tbsp extra virgin olive oil, Tabasco to taste and seasoning. Cover and let the flavours infuse. Serve spooned on the soup with soured cream and chopped coriander.

Beetroot soup with goat's cheese

Beetroot is very sweet so it needs something tart, hence the Bramley apples. The slightly sour, farmyard flavour of goat's cheese is perfect against that sweetness and completely elevates an inexpensive soup (just look at the beauty of it for a start). A swirl of soured cream or Greek yogurt and a scattering of dill is lovely too, though. You can also serve this hot.

Serves 8

60g (2oz) butter
2 onions, chopped
2 carrots, chopped
2 celery sticks, chopped
6 garlic cloves, chopped
800g (1lb 12oz) beetroot, trimmed
   and sliced

1 small Bramley apple, peeled, cored
   and sliced
1.5 litres (2½ pints) chicken stock
salt and pepper

TO SERVE

soured cream
dill sprigs
125g (4½oz) mild goat's cheese

1 Melt the butter in a large, heavy-bottomed saucepan and add the onions, carrots, celery and garlic. Add a splash of water, cover and sweat for 15 minutes until the onions are soft. Add the beetroot (I don't bother to peel it) and apple, cover and sweat for 15 minutes. Pour on the stock and season. Bring to the boil, then simmer until the beetroot is completely tender. Leave to cool, then purée.

2 Serve hot or cold with a dollop of soured cream on top and dill sprigs, then crumble the goat's cheese and add some to each serving.

ALSO TRY...

Beetroot soup with salmon Make the soup as above and garnish with soured cream, sprigs of dill and flaked leftover cooked salmon, or, if you have a piece of raw salmon, cut the flesh into tiny dice, moisten with a little light-tasting olive oil and lemon juice, add salt, pepper and chopped dill and spoon on to the soup along with soured cream.

Parsnip and smoked haddock soup

The saltiness of the fish is lovely against the sweet parsnips. This is also very good –
and makes a complete meal – with a poached egg on top.

Serves 6

35g (1¼oz) butter
1 onion, chopped
3 garlic cloves, finely chopped
800g (1lb 12oz) parsnips, chopped
700ml (1¼ pints) light chicken stock
  or water
750g (1lb 10oz) smoked, undyed haddock
  fillet, skinned

3 tsp ground cumin
salt and pepper
150ml (5fl oz) milk or double cream, plus
  more to serve
1 tbsp chopped flat leaf parsley or chives

1 Melt the butter in a heavy-bottomed pan and add the onion, garlic and parsnips. Stir
to coat in butter, then add a splash of water and reduce the heat. Cover and sweat over
a very low heat for 20 minutes. You will need to add a splash of water every so often to
keep the vegetables from catching.

2 Put half the stock or water into a sauté pan and bring to the boil. Reduce the heat
and poach the fish in this liquid until just cooked (about 5 minutes). Drain off and
reserve the poaching liquor. Break the fish into big flakes, being careful to remove any
remaining bones. Once it is cool, refrigerate.

3 Stir the cumin into the parsnips and cook for 1 minute. Season (go easy on the salt),
add the fish poaching liquor, the remaining stock or water and bring to the boil.
Reduce to a simmer and cook until the parsnips are completely soft. Leave to cool.

4 Purée the soup, add the milk or cream and fish and check the seasoning. Reheat
gently before serving. Sprinkle with parsley or chives and add a swirl of cream to
each bowl.

ALSO TRY...

Smoked haddock, bacon and butter bean chowder Melt 30g (1¼oz) butter in
a large, heavy-bottomed pan and fry 125g (4½oz) bacon lardons until golden. Add
2 leeks, cut into rings and well washed, and a splash of water, cover and sweat over
a medium heat until soft (15 minutes). At the same time put 450g (1lb) smoked
haddock into a pan and cover with 400ml (14fl oz) milk. Bring to the boil, then
reduce the heat immediately and let the fish poach gently for about 5 minutes. Add
600ml (1 pint) chicken stock and 125g (4½oz) cooked and rinsed butter beans to the
leeks. Break the fish in the milk into large flakes (remove the skin if there is any),
then add the milk and fish to the leeks and beans. Season with pepper (you shouldn't
need salt), add 2 tbsp cream, if you have it, and heat through. Serve in warmed bowls
with chopped parsley on top. Serves 4.

Chicken, coconut and ginger soup with lime, basil and mint

Practically a storecupboard soup. You can use cold pork instead of chicken and change the herbs, using just basil or mint alone, or coriander.

Serves 8

1 large onion, sliced into crescent moon-shaped slices
4 tbsp groundnut oil
2.5cm (1in) square of fresh root ginger, peeled and finely chopped
4 red chillies, deseeded and finely chopped
4 garlic cloves, finely chopped
1.4 litres (2½ pints) chicken stock
2 x 400g cans coconut milk

300g (10½oz) small waxy potatoes, halved
1 tbsp fish sauce
1 tbsp soft light brown sugar
juice of 2 limes
1 aubergine, cut into chunks
250g (9oz) cooked chicken, cut into chunks
15g (½oz) basil leaves
10g (¼oz) mint leaves

1 Sauté the onion in half the oil until just colouring. Add the ginger, chillies and garlic and cook for 1 minute. Add the stock and bring to the boil. Reduce the heat to a simmer and stir in the coconut milk. Add the potatoes, fish sauce, sugar and half the lime juice. Simmer until the potatoes are just cooked (about 12 minutes).

2 Sauté the aubergine in the remaining oil until golden, then add to the soup while the potatoes are still cooking. Add the chicken and heat thoroughly. Tear in the basil and mint and add the remaining lime juice. Taste – it shouldn't need anything – and serve.

ALSO TRY...

Squash and coconut soup Cut 2kg (4lb 8oz) peeled squash into chunks, and put into a roasting tin. Drizzle with 4 tbsp oil and seasoning. Roast in a preheated oven at 200°C/400°F/gas mark 6 for 20–25 minutes, until tender and slightly caramelized. Heat 2 tbsp oil in a large saucepan and gently cook 2 onions and 2 celery sticks, both roughly chopped, until soft but not coloured. Add 2 garlic cloves, crushed, 1 red chilli, deseeded and finely sliced, 1cm (½in) fresh root ginger, peeled and chopped, and cook for another 2 minutes. Add the squash, 1 litre (1¾ pints) chicken stock, seasoning and 2 x 400g cans coconut milk. Bring to the boil and simmer so everything can heat through and the flavours can meld. Leave to cool, then purée. Reheat and add the finely grated zest of 1 lime and the juice of 2, ½ tbsp fish sauce and 2 tbsp soft light brown sugar. Taste for seasoning. Stir in torn basil and mint leaves.

Prawn, squash and coconut soup Make as for Squash and Coconut Soup (above), but stir in some prawns – cooked or raw – at the end. Cooked prawns need only heating through; raw prawns will cook in 3 minutes or so.

Sweet potato and coconut soup Make Squash and Coconut Soup (above), replacing the squash with peeled sweet potato.

Swedish spinach soup with egg butterballs

The egg butterballs melt deliciously into the soup.

Serves 6

FOR THE BUTTERBALLS
115g (4oz) butter
yolks of 3 hard-boiled eggs
salt and pepper

FOR THE SOUP
25g (1oz) butter
1 onion, finely chopped

40g (1¼oz) long-grain white rice
1 litre (1¾ pints) chicken stock
500g (1lb 2oz) spinach
150ml (5fl oz) double cream
juice of ½ lemon

1 Make the butterballs first. Mash the butter and yolks together (use the egg whites for egg mayonnaise sandwiches) and season. Roll into 2.5cm (1in) balls, put on a plate, cover with clingfilm and refrigerate.

2 For the soup, melt the butter in a large saucepan and sweat the onion, covered, over a low heat. Add a splash of water and make sure the pan doesn't get dry. The onions take 10 minutes to become soft but not coloured. Add the rice and stock and bring to the boil. Simmer for 15 minutes. Add the spinach, pressing and turning as it wilts. Bring to the boil, season and cook for 6 minutes, stirring. Cool.

3 Purée in a blender and add the cream. Return to a saucepan to heat, add a squeeze of lemon juice and taste for seasoning. Serve hot with the butterballs on top.

ALSO TRY...

Spinach soup with Thai butter Make the soup as above but use an extra 150ml (5fl oz) stock instead of cream. To make the Thai butter, mash 75g (2½oz) slightly softened butter with 4 heaped tbsp finely chopped coriander, 1 garlic clove, crushed, the finely grated zest and juice of ½ lime, 2 tsp fish sauce, ½ tsp ground ginger and pepper. Mix in 1 red chilli, deseeded and very finely chopped. Chill and serve in melting chunks on the hot soup.

Spring greens and roast garlic soup Preheat the oven to 190°C/375°F/gas mark 5. Put 3 heads of garlic in a small roasting tin, drizzle with olive oil and season. Pour in a little water and roast for 40–50 minutes until tender. Melt 40g (1½oz) butter in a large heavy saucepan and gently cook 1 onion, 2 bunches spring onions and 250g (9oz) potato, all chopped. Stir to coat in the butter, then add a splash of water, cover, reduce the heat and sweat for 15 minutes. Remove the tough ribs from 500g (1lb 2oz) spring greens and slice the leaves. Add to the pot with a splash of water and seasoning. Stir, cover and sweat for 10 minutes. When the garlic is cooked, squeeze the soft pulp from each clove. Add this and 1.2 litres (2 pints) chicken stock to the soup and bring to the boil. Cool. Purée. Check the seasoning. Serve hot, with a drizzle of cream on top, if you like. Serves 8.

Cold weather soupe au pistou

I often make *soupe au pistou* (see below) in summer. I missed it during autumn and winter, so I adapted it using cold weather vegetables and wintry pesto.

Serves 8

FOR THE SOUP
4 generous tbsp olive oil
1 onion, finely chopped
1 large carrot, chopped
1 celery stick, finely chopped
1 leek, sliced
250g (9oz) peeled butternut squash, cubed
1 small fennel bulb, sliced
1 potato (about 150g/5½oz), in small chunks
salt and pepper

2 litres (3½ pints) chicken or veg stock
400g can cannellini or borlotti beans

FOR THE PESTO
50g (1¾oz) walnuts
50g (1¾oz) pine nuts
1 garlic clove, crushed
30g (1¼oz) flat leaf parsley leaves
150ml (5fl oz) extra virgin olive oil
50g (1¾oz) Parmesan cheese, grated

1 Heat the oil in a large, heavy saucepan. Add the onion and carrot and sauté for 5 minutes. Add the other vegetables, season and sauté for 10 minutes. Pour in the stock and simmer for 5 minutes. Drain and rinse the beans. Add and cook for 5 minutes.

2 To make the pesto put the nuts, garlic and parsley into a food processor with seasoning and half the oil. Pulse-blend, then stir in the remaining oil and the Parmesan. Top the soup with spoonfuls of pesto, serving the rest alongside.

LEFTOVERS...

Parsley and walnut pesto is great with spaghetti (add chunks of ricotta to make it go further). It's also good with pasta, goat's cheese and fried radicchio.

ALSO TRY...

Summer soupe au pistou Gently cook 1 leek, 1 large potato and 1 celery stick, all chopped, in olive oil for 5 minutes, stirring. Add 1.7 litres (3 pints) chicken stock, season and cook for 10 minutes. Add 2 courgettes, chopped, 225g (8oz) green beans, topped, 225g (8oz) drained canned haricot beans and 12 cherry tomatoes, quartered. Cook for 5 minutes, uncovered, then add 2 tbsp chopped parsley. Put 2 bunches basil, 3 garlic cloves, salt and pepper in a blender, whizz and add 125ml (4fl oz) extra virgin olive oil. Top the soup with spoonfuls of pistou and grated Parmesan. Serves 4–6.

Hot-and-sour soup Put 2 lemon grass stalks, shredded and 2.5cm (1in) fresh root ginger, finely chopped, 2 shallots, sliced, 6 spring onions, chopped, 3 red chillies, deseeded and finely sliced, and 4 kaffir lime leaves into 3 litres (5¼ pints) chicken stock. Simmer for 10 minutes. Add 115g (4oz) oyster mushrooms, sliced, 500g (1lb 2oz) shredded cooked chicken, 2 tbsp fish sauce and 2 tsp soft light brown sugar and gently heat for about 3 minutes. Stir in 40g (1½oz) chopped coriander and the juice of ½ lime. Taste. Add more lime juice, sugar, fish sauce or chilli, to taste. Serves 6.

Where the wild things are

The idea of wild food has become more appealing over the last few years. It's free, it forms part of our increasing attachment to the countryside and concern for the planet, and it fits in with an idealized, somewhat romantic notion of a rural 'lifestyle'. There are pluses in the first two parts of that sentence, but a negative in the last. Foraging is the ecologically aware foodie's badge of honour. It is 'fashionable', and that's always a worry, as it suggests a fleeting and insincere fad. So listen up. You don't need to take special classes, own a crumbling country pile, or tote a gun to enjoy wild food. I have never shot an animal, but I've always eaten 'wild food', even though I didn't look at it that way.

Every year I go blackberry picking (one of the greatest seasonal pleasures of my childhood). I wait for the first frost to attack sloes before gathering them for sloe gin, and I stand at the bottom of trees while nimbler friends chuck down crab apples. If you live in, or can get to, the countryside, you can pick blackberries, sloes, crab apples, rosehips, elderflowers, nettles, sorrel, wild garlic and rocket, among many other free delights. If you have a good butcher nearby you can – cheaply – buy pheasant and rabbit.

Apart from the fact that it's free, why bother with wild food? Well, it seems mad – almost wasteful – not to use a resource that is just sitting there. I find it hard to look at blackberries that have rotted in the hedgerow. Nettles and wild garlic are abundant. Why leave those crab apples on the branch when they can be turned into a jelly to accompany six months' worth of roast pork? But the most compelling reason is that it's a huge pleasure – a thrill, in fact – to gather wild stuff. You are literally getting your hands dirty, often stained and scratched as well, as you try to reach a particularly hard-to-get-at cluster of blackberries, or another handful of wet, heady garlic leaves. And it feels great to take the lid off some pot-roasted rabbit and know you have cooked meat that is just out there for the taking.

I haven't covered wild mushrooms in this chapter because it takes special knowledge to gather them (and avoid poisoning yourself), and those collected by others are very expensive. I have included dishes for rabbit and pheasant, but not partridge, because most other game, if you don't shoot it yourself, is expensive.

The greens – wild garlic leaves, rocket and sorrel – can be found in April and May and nettles (use only the young shoots) in March and April; fragrant elderflower blossoms are everywhere (once you can identify them you'll realize) for six weeks from the beginning of June; blackberries are around in August and September, crab apples in September and October, and rosehips and sloes in October and November. Abundance is yours. Fill your boots.

Wild greens soup

You really need to gather the nettles when they are young, otherwise the leaves are coarse and the flavour much less pleasant. The sting goes out of nettles as soon as they are heated. You can also make this soup partly with lettuce or spinach, but making it with nettles feels, well, as if you are really cooking and getting your hands dirty. It's really good with the addition of butterballs (see page 227).

Serves 6

½ **carrier bag of young nettles (about 650g/1lb 7oz), or nettles with other wild leaves such as sorrel or wild rocket**
55g (2oz) butter
1 large onion, finely chopped
1 large carrot, diced
2 large garlic cloves, crushed
40g (1½oz) long-grain white rice
1 litre (1¾ pints) well-flavoured chicken stock

salt and black pepper
freshly grated nutmeg
juice of ½ lemon
100ml (3½fl oz) double cream, plus more to serve

TO SERVE
double cream and snipped chives or soured cream and goat's cheese (optional)

1 Go through the nettles, discarding any really tough stalks. Wash the nettles and other leaves thoroughly. Melt the butter in a large pan and sweat the onion and carrot until soft but not coloured. Add the garlic and cook for another minute or so, then add the rice and stir around. Add the stock and simmer for 10 minutes to cook the rice, then add the nettles, pushing them down into the pot (they will wilt a lot and reduce). Bring to the boil and simmer for 5–10 minutes, until the nettles are really tender. Season.

2 Allow to cool, then purée the soup in a blender. Pour back into a saucepan, heat through and add the nutmeg, lemon and cream. Stir everything together well and taste for seasoning.

3 Serve with an extra swirl of cream on top and some snipped chives, or a dollop of soured cream and crumbled goat's cheese.

Wild garlic and goat's cheese omelette

I remember the day I first came across wild garlic. I was visiting a stately pile with huge gardens in Gloucestershire and I couldn't understand what the smell was. Now I make forays to the countryside just to collect it. The leaves have a lovely, subtle garlic flavour which an omelette shows off perfectly. Leave out the goat's cheese if you want a pure garlic experience.

Serves 2

good handful of wild garlic leaves (about 50g/1¾oz)
salt and pepper

4 large eggs, lightly beaten
25g (1oz) butter
50g (1¾oz) goat's cheese, crumbled

1 Shred the garlic leaves finely. Season the eggs. Heat half the butter in a nonstick frying pan. Add half the wild garlic and wilt for about 20 seconds, then add half the eggs. Leave for about 15 seconds, then tilt the pan, gently scraping up the bits of the omelette which have set round the edges into the middle of the pan, allowing the uncooked eggs to run into the spaces left behind.

2 When the omelette is still liquid on top but set underneath, put half the cheese on one half. Fold the other half over the filling, let the cheese melt for 20 seconds or so, then turn the omelette out on to a plate (preferably warmed, but we live in the real world, and not many people heat a plate for an omelette.)

3 Repeat with the rest of the ingredients to make another omelette. Serve immediately.

Pheasant with beer, carrots and honey

Pheasant can be incredibly cheap once the season is under way. I tend not to like it too highly flavoured (very girly, but there we are). Your butcher should be able to tell you how long the pheasant has been hung. That will give you an indication of how strong it will taste. The birds can be hung for up to 7 days, the flavour becoming more gamey the longer they hang. Cooking pheasant may sound like a big deal, but the pot-roasted recipes here and on page 236 are a doddle, as well as lovely and moist. They go well with something gutsy, such as a dish of barley (see page 126). Some recipes suggest 1 pheasant feeds 4; not in my house…

Serves 2 greedy people

25g (1oz) butter
1 oven-ready pheasant
1 large onion, sliced into slim
    half-moon-shaped slices
50g (1¾oz) bacon lardons
6 medium carrots

salt and pepper
350ml (12fl oz) beer
1½ tbsp honey
4 thyme sprigs, plus the leaves from 1 more
    to serve

1 Preheat the oven to 190°C/375°F/gas mark 5. Melt the butter in a heavy-bottomed flameproof casserole (a small one, which will just fit the bird) and brown the pheasant all over on a medium heat. Lift out and set aside.

2 Add the onion and the bacon to the pot and cook it over a medium heat until the onion is soft and pale gold, about 5 minutes. Add the whole carrots and stir them around in the buttery juices. Put the pheasant back in the pot, with any of the juices which have run out of it, season, add the beer, honey and thyme and bring to the boil. Cover the pot tightly and put into the oven for 40 minutes, removing the lid for the last 15 minutes. Baste the bird a few times while cooking (pheasant can dry out very easily, so you need to keep it moist). Push a skewer into the thickest part of the thigh; if there are any pink juices put it back in the oven for a few minutes longer.

3 Sprinkle over some more thyme leaves and serve at the table in its cooking pot.

ALSO TRY…

Pheasant with red wine and sour cherries Boil 500ml (18fl oz) red wine and 250ml (9fl oz) stock, separately, until they are reduced by half. Set aside. As in the main recipe above, brown the pheasant in butter, then remove it and sauté 2 onions. Add 2 garlic cloves, chopped, and sauté for a further 2–3 minutes. Put the pheasant back, along with any juices which may have run out of it, and add the wine and stock, 3 thyme sprigs, a bay leaf, a 5cm (2in) cinnamon stick, seasoning and 100g (3½oz) dried sour cherries. Add a slug of port if you have any lurking. Continue to cook as above. If it looks as if there is too much juice at the end, remove the pheasant, boil the juices so they reduce, then return the pheasant to heat through.

Pheasant with cider and apples As for Pheasant with Beer (see page 234), brown the pheasant, then remove, and sauté 1 onion, sliced, and 75g (2½oz) bacon lardons. Put the pheasant back on top of these and add 300ml (½ pint) dry cider. Bring to the boil, season, add 4 thyme sprigs, reduce the heat and cook as on page 234. While waiting for the pheasant to finish cooking, sauté 2 tart eating apples (cored and cut into wedges) in 15g (½oz) unsalted butter, sprinkling with a little caster sugar once just soft. When the pheasant is cooked, remove it from the pan, cover with foil and keep warm in a low oven. Quickly bring the juices to the boil and add 100ml (3½fl oz) double cream and 2 tsp Dijon mustard. Boil until the juices coat the back of a spoon. Check the seasoning. Put the apples and pheasant into the sauce and heat through. Serve in the pot.

Pheasant with Savoy cabbage and bacon As for Pheasant with Beer (see page 234), brown the pheasant in butter and set it aside. Add 2 tbsp olive oil to the pan, 6 shallots, peeled and sliced, 1 carrot and 1 stick celery, both diced, and 100g (3½oz) bacon lardons. Cook until golden, then add 1 small Savoy cabbage, shredded, 6 juniper berries, crushed, and another 40g (1½oz) butter. Season and turn the cabbage to get it coated in butter (don't worry if it seems like a lot of cabbage – it shrinks considerably). Add 200ml (7fl oz) chicken stock and 3 thyme sprigs and bring to the boil. Immediately reduce the heat to low, return the pheasant to the casserole, cover and cook as on page 234.

Georgian pheasant with tea, grapes and hazelnuts Toast 30g (1¼oz) blanched hazelnuts until pale gold, then pound roughly (use a mortar and pestle or put the nuts in a bag and bash with a rolling pin) so some are ground and others in chunks. Cover 100g (3½oz) raisins with 150ml (¼ pint) cold tea and bring to the boil. Remove from the heat and leave to plump up for half an hour. Brown the pheasant in butter, then remove from the pan and sauté 1 onion, finely chopped. Add 2 garlic cloves, crushed, and sauté for another couple of minutes. Return the pheasant to the pan with any juices which have run from it. Add the raisins and tea, 100g (3½oz) black and green grapes, halved and deseeded, most of the nuts, 200ml (7fl oz) port, 50ml (2fl oz) red grape or orange juice and a few bay leaves. Bring to the boil, then immediately reduce the heat. Continue to cook as in the main recipe (see page 234). It's traditional, but optional, to add fresh tangerine segments once the pheasant is cooked. If the liquid hasn't thickened enough (though some grapes should burst and thicken the sauce), remove the pheasant, reduce the liquid by boiling and return the pheasant to heat through. Stir in 1 tbsp finely chopped parsley and sprinkle the remaining nuts on top.

Pigeon, hazelnut and blackberry salad

Pigeon breasts aren't too gamey and make a grand salad.

Serves 4

FOR THE SALAD
4 pigeon breasts
olive oil
salt and pepper
6 juniper berries, crushed
15g (½oz) unsalted butter
150g (5½oz) blackberries
½ tsp caster sugar (optional)

200g (7oz) salad leaves (baby spinach,
    watercress or lamb's lettuce)
50g (1¾oz) hazelnuts, halved and toasted

FOR THE DRESSING
smidgen of Dijon mustard
1 tbsp red wine vinegar
1 tsp crème de cassis
2 tbsp olive oil
5 tbsp hazelnut oil

1 Mix the pigeon with 2 tbsp olive oil, salt, pepper and the juniper berries and allow to marinate for a few hours.

2 To make the dressing, put the mustard and wine vinegar into a cup, season and whisk in the remaining ingredients. Taste for seasoning.

3 Heat a griddle or frying pan until very hot, then cook the pigeon for 2 minutes on each side in the olive oil clinging to them. They should be rare; cut into one to check. Put on a warmed plate, cover with foil and leave to rest for 5 minutes.

4 Add the butter to the same pan and heat until foaming. Toss in the blackberries and roll in the warm butter to soften slightly. Add the sugar, if using (I love that sweet-savoury thing).

5 Using a fine, very sharp knife, cut the breasts into neat slices. Toss the leaves and nuts with most of the dressing, then arrange on 4 plates. Spoon on the blackberries and lay the pigeon on top. Drizzle with the remaining dressing and serve.

ALSO TRY...

Venison with blackberries Put 150g (5½oz) blackberries in a pan with 5 tbsp crème de cassis or crème de mûre and simmer for 10 minutes. Set aside. Heat 25g (1oz) butter and sauté 3 shallots, finely chopped, until soft but not coloured. Add 300ml (½ pint) red wine and 150ml (¼ pint) red wine vinegar and cook until reduced to about 5 tbsp. Add 350ml (12fl oz) well-flavoured chicken or game stock and bring to the boil. Reduce until slightly syrupy. Stir in the blackberries and juices and taste for seasoning. Season 6 x 2cm (¾in) thick venison steaks. Heat 30g (1¼oz) unsalted butter and 1 tbsp groundnut oil in a frying pan. Sear the steaks on each side over high heat to colour, then reduce the heat and cook until rare (about 3 minutes each side). Reheat the sauce and beat in 50g (1¾oz) very cold unsalted butter, diced; it will become glossy and thicken. Cut each steak into 4 to reveal the lovely pinkness inside and serve on warmed plates with the sauce.

Rabbit with mustard and tarragon

There isn't masses of meat on a rabbit, but what is there has great flavour and my butcher practically gives it away. So why don't we eat more? I guess it's the 'bunny in the pot' thing. Try to get over it; it's mad not to eat food that is healthy, cheap and abundant. This recipe is an old-fashioned French classic and delivers a bit of relatively inexpensive luxury.

Serves 3–4

salt and pepper

1.5kg (3lb 5oz) rabbit joints

25g (1oz) unsalted butter

1 onion, finely chopped

500ml (18fl oz) chicken stock

100ml (3½fl oz) double cream

4 tsp Dijon mustard

good squeeze of lemon juice

leaves from 8 tarragon sprigs

1 Season the rabbit. Heat the butter in a sauté pan and brown the joints all over. Remove and set aside. In the same pan, cook the onion until soft and pale gold. Add the stock, bring to the boil, reduce to a gentle simmer and return the rabbit. Simmer, covered, for 20 minutes, then take the lid off and cook for another 20 minutes.

2 Remove the rabbit from the pan, put in a warm dish and cover. Add the cream to the stock and reduce by about half. Add the mustard, lemon juice and half the tarragon. Reduce again until it is the consistency of single cream; do taste, though – you don't want the sauce to be sticky or over salty. Return the rabbit to heat through and stir in the rest of the tarragon just before serving. Lovely with boiled waxy potatoes or ribbons of egg pasta.

ALSO TRY...

Rabbit with bacon and watercress-and-lemon dumplings Preheat the oven to 190°C/375°F/gas mark 5. Heat 1 tbsp olive oil in a shallow, ovenproof pan and cook 2 small onions, sliced, until soft but not coloured. Add 2 garlic cloves, sliced, and cook for 1 minute. Season. Rub 1.5kg (3lb 5oz) rabbit joints with olive oil, season and wrap a piece of bacon around each. Set on the onions and drizzle with oil. Tuck in 4 thyme sprigs, pour on 250ml (9fl oz) dry white wine or stock and simmer for 20 minutes. Make the dumplings by sautéing ½ onion, very finely chopped, and 1 garlic clove, crushed, in 40g (1½oz) butter. Put in a bowl and add 2 tbsp finely chopped parsley, 80g (3oz) watercress, chopped, 80g (3oz) white breadcrumbs, the finely grated zest of ½ lemon plus a good squeeze of juice, the leaves from 4 thyme sprigs, 1 large egg, beaten, and seasoning. Bring the mixture together and form about 12 little golf-ball-sized dumplings. Tuck the dumplings in around the joints. Roast for 20 minutes.

Elderflower and berry jellies

Jellies with fruit suspended in them are quite magical, but one made with the scent of elderflowers is glorious. You can choose just one type of berry for this rather than a mixture if you prefer.

Serves 6

5 large or 10 small sheets gelatine (about 15g/½oz)
425ml (¾ pint) white wine
4 tbsp caster sugar
150ml (¼ pint) elderflower cordial

400g (14oz) berries (raspberries, loganberries, blueberries, redcurrants, whitecurrants and blackcurrants, all stems removed)

1 Put the gelatine into a shallow bowl and cover with water. Soak for 5 minutes, until completely soft. Scoop up the gelatine and gently squeeze out the excess water.

2 Meanwhile, heat the wine with the sugar, stirring gently to help the sugar dissolve. The wine shouldn't get any hotter than hand warm. Add the soaked gelatine and stir to dissolve. (Gelatine can't go into boiling liquid or it will lose its setting properties.) Add the elderflower cordial and stir.

3 Divide the berries between 6 little glasses and pour over the liquid. Put in the refrigerator to set. There is a lot of fruit here, so it shouldn't bob too much to the top as it is tightly packed into the jelly, but if it does just push it down gently as the jellies are setting. It's best to make these the day before so that they have time to set. Serve with cream on the side.

Raspberry and elderflower sorbet

This has a very intense flavour. It's delicious with vanilla ice cream.

Serves 4
450g (1lb) raspberries
100g (3½oz) granulated sugar, plus 2 tbsp
5 tbsp elderflower cordial

1 Put the raspberries in a large bowl with 2 tbsp of the sugar. Leave for an hour. Put the remaining sugar in a saucepan with 55ml (2fl oz) water and heat gently, stirring to help the sugar dissolve. Simmer for 2 minutes. Leave to cool.

2 Put the berries in a food processor and whizz, then sieve. Mix the purée with the cooled syrup and the cordial. Cover and chill, then freeze in an ice cream machine according to the manufacturer's instructions, or still-freeze in a shallow container, beating the mixture to break up the crystals 3 or 4 times during the freezing process.

ALSO TRY…

Elderflower cordial This is a simple and lovely thing to do. Leave the house with some bags and a pair of scissors and return smelling of heaven. Use only very fresh flowers. Gather 20 heads of elderflower. Shake them gently to get rid of any little insects. Put 1.8kg (4lb) granulated sugar into a pan with 1.2 litres (2 pints) water. Bring to the boil, stirring to help the sugar dissolve. Pare the zest of 3 large unwaxed lemons in wide strips and put into a large bowl with the elderflowers. Slice the lemons and add to the bowl. When the syrup has boiled, pour it over and stir in 75g (2½oz) citric acid. Cover with a cloth and leave for 24 hours. Next day, preheat the oven to 150°C/300°F/gas mark 2. Thoroughly wash and rinse some glass screw-top bottles and put them in the oven for 15 minutes to dry. Remove and leave to cool for 15 minutes. Sterilize the lids by boiling in water for a few minutes, and rinse any funnels or bowls with boiling water before you use them. Taste the juice around the flowers and add a little more lemon juice if needed. Strain the cordial through a sieve lined with clean muslin or a new J-cloth and pour into the sterilized bottles. Cover and keep in the refrigerator for up to 5 weeks. Makes about 2 litres.

Elderflower and lemon creams Basically a lemon posset with added elderflower. It's great with poached rhubarb or gooseberries. Put 500ml (18fl oz) double cream and 100g (3½oz) caster sugar into a heavy saucepan and slowly bring to the boil, stirring to dissolve the sugar. Reduce the heat slightly and bubble for 3 minutes, no more, and don't let it boil over. Pour the warm cream into a bowl and whisk in the juice of 2 large lemons. It will thicken; mix to remove any lumps. Stir in 4 tbsp elderflower cordial. Pour into a jug and cool a little. Divide between 6 small glasses and leave to cool completely, cover with clingfilm then refrigerate. It will set in about 3 hours, but it's a good idea to make this the day before it's needed. Serves 6.

Blackberry and nectarine jam

You really need to find a good patch of wild blackberries if you are going to make this, as shop-bought ones are just too expensive. If picking your own proves impossible, raspberries are great in this too, though going to a pick-your-own fruit farm is the only way to make it without breaking the bank. This is good with peaches and apricots too; get them from a market at the end of the day, when you can pick up a bargain. Sterilize your jam jars as you would the bottles for my Elderflower Cordial (see page 242). This recipe is for a glut of fruit. If you don't want to make so much, halve the quantities of everything except the lemon juice.

Makes about 3.5kg (7lb 12oz)

1.5kg (3lb 5oz) nectarines
1.5kg (3lb 5oz) blackberries

juice of 1½ lemons
1.5kg (3lb 5oz) preserving sugar

1 Halve and stone the nectarines and cut the flesh into chunks. Pick over the blackberries, removing any stalks or withered leaves. Put the fruit into a preserving pan with the juice of 1 of the lemons and 300ml (½ pint) water. Bring to the boil, then reduce to a simmer and let the fruit cook for about 15 minutes, or until tender.

2 Add the sugar and stir to help it dissolve, then bring to the boil and keep on a steady boil. Skim off any scum that rises to the surface during this time.

3 It's important to test for the setting point about 5 minutes after your sugar has dissolved, as cooking the jam for longer than it needs will impair the flavour. Some jams take as little as 3 minutes to reach setting point, others can take 15. You can use a sugar thermometer (they're not expensive) or – a failsafe low-tech way – put a spoonful of the boiling jam on to a plate and then stick it very quickly in the freezer for about 2 minutes. Push the jam lightly with your finger. If it wrinkles slightly, the jam is at setting point and ready to be potted. If you have a sugar thermometer, the setting point for jam is 104°C (220°F) so test on that. Add the remaining lemon juice, pot the jam in warm sterilized jars and seal.

Blackberry and brown sugar loaf

This is based on a recipe from the inspirational American food writer John Thorne. He uses raspberries, so you can make it with those in the summer. A lovely, no-nonsense teatime cake.

Serves 8–10

175g (6oz) unsalted butter, softened

175g (6oz) soft light brown sugar

2 large eggs, beaten until frothy

2 heaped tbsp soured cream

1 tbsp grated lemon zest

pinch of ground cinnamon

250g (9oz) plain flour, sifted

1 tsp baking powder

200g (7oz) blackberries

icing sugar, to dust

1 Preheat the oven to 160°C/325°F/gas mark 3. In an electric mixer beat the butter until light, then add the sugar and beat until fluffy. Add the eggs a little at a time and beat until creamy. Turn the speed down to low and add the soured cream, zest, cinnamon and flour. Beat until the mixture just comes together.

2 Sift the baking powder over the top, sprinkle on the blackberries and gently fold these into the mixture with a metal spoon, breaking them up as little as possible. Spoon into a buttered 23x13cm (9x5in) loaf tin, smooth the top and bake in the oven for 45–50 minutes, or until a fine skewer inserted into the centre of the loaf comes out clean.

3 Let the loaf cool in the tin for about 15 minutes, then run a fine knife round the edges and turn it out on to a wire rack. Turn it right side up and leave to cool completely. Sift a light dusting of icing sugar over the top.

ALSO TRY...

Blackberry, apple and maple brown betty A great, down-home American dessert that's even easier to make than crumble. Preheat the oven to 180°C/350°F/gas mark 4. Mix 150g (5½oz) soft light brown sugar with ½ tsp each ground mixed spice and ground ginger. Mix 3 tbsp of this with 250g (9oz) stale cake crumbs and pour over 100g (3½oz) melted butter. Slice 1 cooking apple thinly and mix with 500g (1lb 2oz) blackberries along with the remaining sugar and spice mixture. Butter a gratin or pie dish and put in half the crumbs. Pile the fruit on top and pour over 25ml (1fl oz) maple syrup. Put the remaining crumbs on top and bake, loosely covered with foil, for 20 minutes. Remove the foil and bake for another 20 minutes or so, until the fruit is tender and the top golden. Serve with whipped cream or vanilla ice cream. Serves 6.

Blackberry and ricotta hot cakes with honey

An amalgam of an American and an Italian recipe. Great for brunch, and for ekeing out a small stash of blackberries.

Serves 4

FOR THE HOT CAKES
250g (9oz) ricotta cheese
3 eggs, separated
25g (1oz) unsalted butter, melted, plus
   more for frying
40g (1½oz) caster sugar
½ tsp vanilla extract

finely grated zest of 1 orange
50g (1¾oz) plain flour, sifted
125g (4½oz) blackberries

TO SERVE
icing sugar, to dust
honey, to drizzle

1 Mash the ricotta in a bowl with the egg yolks, 1 of the egg whites, the melted butter, sugar, vanilla and zest. Fold in the flour. Beat the remaining 2 egg whites until stiff, then carefully fold them into the mixture, followed by the blackberries.

2 Melt a little knob of butter in a nonstick frying pan over a medium heat and spoon in enough batter to make a round about the size of your palm. You can do 2 or 3 hot cakes at a time. After a couple of minutes, when you can see the underside is golden (do a bit of gentle levering with a palette knife) and set, carefully turn the cakes over. Cook for 2 minutes on the other side, then remove from the pan and keep them warm.

3 Add more butter to the pan as needed to cook the rest of the hot cakes and try not to let it burn. If it does, discard the burnt butter and start again with fresh stuff. Sift icing sugar over the top of each cake before serving and drizzle with a little honey.

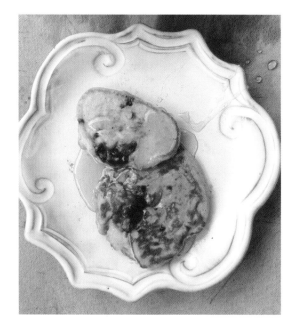

Sweet fruitfulness

Fruit is the food that most makes me feel we have been given an embarrassment of riches, and also the one that firmly anchors us to the seasons. A visit to an orchard when the trees are so heavy with fruit that their branches are pulled to the ground can make you gasp at the plenty we enjoy. Even the word 'ripe' suggests fullness, perfection, sensual pleasure. Fruits dazzle – the crimson flesh of a plum, or the red blush on the curves of an apricot – and they burst with a taste for which we yearn: sweetness.

I love it when friends who grow fruit bring presents from their gardens or allotments: Victoria plums in summer, fat golden quinces in November, even huge bags of Bramley apples so ripe that they have to be cooked immediately. Gluts of fruit are a challenge. You can initially think, when faced with a large quantity of pears: what on earth will I do with them? But spend a Sunday morning cutting and boiling before ladling pear chutney into clean jars and it will be worth it. To capture abundance by making preserves gives a special kind of thrill.

Of course many fruits are now taken for granted and grown for high yield and shelf life, not quality. With so many varieties of apples in the world, supermarkets still fill bays with bland Golden Delicious, and we can eat strawberries in January (jolly red and a perfect shape, but they often taste of turnips, particularly the ubiquitous Elsanta). When I was a child I kept an eye on the strawberry patch in our neighbour's garden. The scarlet that suddenly appeared against the green leaves and pale straw was magical, and a sure sign of summer. My children do not enjoy this pleasure – they think strawberries are available year round.

Ensuring that fruit tastes of something requires an almost campaigning zeal on all our parts. Buy it at farmers' markets and greengrocers'; they aren't as likely to stock varieties just because thay have a long shelf life and they need your support. When you get a chance, visit a pick-your-own farm both to support it and to find bargain loads of fruit. If we accept only what's on offer in supermarkets, caring growers and flavourful varieties will disappear.

In this chapter there are recipes for fruits that are cheap only at the height of their season, or if you pick your own. Most stone fruits are expensive, but become plentiful and cheaper in August. Other recipes here offer ways to make more of fruit that's never very cheap – cherries, gooseberries, rhubarb – by ekeing it out.

One of the most enjoyable things I do at the height of summer is to slow-bake stone fruits in readiness for breakfast the next morning. When apricots are abundant and on sale in street markets for a song (especially at the end of the day), I carry home bag after bag, mix them with sugar and vanilla and look forward to a bowlful of heaven.

It takes very little to make something special out of fruit. Revel in it.

Strawberry and lemon curd cake

This sponge is also delicious as a cake without the fillings (halve the recipe and start checking after 30 minutes). You can make it in the autumn with ground hazelnuts.

Serves 8–10

FOR THE CAKE
250g (9oz) self-raising flour
350g (12oz) caster sugar
½ tsp salt
150g (5½oz) ground almonds
3 large eggs
175g (6oz) plain low-fat yogurt
1 tsp vanilla extract
2 tsp almond extract
225g (8oz) butter

FOR THE TOPPING AND FILLING
800g (1lb 12oz) strawberries
5 tbsp caster sugar
finely grated zest and juice of ½ lemon
200g (7oz) mascarpone
200ml (7fl oz) double cream
10 heaped tbsp lemon curd
icing sugar, to taste, plus more to dust

1 Preheat the oven to 180°C/350°F/gas mark 4. Sift the flour on to the sugar and salt, then stir in the almonds. Whisk the eggs lightly with a third of the yogurt and the vanilla and almond extracts. Using a food processor, or hand-held electric beater, cream the butter until pale and fluffy. Gently beat in the remaining yogurt and, with the machine on a very low speed, add the dry ingredients alternately with the eggs. Beat on a medium speed for 1–2 minutes.

2 Butter and base-line a 23cm (9in) springform cake tin (it should be 7.5cm/3in deep) and spoon in the batter. Bake for 50 minutes; a skewer pushed into the centre should come out clean. Leave to cool slightly, then turn out on to a wire rack and leave to cool completely. The sponge is very delicate, so carefully, with a broad, sharp knife, cut it horizontally into 3 layers.

3 Wash and hull the strawberries and cut into halves and quarters (reserve good-looking small berries for decoration). Sprinkle the cut strawberries with the sugar, zest and juice, stir and leave to macerate for 15 minutes. Beat the mascarpone to loosen it a bit. In a separate bowl whip the cream until it holds its shape well. Combine the cream, mascarpone, lemon curd and icing sugar to taste.

4 Spread the bottom layer of cake with half the cream, then half the strawberries. Repeat with the next layer. Put the top layer on. Arrange a small pile of perfect strawberries in the middle and sift over a light dusting of icing sugar. Keep in the refrigerator until about 20–30 minutes before serving. It's best eaten on the day it's made.

ALSO TRY…

This cake is good with all other berries (blackberry and lemon curd is particularly lovely). Try orange curd or a few spoonfuls of elderflower cordial instead of lemon curd, or make the filling using all cream instead of mascarpone if you prefer.

Strawberry and rose ice cream

Ice creams made with fruit and cream seem purer and more intense than those with a custard base, and are easier to make. If you aren't partial to floral scents in food leave out the rosewater; you'll still have a lovely ice cream.

Serves 6
450g (1lb) strawberries, hulled
juice of ½ lemon
115g (4oz) caster sugar
5 tbsp rosewater
250ml (9fl oz) whipping cream, chilled

1 Chop the strawberries roughly and mix with the lemon juice, sugar and rosewater. Leave to stand for an hour until the sugar has dissolved and the fruit has softened.

2 Whip the cream until it forms soft peaks. Purée the strawberries and all their juices in a blender or food processor. Stir the strawberry purée into the cream, then mix everything together.

3 Churn in an ice cream machine, or pour into a shallow container and still-freeze. If still-freezing, you need to take the ice cream out of the freezer every couple of hours (do this 3 or 4 times) and fork the frozen stuff around the outside into the rest of the mix, to make it smooth.

ALSO TRY...

This is a simple ice cream and therefore very adaptable. You can replace the strawberries with raspberries or blackberries (the blackberry version is better without rosewater), but taste the mixture before freezing; the raspberry version will need a little more sugar as raspberries are a tarter fruit. Raspberry or blackberry purées need to be sieved (because they have so many seeds) before being mixed with the cream.

Cherry and almond croûtes

This is just about the easiest pudding in the world, basically baked fruit on toast. You don't have to use brioche – other breads are good, but you just get different results. However, don't cut them too thinly or you'll get charred bread rather than golden croûtes. This is a good way of using up the end of a loaf, and of getting rid of that stash of marzipan (bought only at Christmas) hanging around in the cupboard. Your croûtes don't have to be boozy; use fruit juice to moisten the bread, or spread the bread and dot the fruit with butter. Leave the stalks on (and therefore the stones in) a few of the cherries: it looks pretty. But warn your guests; especially those with dentures!

Serves 4

4 slices brioche

75ml (2½fl oz) kirsch

juice of ½ lemon

135g (4¾oz) marzipan, broken into chunks

400g (14oz) cherries, pitted

4 tsp caster sugar

25g (1oz) flaked almonds

icing sugar, to dust

TO SERVE

thick cream

1 Preheat the oven to 180°C/350°F/gas mark 4. Put the brioche on to a baking tray. Sprinkle half the kirsch and lemon juice over the slices and scatter with the marzipan. Put the cherries on top, sprinkle the rest of the lemon juice and kirsch over, then dust with the caster sugar and add the almonds.

2 Bake for 30 minutes. The cherries should be tender and the bread and marzipan golden. Leave to cool a little, then sift icing sugar over each piece and serve with thick cream.

ALSO TRY...

You can make croûtes with apricots, peaches, nectarines and plums as well, as long as they are ripe (if the fruit is hard, the bread gets too toasted by the time it becomes tender). Plums and apricots should be halved or quartered, depending on ripeness, and peaches should be sliced. Almond liqueur can be used instead of kirsch.

Guignolet, or cherry wine

Fruit liqueurs and 'wines' are a wonderful way of capturing summer – doesn't cherry wine seem lovely, even before you've tasted it? – and they are the easiest kind of 'preserve' you can make. Cherries are usually expensive, but every so often you come across a mountain being sold cheaply in a street market. That's the time to make this. Cherry wine is a French aperitif. Serve it chilled in small glasses (a fresh cherry hanging on the side of the glass doesn't go amiss! – it is, after all, a pretty and romantic drink). You can add sparkling white wine to make a sort of cherry kir, or sparkling water to make a spritzer.

Makes about 1.2 litres

500g (1lb 2oz) unblemished pitted cherries
1 bottle light red wine

300g (10½oz) caster sugar
75ml (2½fl oz) kirsch

1 Heat the cherries in a saucepan with the wine and sugar, stirring to help the sugar dissolve. Bring just up to the boil, then turn down the heat and simmer gently for 5 minutes. Cool, add the kirsch, cover and leave for 2 days.

2 Strain and pour into sterilized bottles (see page 242) and add a screw top or cork. The boozy cherries left behind are delicious with chilled rice pudding, or used to make a filling for a summer sponge (spoon them on to a layer of whipped cream, or a mixture of mascarpone and crème fraîche).

ALSO TRY...

Apricot liqueur Put 450g (1lb) apricots, halved and stoned, into a saucepan with 450g (1lb) granulated sugar and 700ml (1¼ pints) dry white wine and proceed as above. Take the pan off the heat. Add 5 tbsp kirsch or amaretto and 300ml (½ pint) vodka. Put into a bowl or jug, cover and leave for 6 days. Strain (I filter it twice through cheesecloth as the apricots do disintegrate a bit) and put into clean, sterilized bottles. Add tops and leave for a month before using. The boozy apricots can be used just like the cherries above, and they also make a lovely fool. The liqueur itself should be served in small glasses – I prefer it chilled – or mixed with white wine or sparkling white wine to make an apricot kir.

Dorothy Allhusen's cherry salad

This sounds quite odd but is totally delicious. It's based on a dish from Dorothy Allhusen's lovely tome, *A Book of Scents and Dishes* (1926). She doesn't use balsamic vinegar, but I like the sweetness it imparts. Dorothy suggests serving it with cold roast beef. I also serve it with roast chicken, roast lamb and grilled goat's cheese on toast.

Serves 4

500g (1lb 2oz) cherries, pitted

2 tbsp brandy

2 tsp balsamic vinegar

4 tbsp olive oil

salt and pepper

juice of ½ lemon

2 tbsp roughly chopped flat leaf parsley

1 Put the cherries into a shallow bowl and add the other ingredients.

2 Stir everything together gently and leave to macerate for about an hour before serving. These are good the next day too; the cherries become slightly softer but the flavours have permeated the flesh. If you do want to serve them next day, don't add the parsley until about an hour before serving, otherwise it loses its bright colour.

ALSO TRY...

Chicken and cherry salad with creamy tarragon dressing Mix ½ tbsp white wine vinegar, ½ tsp Dijon mustard and salt and pepper in a cup. Whisk in 4 tbsp light olive oil, 1 tbsp water and 1 tbsp single cream. Add the leaves from 3 tarragon sprigs, chopped, and about ½ tsp caster sugar. Mix and taste for seasoning and a good balance of sweet and sour. Toss with about 350g (12oz) cooked chicken, neatly sliced, 250g (9oz) cherries, pitted, 125g (4½oz) salad leaves (watercress is very good) and 25g (1oz) toasted flaked almonds. Serve straight away. Serves 2.

Gooseberry 'pots'

This recipe was sent to me by Margaret Drummond, a reader of my newspaper cookery column. It originally comes from a very old book, where they suggest using it as a filling for a 'coffin' of pastry (basically a pie), but I'd rather have it like this. It has the feel of an old-fashioned English nursery pudding and is a great way to use up a horde of gooseberries.

Serves 4

500g (1lb 2oz) gooseberries, topped and tailed
100g (3½oz) caster sugar
2 tbsp sweet cider, sweet wine or apple juice

75g (2½oz) white breadcrumbs (not too fine)
30g (1¼oz) unsalted butter
2 large egg yolks

1 Put the gooseberries in a pan with the sugar and cider, wine or juice and cook over a low heat until half-stewed (7–10 minutes). Add the breadcrumbs and cook for another 3–4 minutes. The mixture should be quite thick.

2 Take the pan off the heat and beat in the butter and yolks. Taste for sweetness. Leave to cool to room temperature, then put into little glasses and chill. Serve topped with whipped cream, or good bought or home-made cold custard.

ALSO TRY...

Stewed gooseberries Lovely to have in the refrigerator. You can eat them for breakfast (that tang is great first thing in the morning), or serve as an easy dessert with rice pudding (perhaps flavoured with elderflower cordial) or with good, thick, yellow cream and shortbread or a big, blousy meringue. Don't forget their potential in trifle (see page 261). They also make a great fruit fool: combine them with custard and whipped cream or Greek yogurt and a couple of tablespoons of elderflower cordial.

Gooseberry and elderflower mess A play on Eton mess, but even better as gooseberries are so much tarter than the traditional strawberries. Don't stir in your crushed meringues until just before serving, or they will go soggy. Poach 450g (1lb) gooseberries in 100ml (2½fl oz) water and 75g (2½oz) caster sugar. When they are tender, remove the gooseberries with a slotted spoon. Roughly smash up 100g (3½oz) meringues and gently combine them with 200ml (7fl oz) cream, whipped, 100g (3½oz) Greek yogurt, the gooseberries, 2 tbsp lemon curd and 3 tbsp elderflower cordial. Pile into glasses and garnish with mint leaves.

Scottish pear and raspberry trifle

I had this in a small hotel in Westray, the island just next to Orkney. Sharp raspberries are lovely with the sweet muskiness of pears.

Serves 6

75g (2½oz) caster sugar
strip of lemon zest
2 pears, peeled, halved and cored
3½ tbsp whisky
light egg sponge, bought or home-made

200ml (7fl oz) whipping cream
2 tbsp icing sugar
seeds from ½ vanilla pod, or ½ tsp pure
  vanilla extract
200g (7oz) raspberries

1 Put 120ml (4fl oz) water and the caster sugar in a saucepan and gently heat, stirring to help the sugar dissolve. Add the zest and pear halves and poach until just tender. How long this takes will depend on the pears, but start checking after 12 minutes.

2 Drain the pears and leave them and their liquid to cool. Add the whisky to the liquid. Break the sponge into chunks, spread on a plate, and spoon over about three quarters of the poaching liquid. Leave to soak in really well.

3 Assemble the trifles in individual glasses at the last minute. Whip the cream lightly, adding the icing sugar and vanilla. Cut the pears lengthways into slices. Add a layer of sponge to each glass, then sliced pears, raspberries, a trickle of the remaining poaching syrup and a good spoon of cream. Repeat, finishing with fruit on top, and serve.

ALSO TRY...

There is nothing trifling about trifles. They are one of the glories of British cookery, far greater than the sum of their parts. The basic idea of a trifle is so good that it's a shame to be restricted by rules. I make trifles without custard (as above), with crushed ginger snaps or amaretti biscuits instead of cake, with cooked fruit and fresh fruit. Curds and marmalade can be used instead of jam, and indeed there is not always the need for jam at all. When it comes to alcohol I have used Muscat, sherry, calvados and rum. These are all riffs on the basic idea. Go where you will...

Gooseberry and Muscat trifle With stewed gooseberries, custard, cream and Muscat-soaked cake.

Plum and ginger trifle Make with crushed ginger biscuits or gingerbread (whisky or brandy is good as the moistening agent here), poached plums, cream and custard.

Apple and calvados trifle Make with stewed Bramleys, cream, custard and calvados-soaked cake.

Caramelized orange trifle Make with cake spread with marmalade and soaked in whisky or cointreau, custard, cream and segments of orange in caramel.

Gooseberry meringue pie

This has more tang than lemon meringue pie and a good substantial filling (making it more satisfying).

Serves 8

FOR THE PASTRY

275g (9¾oz) plain flour, plus more to dust
155g (5½oz) butter, cubed
pinch of salt
2 tbsp caster sugar
1 egg yolk, mixed with 1 tbsp very
   cold water

FOR THE FILLING

900g (2lb) gooseberries, topped and tailed
200g (7oz) caster sugar
5 tbsp cornflour
4 large egg yolks

FOR THE MERINGUE

3 egg whites
175g (6oz) caster sugar, plus more
   to sprinkle

1 To make the pastry, put the flour, butter and salt into a food processor and whizz until the mixture resembles breadcrumbs. Add the sugar and whizz again, then gradually add just enough egg and water to bring it together into a ball. Wrap in clingfilm and refrigerate for an hour or so.

2 Preheat the oven to 190°C/375°F/gas mark 5. Roll the pastry out on a floured surface and use to line a 24–25cm (9½–10in), 3½cm (1½in) deep, metal tart tin with a removable base. Prick the base with a fork and line with greaseproof paper and baking beans. Bake blind for 15 minutes, then remove the paper and beans and bake for another 10 minutes. It should be a pale biscuit colour.

3 Meanwhile, put the gooseberries in a pan with 2 tbsp water and the sugar. Cover and gently heat, stirring to help break the gooseberries down and coax out the juice. Cook over a medium heat until tender. Some will stay whole, some will become mushy. Strain through a sieve into a bowl and put the liquid back into the saucepan. Simmer until it has reduced to about 200ml (7fl oz).

4 Mix 5 tbsp of the reduced gooseberry liquor with the cornflour, stirring until really smooth. Pour this back into the liquor in the saucepan and return the drained gooseberries. Bring to the boil and stir vigorously while the mixture is thickening. Add the egg yolks and stir well to combine. It will be thick but still just pourable. Pour into the pastry case and leave to cool.

5 Put the egg whites in a large, clean bowl and beat until you have medium peaks (when you hold up the beaters, the peaks just slightly droop). Beat in 1 tbsp of the sugar at a time until you have a stiff, glossy mixture. Spoon this over the tart, making sure you don't leave any gaps and being careful to cover the rim of pastry. Bake for 25 minutes, until golden brown on top.

Early autumn salad of blackberries, raspberries, melon and lemon thyme

A lovely pudding. If you can't find lemon thyme, use ordinary thyme.

Serves 6

600ml (1 pint) mixed white wine and
    water, or just water
225g (8oz) caster sugar
3 lemon thyme sprigs, plus more to serve
juice of 1 lemon

1 strip of lemon zest
150g (5½oz) blackberries, stalks removed
    (though some left on looks very pretty)
150g (5½oz) raspberries
½ melon (Ogen or charentais)

1 Put the wine and water mix, sugar, lemon thyme, lemon juice and zest into a pan. Bring slowly to the boil, stirring to help the sugar dissolve. Boil for 4 minutes, or until syrupy; it will thicken as it cools. Leave to cool completely, then strain.

2 Put the berries in a broad, shallow bowl. Cut the melon into slices, remove the skin and cut the flesh into cubes. Add these to the bowl and pour the syrup over. Add a few sprigs of lemon thyme. You can either chill this before serving (though the raspberries will soften), or serve at room temperature.

ALSO TRY…

Strawberries in Beaujolais Slice 450g (1lb) hulled strawberries and put them into a bowl. Sprinkle with 4 tbsp caster sugar, then add enough Beaujolais just to cover. Leave to macerate for 30 minutes to 1 hour; no longer, as the strawberries get too flaccid. Serve, since this is the French way, with crème fraîche.

Peaches in Marsala Slice perfectly ripe peaches into a bowl and add enough sweet Marsala to cover. Cover and refrigerate for about half an hour. Eat.

Sweet ricotta with berries This is simple but looks spectacular. Beat ricotta with a fork, add icing or caster sugar to taste and put in a mound in the centre of a plate. Surround with red berries and let everyone help themselves. If you have cherry or other berry liqueur, drizzle a little over before serving.

Strawberry, clotted cream and rose petal sandwiches Spread brioche slices with clotted cream and slice strawberries thinly. Cover half the brioche slices with these, sprinkling with a little caster sugar. Put rose petals – torn if they're big – on top, then make into sandwiches with the remaining brioche slices. Cut each into 3 fingers and dust with icing sugar. Pile on to a plate and scatter with rose petals.

Moroccan peaches with cinnamon and orange flower water Lay peach slices on a platter and squeeze over lemon or lime juice. Sprinkle with caster sugar and add 1–2 tbsp orange flower water (different brands vary in strength; don't make it too perfumed). Sprinkle on a little ground cinnamon and chopped pistachios or toasted almonds. Chill before serving.

Apricot, peach and blackberry crumble

This is the quintessential British never-fails-to-please pudding. It's also sensible, by which I mean that it isn't expensive and it is a great vehicle for celebrating gluts of fruit. The only thing to remember is that your fruit must cook to tenderness in the time it takes the crumble to become golden. So, when your fruit is particularly unripe, it's a good idea to cook it slightly in advance.

Serves 8

600g (1lb 5oz) apricots, quartered
  and stoned
3 peaches, stoned and sliced
400g (14oz) blackberries
finely grated zest of ½ and juice
  of 1 lemon

150g (5½oz) caster sugar
150g (5½oz) plain flour
125g (4½oz) ground almonds
175g (6oz) butter, chopped
30g (1¼oz) flaked almonds

1 Preheat the oven to 180°C/350°F/gas mark 4. Put the fruit and lemon juice and zest into an ovenproof dish and stir in 40g (1½oz) of the sugar. To make the crumble, mix the flour, remaining sugar and the ground almonds together and rub in the butter until the mixture turns crumbly.

2 Put the crumble on top of the fruit, scatter the flaked almonds on top and bake for 40 minutes. The top of the crumble should be golden and the fruit tender (insert a small, sharp knife to test for this). If your fruit is still a bit hard but your crumble is already golden, cover the top with some foil to stop it getting too dark and bake a little longer.

3 Leave to cool a little and serve with crème fraîche or whipped cream.

ALSO TRY...

Other fruits: You can fall back on good old cooking apples to extend a meagre amount of expensive fruit – raspberry and apple is lovely at the end of the summer, for example – then there is plum or greengage and almond, pear or apple and rhubarb (rhubarb crumbles are good with chopped preserved ginger or grated orange rind), pear and cherry, and gooseberry and apple (the last benefits from a slug of elderflower cordial with the fruit).

Other toppings: The nuts and sugars can be changed too. Brown sugars are lovely in autumn (a little molasses sugar makes a particularly fudgy, dark crumble), and honey or maple syrup can replace some of the sugar in the fruit. Nuts can be quite chunky. You can also replace some of the plain flour with wholemeal, or brown breadcrumbs, in autumn and winter.

Dried fruits: Dried apples, cranberries, sour cherries and apricots (soaked and drained) are all good when mixed with fresh apples and pears.

Apricot and almond upside-down cake

One of my favourite cakes, with a good balance of sweet and tart that really makes the best of apricots, especially those that are lacking in flavour or are underripe.

Serves 8

FOR THE APRICOTS
50g (1¾oz) butter, plus more for the tin
125g (4½oz) caster sugar
7–8 fresh apricots (not too ripe) halved and stoned
1 tbsp runny honey

FOR THE CAKE
150g (5½oz) unsalted butter
150g (5½oz) caster sugar
2 eggs, beaten
100g (3½oz) plain flour
1½ tsp baking powder
100g (3½oz) ground almonds
1 tsp vanilla extract
125ml (4fl oz) full-fat milk

1 Butter a 20–23cm (8–9in) cake tin and prepare the apricots. Put the sugar and 75ml (2½fl oz) water into a small saucepan. Heat slowly until the sugar has dissolved. When the sugar has completely melted bring to the boil and watch until the syrup starts to turn to caramel (it will turn golden first). Swish the pan a bit. Once it becomes caramel (you will know by the smell and colour) take immediately off the heat and add the butter. Stir once the butter has melted. Pour into the tin and place the apricots, close together and cut-side-down, on top. Preheat the oven to 180°C/350°F/gas mark 4.

2 To make the cake, cream the butter and sugar until pale and fluffy, then add the eggs a little at a time, beating well after each addition (add a couple of spoonfuls of flour to the mixture if it starts to curdle). Sift together the flour and baking powder and stir in the almonds. Add the vanilla, then the dry ingredients, alternating with the milk. Spoon this batter over the apricots and bake for 50 minutes. When the cake is cooked, a skewer inserted into the centre should come out clean.

3 Run a fine knife between the cake and the tin and invert on to a plate. If some apricots have stuck to the tin, carefully replace them on the cake.

4 Gently heat the honey. Using a pastry brush or spoon, glaze the top of the cake. The honey will run down the sides to give a lush, homemade look. Leave to cool completely. The cake is lovely with crème fraîche (you can sweeten it slightly) or a mixture of sweetened Greek yogurt and double cream (no need to whip).

ALSO TRY...

Making this with plums: Red-fleshed ones are particularly good for their great colour, or try greengages. You will need to use more or less of these depending on the size of the fruit. If you use red-fleshed plums, make a glaze with melted redcurrant jelly mixed with a little water for a nice shine, instead of honey.

Salsa mish mish

Mish mish is the Arabic for apricot and the fruit is adored in the Middle East and North Africa. You will see it not only in puddings, but in sweet-and-sour meat and poultry stews such as the tajines of Morocco or the khoresht of Iran. Sometimes an apricot sauce is served alongside lamb or chicken and I so like the combination that I wanted to make the sauce into a preserve. This is what I came up with, a kind of Middle Eastern-flavoured relish. It is particularly lovely with a leg of lamb that you have marinated in yogurt and crushed garlic for 24 hours before roasting.

Makes 2 x 450g (1lb) jars

2 tbsp olive oil
1 large onion, roughly chopped
4 garlic cloves, crushed
2 red chillies, deseeded and cut into slivers
4cm (1½in) cube of fresh root ginger, peeled and finely chopped
½ tbsp crushed coriander seeds
seeds from 10 cardamom pods, crushed
5cm (2in) cinnamon stick

150g (5½oz) dried apricots, roughly chopped
350g (12oz) fresh apricots, halved, stoned and chopped
300ml (½ pint) white wine vinegar or cider vinegar
250g (9oz) granulated sugar
4 tbsp roughly chopped coriander leaves (optional)

1 Heat the oil in a heavy-bottomed pan and sauté the onion over a medium heat until soft and pale gold. Add the garlic and all the fresh and dried spices and cook for another 2 minutes, until the spices release their fragrance. Now add all the other ingredients, except the sugar and coriander leaves, and bring to the boil. Reduce to a simmer and cook for about 15–20 minutes, until the fruit is soft.

2 Now add the sugar and stir from time to time to help it dissolve. Continue to cook until the mixture is thick. It has cooked enough when you can pull a wooden spoon across the bottom of the pan and it leaves a channel before closing again. Discard the cinnamon stick.

3 Stir in the chopped coriander if you want to use it (it does discolour slightly over time, but it tastes great). Spoon the relish into hot sterilized jars (see page 242) and seal. (You need to use non-metallic lids that you are sure will not react with vinegar.)
I find this relish is better when it's relatively fresh, so I generally use it up within about 3 months. Keep it in the fridge once opened.

Plums with red wine and rosemary

Based on an idea from the wonderful Italian food writer Anna del Conte in her book *Food From an Italian Kitchen*. Rosemary in plum compote is fabulous, and it's good with poached pears, too.

Serves 6

400ml (14fl oz) red wine
225g (8oz) caster sugar
1 strip of lemon zest
2.5cm (1in) cinnamon stick

6 black peppercorns, lightly bruised
3 rosemary sprigs
900g (2lb) plums (just under-ripe)

1 Put everything except 2 of the rosemary sprigs and the plums in a saucepan, add 200ml (7fl oz) water and heat gently until the sugar dissolves, stirring. Bring to the boil and cook for 2 minutes.

2 Reduce to a simmer and add the plums. Cook very gently until the plums are just soft. (Be careful; they fall apart easily.) How long it takes depends on the size and ripeness of the plums. Carefully remove the fruit with a slotted spoon to a serving dish.

3 Strain the juices (reserve the cinnamon) and pour into a clean saucepan. Boil until syrupy. Leave until cold, then pour over the plums. Add the remaining rosemary and reserved cinnamon. Cover and refrigerate. Serve with yogurt, or sweetened yogurt mixed with double cream.

ALSO TRY...

Wine-poached apples Once I'd made this – when there was nothing much else in the house – I wondered why it wasn't a classic. Put a bottle of red wine in a saucepan with 250g (9oz) caster sugar and 2.5cm (1in) cinnamon stick. Heat slowly, stirring. Cut 6 peeled, cored dessert apples into wedges. Put these into the wine, increase the heat until simmering, then place a circle of baking parchment on top and cover. Poach until tender but not falling apart, about 25 minutes. Remove the apples to a dish and boil the wine until you have 250ml (9fl oz) left. Cool, then pour over the apples. They'll be a fantastic deep red but get even darker as they sit in the syrup. Serve chilled, or at room temperature.

Rose-scented apples Make as for Wine-poached Apples (above) but replace the red wine with white (or mixed apple juice and water) and the cinnamon with 8 crushed cardamom pods. Add rosewater to taste – about 2 tsp – and a squeeze of lemon to the reduced syrup and scatter with chopped pistachio nuts (unsalted) and rose petals.

Garnet quinces Prepare the poaching liquid as for Wine-poached Apples (see above). Peel 6 quinces, halve, core and put them in the wine. Simmer until tender, turning. It could take as much as 1 hour. Remove the cinnamon and let the quinces cool in their liquid (you shouldn't need to reduce it as the pectin in quinces makes the liquor syrupy). Serve with crème fraîche or whipped cream.

Plum jumby tart

Cute name, easy as pie.

Serves 6–8

220g (8oz) self-raising flour
100g (3½oz) butter, plus more for the tin
60g (2oz) caster sugar, plus more to sprinkle
1 egg, beaten
3 tsp vanilla extract

about 10 large or 18 small plums, quartered
  if large, halved if small, and stoned
100g (3½oz) marzipan
15g (½oz) flaked almonds
icing sugar, to dust

1 Preheat the oven to 190°C/375°F/gas mark 5. Put the flour, butter and caster sugar into a food processor and using the pastry blade, blend until you have a breadcrumb-like mix. Add the egg and vanilla and blend again until the pastry comes together. If it doesn't come together, take the pastry out and make it into a smooth ball with floured hands.

2 Butter a 22x30cm (9x12in) Swiss roll tin and press in the pastry. You can do this in chunks; it doesn't have to be particularly even. Put the plums on top, cut side up, packed really closely together. Take the marzipan and break off little chunks. Stick a chunk in the cavity of each plum (this is harder with quartered than with halved plums, but it doesn't have to be neat or exact). Sprinkle 2 tbsp caster sugar over the tart and put into the oven for 30 minutes. About 5 minutes before the end of the baking time, sprinkle with the flaked almonds.

3 Allow to cool a little. Dust with icing sugar and serve either warm or at room temperature. Whipped cream or crème fraîche is good on the side.

ALSO TRY...

Other fruits: You can make this with fresh apricots and sliced peaches or nectarines. Apples take longer to soften so, if you want to use those, slice them quite thinly.

Other glazes: If you want a glossy tart, leave off the almonds and icing sugar and glaze the top thickly with sieved warmed apricot jam or redcurrant jelly, then leave it to set.

Freeform autumn fruit tart with cinnamon sugar

'Freeform' tarts remove the need to fit pastry into a tin, so are much quicker. They're brilliant for less confident pastry cooks, and their appearance suggests plenty and simplicity. The nuts soak up the juices, but you can use breadcrumbs instead.

Serves 8

FOR THE PASTRY

250g (9oz) plain flour, plus more to dust

150g (5½oz) butter, in rough cubes

75g (2½oz) icing sugar, plus more to dust

1 egg yolk

FOR THE FILLING

300g (10½oz) plums, halved and stoned

275g (9¾oz) eating apples, halved and cored (no need to peel)

juice of ½ lemon

75g (2½oz) ground hazelnuts

30g (1¼oz) soft light brown sugar

8 figs, halved

150g (5½oz) blackberries

30g (1¼oz) granulated sugar

TO SERVE

½ tsp ground cinnamon, or to taste

1 To make the pastry, put the flour, butter and icing sugar into a food processor. Using the pastry blade, blend until it forms a breadcrumb-like mixture. Mix the egg yolk with 1 tbsp cold water and add that. Whizz again; the pastry should come together to form a ball, though you may need more water. Wrap in clingfilm and refrigerate for an hour.

2 Slice the plums and cut the apples into thinner slices. Toss with the lemon juice to prevent discolouration. Preheat the oven to 190°C/375°F/gas mark 5.

3 Roll the pastry on a floured surface into a rough circle, about 3mm (⅛in) thick. Put on to a baking sheet lined with baking parchment. Mix the nuts and brown sugar and sprinkle on top, leaving a 4cm (1½in) rim. Put all the fruit on top in a higgledy-piggledy way. Sprinkle over the granulated sugar. Pull the pastry up over the fruit all the way round. Bake for 45 minutes, or until the fruit is tender. The tart should be golden and the fruit soft and slightly caramelized. If the pastry gets too dark before the fruit is cooked, cover with foil.

4 Leave to cool slightly. This tart is better warm or at room temperature as the sugar, nuts and juices under the fruit firm up. Mix a little icing sugar with the cinnamon and dust the top. Lever the tart off the paper with a palette knife, then slide it on to a plate.

ALSO TRY…

Freeform nectarine tart Halve and stone 750g (1lb 10oz) nectarines and thinly slice. Roll out and assemble the tart as above, but use 100g (3½oz) ground almonds instead of hazelnuts. Bake as above. Melt 30g (1¼oz) apricot jam in a small pan with 1 tbsp water. Paint the warm jam glaze thickly all over the fruit.

Try this tart with apricots, peaches or plums. Plums and apricots require more sugar.

Butter and brown sugar roast apples

If you thought a pan of baked apples was the easiest pudding ever, think again. The apples for this aren't even cored. Instead they are simply halved, so retain those lovely plump appley curves, and there is no filling. But this dish is somehow grand in its simplicity; it will really make you appreciate the beauty of apples. A mixture of apple varieties looks very good and, if you can find any with some leaves still attached to the stalks (cultivate friends with apple trees, or look for some at farmers' markets), even better.

Serves 6

6 dessert apples

30g (1¼oz) unsalted butter

2 tbsp granulated sugar

2 tbsp soft light brown sugar

¼ tsp ground cinnamon (optional)

generous grating of nutmeg (optional)

¼ tsp salt

1 Preheat the oven to 180°C/350°F/gas mark 4. Halve the apples. You don't need to core them and you should leave the stalks intact if you can; it looks pretty. Put them into a small roasting tin.

2 Heat the butter in a frying pan until it turns light brown and smells nutty. Don't let it burn. Stir in the sugars, spices (if using) and salt, then pour this over the apples. Turn the apples round to make sure they get well coated.

3 Arrange the apples cut side up and bake in the oven for 30–40 minutes, until tender and slightly caramelized in places.

ALSO TRY...

Honey roast pears with gorgonzola Halve the pears as in the apple recipe above. Put 15g (½oz) butter in a pan, add 4 tbsp runny honey and a pinch of salt and heat until the mixture is melted. Add 2 tbsp granulated sugar. Proceed as above, baking the pears until they are completely tender and golden. Serve each person with 2 pear halves and about 30g (1oz) gorgonzola (or other blue cheese) alongside. Scatter on some very roughly chopped hazelnuts (lightly toasted).

Pear, almond and red wine cake

If you can, poach the pears the day before, then leave them to get a good dark colour while sitting in the wine syrup.

Serves 6–8

FOR THE PEARS
350ml (12fl oz) fruity red wine
200g (7oz) caster sugar
2 strips of lemon zest and juice of ½ lemon
6 pears, peeled, halved and cored
1 tbsp redcurrant jelly (optional)

FOR THE CAKE
200g (7oz) butter
200g (7oz) soft light brown sugar
75g (2½oz) ground almonds
1½ tsp baking powder
300g (10½oz) plain flour, sifted
4 eggs, lightly beaten
2 tsp vanilla extract
125ml (4fl oz) buttermilk

1 To cook the pears, put the wine, caster sugar, zest and juice into a saucepan and bring slowly to the boil, stirring to help the sugar dissolve. Reduce to a simmer, add the pears (they should lie in a single layer) and cook until tender (about 20 minutes). Turn them halfway through.

2 Butter a springform cake tin 23cm (9in) in diameter and 9cm (3½in) deep. Preheat the oven to 170°C/350°F/gas mark 3½. Lift the pears from the syrup with a slotted spoon and carefully arrange them, cut side down, on the bottom of the tin, in a circle like the spokes of a wheel. Alternate the bottoms and tops of each pear half. Reserve the cooking liquid.

3 Cream the butter and brown sugar until pale and fluffy. Mix the almonds and baking powder with the flour. Gradually add the eggs to the creamed butter and sugar, beating well after each addition. Sprinkle on a little flour if the mixture looks as though it is curdling. Mix in the vanilla and buttermilk, then fold in the combined flour, baking powder and almonds. Spoon this on top of the pears and bake for 45–50 minutes. A skewer inserted in the centre should come out clean when the cake is cooked.

4 Run a knife between cake and tin and turn the cake out. If any pears stick to the tin, carefully ease them off and replace on the cake.

5 The reserved pear cooking liquid should be quite thick and syrupy. If it isn't, boil a little to reduce. It should also be a good red colour; if not, add 1 tbsp redcurrant jelly and a squeeze of lemon juice and heat to melt the jelly.

6 Pierce the sponge of the cake peeking out between the pears with a skewer. Slowly pour the syrup all over. Most of it will glaze the pears, but some will run down into the cake. Leave to cool. Serve with thick cream, crème fraîche, or a mixture of cream and yogurt.

Cardamom, honey and orange roast apricots

When stone fruits are abundant I am always looking for different things to do with them. Although almonds (as a stuffing, or in the form of a slug of amaretto poured over before baking) are a classic European pairing, eastern flavours also work very well.

Serves 6

about 30 apricots, halved and stoned
crushed seeds from 10 cardamom pods
100g (3½oz) soft light brown sugar
4 tbsp runny honey (preferably orange
  blossom)

125ml (4fl oz) orange juice
juice of ½ lemon

1 Preheat the oven to 180°C/350°F/gas mark 4. Put the apricots into an ovenproof dish, cut side up, so they can lie snugly in a single layer. Sprinkle on the cardamom and sugar. Drizzle on the honey. Pour the orange and lemon juice round the apricots and bake for 20–25 minutes (depending on how ripe your apricots are), or until the apricots are tender and the sugar is slightly caramelized.

2 Serve warm, at room temperature or chilled with whipped cream (a little orange flower water can be added to the cream).

ALSO TRY...

Lime and ginger roasted nectarines Put 6 halved, stoned nectarines in an ovenproof dish with a 2.5cm (1in) square of fresh root ginger, peeled and grated, 175g (6oz) soft dark brown sugar, the juice of 2 limes and 125ml (4fl oz) water. Mix everything together, then lay the fruit cut side up in a single layer. Bake as above for about 45 minutes (it could take longer, depending on the ripeness of the fruit). If it looks as though your nectarines are a bit pale, put some more sugar on them for the last 10 minutes or so of the cooking time. I like these at room temperature or chilled. Serve with crème fraîche or whipped cream.

Roast plums with brown sugar cream Put 16 plums – halved and stoned – into an ovenproof dish with 150g (5½oz) caster sugar, a 2.5cm (1in) square of fresh root ginger, peeled and grated, and a sprinkling of ground cinnamon. Add 100ml (3½fl oz) orange juice and mix everything together. Lay the plums in a single layer, cut side up. Bake as above for about 20–25 minutes (though it depends how ripe your plums are; they need to be tender). Serve warm, at room temperature, or chilled. Mix about 4 tbsp cream with 250g (9oz) Greek yogurt and sprinkle the top with 6 tbsp soft dark brown sugar. Leave the sugar to form a kind of gooey crust (it takes about half an hour). You can stir this to 'marble' the sugar through the cream or leave as it is. Serve with the plums.

Paradise jelly

I found this recipe in an ancient book, *The Old Yankee Cookbook*, which I picked up in a second-hand shop. The jelly is a beautiful red-amber colour and is very good with turkey, chicken and pork. If you can't get hold of any quinces, you can make this with just apples and cranberries.

Makes about 3kg (6lb 10oz)
4 large quinces
1.5kg (3lb 5oz) cooking apples
750g (1lb 10oz) cranberries
granulated sugar (you'll need about 2kg/4lb 8oz)

1 Chop the quinces and cooking apples into big chunks. There is no need to peel or core them. Put in a large pan with the cranberries and cover with water. Bring to the boil, then reduce the heat and cook until soft. It will take about an hour.

2 Hang a jelly bag over another large pan and put the fruity mush into the bag. Let the juice drip from the suspended bag overnight.

3 Measure the juice that you have collected. Add 500g (1lb 2oz) sugar for every 500ml (18fl oz) of liquid. Bring to the boil slowly, stirring every so often to help the sugar dissolve and skimming any scum that rises to the surface. Once the jelly is boiling test for the setting point: put a teaspoon of the juices on to a saucer. If, once cold, the liquid sets and wrinkles when pushed with a finger, it is ready to pot. You can check for the setting point using a sugar thermometer too.) The setting point for jam and jelly is 104°C/220°F).

4 Ladle the jelly into hot, sterilized jars (see page 242). You will find a funnel handy here. Quickly cover the surface of each with a round of waxed paper and seal with screw tops.

Les Jacques

From the Périgord region of France, these are thin, like crêpes, but have apples cooked inside. They are lovely with pitted cherries too: sauté them briefly in butter and a bit of sugar then spoon them over each crêpe.

Serves 4

125g (4½oz) plain flour
2 tbsp caster sugar, plus more to dust
pinch of salt
2 large eggs
½ tbsp eau de vie or brandy (optional)
150ml (¼ pint) milk

50g (1¾oz) unsalted butter
4 eating apples, peeled, cored and cut
  into wedges
juice of ½ lemon
icing sugar, to dust

1 Put the flour, caster sugar and salt into a bowl and make a well in the centre. Beat the eggs lightly with a fork and put into a jug with the alcohol (if using), 150ml (¼ pint) water and the milk. Gradually pour the liquid into the well, beating in the dry ingredients. Mix thoroughly so there are no lumps. Leave to rest for at least 30 minutes (1½ hours is ideal) for a lighter batter.

2 Melt half the butter in a frying pan and sauté the apples in batches until just tender, but not completely soft. Be careful not to burn the butter; if you do, throw it out and use more fresh butter. Sprinkle with caster sugar as you go to get bits of caramelization. When they are done, squeeze the lemon juice over them.

3 Melt a knob of butter in a nonstick frying pan (ideally 15–20cm/6–8in across). Ladle in a very thin layer of batter, swirling so it goes to the edges. Put slices of apple on top, then cover with another really thin layer of batter. Once that starts to set, turn over carefully. Dust icing sugar over each pancake as it is cooked. Serve with crème fraîche.

ALSO TRY...

Russian apple pancakes Mix 150g (5½oz) sifted plain flour with 25g (1oz) soft light brown sugar, ½ tsp salt and 1 tsp baking powder. Beat 2 eggs with 200ml (7fl oz) full-fat milk and 100g (3½oz) yogurt in a bowl. Gradually mix the liquid ingredients into the dry. Coarsely grate 3 tart apples, peeled and cored. Stir these into the batter along with the finely grated zest of 1 lemon. Heat a knob of unsalted butter and ½ tbsp sunflower oil in a nonstick frying pan. Add a couple of tablespoons of batter (the pancakes should be about 7cm/3in across). Cook over medium heat until set on one side. You should see little holes forming. You can cook several pancakes at a time, depending on the size of your pan. Flip each over and cook the other side. Add more butter and oil as you go. Serve dusted with icing sugar, with soured cream and runny honey on the side. Serves 6.

Chilled Bramley apple and rice pudding

This is adapted from a recipe by Claire Clarke, pastry chef at The French Laundry in California. It's hard to believe humble ingredients can be taken to these heights.

Serves 6

FOR THE RICE

150g (5½oz) short-grain rice

700ml (1¼ pints) full-fat milk, plus more if needed

30g (1¼oz) caster sugar

75ml (2½fl oz) double cream

grated nutmeg or ground cinnamon

FOR THE APPLES

3 Bramley apples, peeled, cored and sliced

100ml (3½fl oz) dry or sweet cider

caster sugar, to taste

FOR THE SYRUP

150g (5½oz) caster sugar

TO SERVE

the remainder of your carton of double cream (you'll probably have bought a 284ml pot), lightly whipped and sweetened to taste

1 Cover the rice with water in a saucepan and bring to the boil. Boil for 4 minutes, drain and rinse. Return the rice to the pan and add the milk and sugar. Bring to the boil, then reduce the heat and cook for about 25 minutes, stirring from time to time. You may need more milk. You should end up with a sloppy mixture that still holds its shape, with soft grains. Remember, it will firm up as it cools. Leave until cold.

2 Put the apples in a pan with the cider and set over medium-low heat. Cover and cook until completely soft, stirring to break them down every so often. Make sure they don't boil dry. Once they're cooked add sugar to taste (they should still be on the tart side, but not unpalatably so).

3 To make the syrup, put the sugar into a pan with 100ml (3½fl oz) water. Heat slowly until the sugar has dissolved. When the sugar has completely melted bring to the boil and watch until the syrup turns to caramel (it will turn golden first). Swish the pan a bit. Once it becomes caramel (you will know by the smell and colour) immediately add about 8 tbsp water and swish around. It will splutter. Stir so the caramelized sugar dissolves in the water.

4 Leave everything to cool, then stir the cream into the rice. If the mixture still seems rather stodgy, add more cream or milk. Season with nutmeg or cinnamon.

5 Layer the components up in glasses. Start with some apple, then add caramel, then rice pudding, then caramel. Repeat. Spoon whipped cream on top and drizzle with caramel. Refrigerate until serving.

ALSO TRY...

Make this in the summer with apricots – they are nice and tart – using white wine and perhaps a little almond liqueur to cook the fruit, rather than cider.

Blood orange and cardamom jellies

Blood oranges are available only for a short time; at other times of the year make this with ordinary oranges. Serve in pretty glasses (Moroccan tea glasses are lovely).

Serves 8

FOR THE JELLIES
4 blood oranges
950ml (1¾ pints) blood orange juice
juice of ½ lemon
ground seeds from 10 cardamom pods
75g (2½oz) caster sugar
20g (¾oz) leaf gelatine

FOR THE CANDIED PEEL
2 oranges (preferably blood oranges)
225ml (8fl oz) blood orange juice
100g (3½oz) caster sugar

TO SERVE
sweetened whipped cream

1 To make the jellies, cut a thin slice off the top and bottom of each orange. Set on its base and, with a very sharp knife, remove the peel and pith in strips, working from top to bottom. To remove the segments, cut between membrane and flesh with a fine, sharp knife and carefully slide each segment out.

2 Put the orange and lemon juices, cardamom and sugar in a saucepan and heat gently, stirring to help the sugar dissolve. Put the gelatine in a dish and cover with water. Leave to soak for 3–5 minutes until soft. Squeeze out the excess liquid and add the gelatine to the warm juice, stirring to dissolve. Divide the orange segments between 8 glasses, then pour in the jelly. Leave to cool, then refrigerate.

3 For the candied peel, finely pare the zest of the oranges (avoid the white pith) and cut into fine julienne strips. Put in a saucepan with the orange juice and sugar. Heat gently until the sugar has dissolved, then simmer until the liquid has almost evaporated (about 30 minutes). Scoop the zest out with a fork, gently separate and lay on baking parchment. Put somewhere warm to dry. Top the jellies with whipped cream and the candied peel.

ALSO TRY...

All you have to remember is that it takes 25g (1oz) gelatine to set 1.2 litres (2 pints) liquid and any juice can be turned into jelly. The only thing which mucks up this ratio is alcohol (it inhibits gelatine's setting properties), so closely follow any jelly recipes you see which include alcohol.

Orange and rosemary jellies Citrus juice with rosemary is deliciously fresh and herby. Make as above but, instead of cardamom, add 2 rosemary sprigs to the juice before heating. Discard these before you add the gelatine. You can use grapefruit or pink grapefruit juice instead, but you will need more sugar.

Apple and blackberry jellies Make as above but use clear apple juice, the juice of a whole lemon and, instead of cardamom, a cinnamon stick (discard it before adding the gelatine). Add whole blackberries before the jelly sets.

Sugar-crusted lemon loaf cake

Classic lemon loaf cake and you don't even need an electric mixer to make it. This is good in the dark wintry months when citrus fruits are at their best and you need something sharp to prick your tastebuds. Any stale cake – hard to believe that is possible but it does sometimes happen – is great in a trifle.

Serves 8

FOR THE CAKE

125g (4½oz) butter, diced, plus more for the tin

225g (8oz) self-raising flour, sifted

a pinch of salt

125g (4½oz) caster sugar

2 large eggs, beaten

2 unwaxed lemons

FOR THE TOPPING

juice of 2 lemons

100g (3½oz) caster sugar

1 Preheat the oven to 180°C/350°F/gas mark 4. Butter a 900g (2lb) loaf tin and line with greaseproof paper. Mix the flour and salt together in a large bowl and rub in the butter with your fingers until the mixture resembles breadcrumbs, then stir in the sugar. Add the eggs and the grated rind and juice of the lemons. Mix together until you have a soft batter, but don't overwork the mixture.

2 Spoon the batter into the loaf tin and bake for 45–55 minutes, or until golden and well risen and a skewer inserted in the centre comes out clean. Leave to cool for 10 minutes in the tin. Meanwhile, stir the lemon juice and sugar for the topping together. Prick the cake surface with a skewer or fork, then slowly pour the sugar and lemon mix over it. This will sink in, but some of the sugar will settle to make a nice, crunchy, sugary crust on the surface.

ALSO TRY...

You can make the same kind of cake with limes; just use twice the amount of fruit.

Rhubarb and lemon curd bread and butter pudding

This does work – and is delicious because of the contrast of sweet and tart – as long as you cook the rhubarb very carefully. It must still hold its shape. Don't throw away the rhubarb syrup; instead, keep it and use like a cordial, topping it up with sparkling water.

Serves 6–8

425g (15oz) rhubarb
150g (5½oz) caster sugar
300ml (½ pint) full-fat milk
300ml (½ pint) double cream
pinch of salt
½ tsp vanilla extract

3 eggs, plus 1 egg yolk
30g (1¼oz) butter
about 250g (9oz) bread (soft white rolls, sliced, are particularly good)
about 8 tbsp lemon curd
icing sugar, to dust

1 Trim the rhubarb and cut it into 3cm (1¼in) lengths. Heat 100ml (3½fl oz) water in a pan with 50g (1¾oz) of the sugar. Bring to the boil and add the rhubarb. Simmer for 1½ minutes, then carefully drain the rhubarb, and reserve the syrup for another use (see recipe introduction). Set the rhubarb aside to cool.

2 Bring the milk, cream and salt to the boil in a heavy-bottomed pan. Add the vanilla. Beat the eggs, extra yolk and the remaining sugar together. Pour the warm milk and cream on to this, stirring all the time.

3 Slice the bread, butter it and spread with lemon curd, then layer it, buttered side up, in an ovenproof dish. Put the rhubarb on top of the bread as you go. Pour on the egg and cream mixture through a sieve and leave to sit for half an hour – this just makes the pudding lighter. Meanwhile, preheat the oven to 180°C/350°F/gas mark 4.

4 Put the dish into a roasting tin and add enough boiling water to the tin to come halfway up the sides of the dish. Bake for 40–45 minutes, or until the pudding is puffy and set on the top and golden in colour. Leave to cool slightly, dust with icing sugar and serve with crème fraîche, or cream mixed with Greek yogurt.

Crusts and crumbs

I hate throwing bread away. There seems such potential in it, and I'm very aware what a fundamental foodstuff it is: the staff of life. In North Africa it's the one food that will be eagerly retrieved if dropped, then wiped and kissed – it is so prized – yet most of us chuck out the end of a loaf without a second thought. But it's worth considering what you can do with that bit.

Using bread well means you can afford to pay a little more for better-quality loaves. I used to baulk at the price of good sourdough, but if you use it all you've had the pleasure of bread that is both worth eating and makes you feel fuller. If you don't believe me, compare how you feel after eating a bit of good coarse country bread from a bakery to how you feel after a slice of the sorry processed stuff that passes for bread in Britain.

Once bread has lost its soft freshness it passes through different phases. It can be toasted – good toast is a glorious edible platter – but it doesn't end there. A stuffing made from breadcrumbs is the most obvious way to use old bread, and sage and onion is just the start. Go Caribbean and mix breadcrumbs with lime zest, thyme, spring onion, chilli and rum and use it to stuff a chicken, or toss breadcrumbs with sautéed aubergine, dates and coriander for a Middle Eastern-inspired filling for lamb. You just need enough fat (butter or oil) to bind and keep the bread moist. And you don't have to stop at stuffing meat. Roasted tomatoes, aubergines, peppers and mushrooms can all be enhanced by flavoursome crumbs.

Think beyond stuffing and you'll hit on some of the chicest platefuls around. The trendiness of 'peasant cooking' has seen us exalt dishes that were created specifically to use up leftover bread. There's the Italian bread salad, panzanella (the Italians are good at counting every crumb), bread and butter pudding, pain perdu, summer pudding, and spaghetti with fried crumbs. Bread's ability to soak up other flavours, to be soft or crispy, to thicken without altering the character of a dish, make it one of the most useful leftovers. See that sausage and bean casserole that isn't rib-sticking enough, or that puréed mushroom soup that is a bit thin? Throw in a handful of breadcrumbs and watch these dishes come together.

I have included only one recipe for making your own bread. There are many other books, from writers more qualified than me, about how to make bread at home. I urge you to consult those and try it. But I wanted to include a recipe for pizza, partly because it is more than just bread, but also because making your own pizza saves you masses of money.

Beyond that, you just need to try to make every loaf earn its keep. It's a simple message: buy good bread and use it well.

290 CRUSTS AND CRUMBS

Southern Italian cauliflower with fried breadcrumbs, capers and anchovies

Much of Italian food has to do with making the best of very little, or using up what is past its peak. Italians transform the old into the new by using hunger, ingenuity and their palates. Bread is one of the things they deal with very well. Stale breadcrumbs – toasted, or fried in olive oil – are common in southern Italy and are often used instead of Parmesan to top pasta or vegetables. I particularly love the Sicilian way here, which teams breadcrumbs with the island's trademark sweet-savoury ingredients: raisins, capers and nuts. Cauliflower has never tasted so good. A cracking dish can be made by tossing the cauliflower into pasta (add olive oil, salt and pepper) before scattering with the flavoured breadcrumbs. You won't miss the Parmesan.

serves 4 as a side dish

1 cauliflower, broken into florets
30g (1¼oz) stale ciabatta or focaccia
2 tbsp olive oil
4 garlic cloves, very finely sliced
1 tbsp capers, rinsed
½–1 tsp dried chilli flakes, to taste
8 cured anchovies, drained and
  roughly chopped

40g (1½oz) raisins or currants, or both,
  soaked in just-boiled water for 15 minutes
  and drained
3 tbsp chopped flat leaf parsley
25g (1oz) pine nuts, toasted
salt and pepper
squeeze of lemon juice
4 tbsp extra virgin olive oil

1 Cook the cauliflower in boiling lightly salted water until just tender. Prepare the topping while it's cooking.

2 Make the bread into coarse crumbs; I use the pulse button of the food processor. Heat the oil in a large frying pan and fry the breadcrumbs until golden. Add the garlic and cook for another minute, then add the capers, chilli, anchovies, dried fruit, parsley and pine nuts. Drain the cauliflower really well (if it's wet it ruins the breadcrumbs).

3 You can now either put the cauliflower in a serving dish and scatter with the breadcrumb mix, or add the cauliflower to the pan, toss with the crumbs and heat for a couple of minutes to give the cauliflower a bit of colour. Season (easy on the salt because of the anchovies), squeeze some lemon juice over and drizzle with the extra virgin oil. Serve immediately.

ALSO TRY...

Plain breadcrumbs fried in olive oil – without any additions – on pasta. It's particularly good tossed with garlic and chilli.

Using the fried breadcrumb mix above to scatter on broccoli, cabbage, green beans, roast tomatoes or peppers and roast fish.

Adding chopped green olives to the breadcrumbs for the main dish.

Spring panzanella

A good way not only to use up bread but to extend ingredients that aren't that cheap. Chunks of ricotta are a very good addition, adding lovely texture, or try finely grated lemon zest.

Serves 6

350g (12oz) ciabatta bread, torn into 2.5cm (1in) chunks

1 shallot, chopped

salt and pepper

3 tbsp olive oil

300g (10½oz) fresh peas (podded weight)

300g (10½oz) fresh broad beans, (podded weight)

400g (14oz) asparagus, trimmed

large bunch of basil, leaves only

1 garlic clove, crushed

about 35ml (generous 1fl oz) extra virgin olive oil

3 tbsp balsamic vinegar (white if you can get it)

75g (2½oz) Pecorino or Parmesan cheese, shaved

1 Preheat the oven to 180°C/350°F/gas mark 4. Toss the bread in a roasting tin with the shallot, seasoning and oil. Bake for about 15 minutes, or until the pieces of bread are golden and crunchy.

2 Cook the peas and broad beans in boiling, lightly salted water (I do it in separate pans as they cook at slightly different rates) until just tender, then drain. Slip the skins from the beans when cool enough to handle. Meanwhile, cook the asparagus in boiling, lightly salted water for 3–4 minutes, or until just tender. Run cold water over it to set the colour, but don't make it completely cold. This salad can be served at room temperature but I like it slightly warmer if I can manage to leave the cooking until the last minute.

3 Put the bread chunks into a large, broad, shallow bowl. Now add the asparagus, peas, broad beans, basil and garlic. Season well. Pour on the extra virgin oil and balsamic vinegar and add the cheese. Toss gently and serve.

Sourdough tartines with labneh and spiced roast tomatoes

Bread doesn't have to be just a filler. A good sandwich is one of the best things you can eat. But you need great bread with a strong identity and a good flavour, such as sourdough. Most sourdough loaves seem prohibitively expensive, but they have such great keeping qualities that thay are worth buying. The woman who makes the most famous sourdough in the world, Apollonia Poilâne from Poilâne in Paris, told me to keep it under a tea towel, spraying the towel every so often with water. Like this it is fine for three days, after which it is good for toasting for another two or three. And the sour, tangy flavour is incomparable. A small café beside the Poilâne bakery got me hooked on sourdough 'tartines' (basically open sandwiches). You can have diet-friendly versions spread with low-fat cream cheese topped with thinly sliced raw salmon with lemon and dill, or more indulgent blue cheese with toasted walnuts and slices of sautéed pear. Tartines are also a great way to use up leftovers: try flaked salmon and crushed broad beans with olive oil and lemon juice; chicken with mango, watercress and curry mayo; pork with spinach and sautéed apples. Tartines are certainly grand enough to give friends for lunch (and perfect if there's only two of you).

Serves 4

250g (9oz) Greek yogurt
1 garlic clove, crushed
a little salt
12 plum tomatoes
4 tbsp olive oil
2 tbsp balsamic vinegar

1½ tsp harissa
2 tsp soft dark brown sugar
4 slices of sourdough bread
coriander leaves and extra virgin olive oil,
    to serve

1 Make the labneh the day before you want to use it. Line a sieve with clean muslin or a new J-cloth and set it over a bowl. Mix the yogurt with the garlic and salt and put it into the cloth. Tie the cloth up and refrigerate the whole thing. The yogurt will lose moisture over the next 24 hours, gaining a firmer texture, but help it along by giving it a good squeeze once or twice.

2 Preheat the oven to 180°C/350°F/gas mark 4. Halve the tomatoes lengthways and put them in a small roasting tin. Mix together the olive oil, balsamic vinegar and harissa, season and pour over the tomatoes. Turn them over to coat, ending with them cut-side up. Sprinkle with the sugar and roast for 40–45 minutes, until slightly shrunken. You can serve them warm or at room temperature.

3 Toast the sourdough. Unwrap the labneh, spread it on to each slice of bread and top with the roast tomatoes (and any of their juices). Sprinkle with the coriander and drizzle with extra virgin olive oil before serving.

Yoghurtlu kofta kebab

I can't say I first ate this Turkish classic overlooking the Bosporus. It was actually in a cheap restaurant in north London, but I immediately tracked down several recipes for it. A great mix of temperatures and textures, it's one of the best meals you can make and for less than the price of a takeaway curry.

Serves 4

FOR THE KEBAB

800g (1lb 12oz) minced lamb
1 onion, grated
2 garlic cloves, crushed
4 tsp ground cumin
leaves from 1 small bunch parsley, very
   finely chopped
2 tbsp olive oil
2–3 white pitta breads
350g (12oz) plain Greek yogurt
15g (½oz) unsalted butter
1½ tbsp pine nuts

pinch of cayenne, paprika or sumac
coarsely chopped coriander or mint
   (optional)

FOR THE TOMATO SAUCE

400g can tomatoes in thick juice
1 small onion, finely chopped
2 garlic cloves, crushed
1 red chilli, deseeded and chopped
2 tsp soft light brown sugar
2 tbsp olive oil
salt and pepper

1 Put the lamb in a bowl and pummel it. Add the onion, garlic, cumin and parsley. Season and mix really well. With wet hands, form into rounds slightly smaller than golf balls. Set on a plate, cover and firm up in the refrigerator.

2 Put everything for the sauce in a pan, add 50ml (2fl oz) water and bring to the boil. Reduce to a simmer and cook for 20–30 minutes, stirring. It should be thick, but not like chutney. If it's too thick, add more water. Bring the meatballs to room temperature.

3 Heat the oil in a frying pan and fry the meatballs over high heat, in batches to get a good brown colour. Reduce the heat and cook through (though they're nice rare).

4 Meanwhile, tear your pitta into triangles and toast. Put in a broad, shallow bowl and pour the sauce on. Traditionally yogurt goes next, then the kofta. I prefer yogurt on top, but take your pick. Sizzle the butter and fry the pine nuts for a few seconds, then pour over. Sprinkle with the spice and herbs, if you want.

ALSO TRY...

Chicken fatteh Fry 1 large onion, chopped, in 1½ tbsp olive oil until soft and golden. Add ½ tsp ground cinnamon, ½ tsp ground allspice, ground seeds from 5 cardamom pods and a pinch of dried chilli flakes. Cook for 2–3 minutes, then mix in 400g (14oz) cooked chicken. Season really well and add a squeeze of lemon juice. Toast 4 pitta breads, cut into triangles, and put half in a dish. Moisten with warm chicken stock and extra virgin olive oil. Lay the chicken on, then the remaining crunchy pittas. Add 3 garlic cloves, crushed, to 200ml (7fl oz) Greek yogurt and spread over. Sprinkle with toasted pine nuts, chopped coriander or parsley and drizzle with extra virgin olive oil.

Le bettelman

An Alsace recipe, in which the broken bread creates something almost like a sponge. Make in a dish with lots of surface area as the toasted top is delicious.

Serves 6

350g (12oz) white bread
250ml (8fl oz) full-fat milk
250ml (8fl oz) double cream
150g (5½oz) caster sugar
finely grated zest of 1 and juice of ½ lemon
500g (1lb 2oz) tart eating apples

65g (2oz) butter
4 eggs, lightly beaten
2 tsp vanilla extract
3 tbsp calvados or brandy (optional)
icing sugar, to dust

1 Break the bread into irregular hazelnut-sized chunks and put them into a baking dish. Heat the milk, cream, sugar (reserve 2 tbsp sugar) and zest, stirring to dissolve the sugar. When just under the boil, pour over the bread. Mash, then soak for 15 minutes. Preheat the oven to 180°C/350°F/gas mark 4.

2 Core the apples and cut into chunks. Melt 25g (1oz) of the butter in a large frying pan. Cook the apples over medium-high heat until golden. Toss in the reserved sugar and cook until almost caramelized.

3 Mix the eggs with the vanilla and alcohol, if using. Mix into the bread with the lemon juice and apples and dot with the remaining butter. Bake for 45 minutes. The top should be golden and souffléd. Leave to cool and set for 10 minutes. Sift over icing sugar and serve with crème fraîche.

ALSO TRY...

Cherry, apricot or peach bettelman Make as above, slicing peaches or quartering apricots before sautéing. If you're using cherries, don't cook them much before adding. Use kirsch or amaretto instead of calvados.

Ham and cheese pain perdu Butter two slices of white bread. Sprinkle 25g (1oz) grated Gruyère on one piece, top with a slice of ham and sprinkle on another 25g (1oz) Gruyère. Top with the other bread slice and cut in half. Put 2 beaten eggs in a broad dish with 2 tbsp milk and seasoning. Leave the sandwich to soak in the egg mixture for 5 minutes, turning. Melt a knob of butter in a nonstick pan and fry the sandwich on both sides over a medium heat until golden, then reduce the heat and allow the cheese to melt. Serves 1.

'Sicilian' pain perdu with toasted peaches Make as above without the ham and cheese, adding 1 tbsp double cream, ½ tbsp Marsala and ½ tbsp sugar to the eggs. While the bread's soaking fry a ripe peach, quartered, in butter until toasted. Throw in ½ tbsp caster sugar and cook until caramelized in places. Slosh in some Marsala and bubble to a syrup. Serve with the pain perdu. Sift icing sugar over before serving. If you prefer, serve with roasted or baked stone fruits instead (see page 279). Serves 2.

Canederli

I first had these in a very humble roadside restaurant in northern Italy. I had never heard of 'canederli' and was surprised to learn they were just made with bread, as they were so delicious. They are made the way we would make stuffing for a chicken, but the mixture is rolled into little dumplings and poached. You can also treat them like dumplings and serve them in soup.

Serves 4

FOR THE CANEDERLI
200g (7oz) white bread
125ml (4fl oz) milk
40g (1½oz) butter
1 onion, very finely chopped
100g (3½oz) pancetta, in small chunks
2 eggs, lightly beaten
generous grating of nutmeg
leaves from 4 thyme sprigs

25g (1oz) flat leaf parsley, very
 finely chopped
salt and pepper
chicken stock or water, for poaching
plain flour, to dust

TO SERVE
melted butter or chicken stock
shaved Parmesan cheese

1 Break the bread up into various-sized little chunks and crumbs with your fingers – the food processor does it too finely. Sprinkle with the milk, mix with your hands and leave for 15 minutes or so.

2 Melt the butter in a frying pan and sauté the onion and pancetta until the onion is completely soft. Mix gently with all the other ingredients except the stock and flour, using your hands. Don't overwork the mixture. Season really well; this is very important.

3 Bring a large pan of chicken stock or water to the boil. Meanwhile, wet your hands and shape the bread mixture into balls the size of walnuts. Roll very lightly in the flour and shake off excess. Once the stock is boiling, reduce to a steady simmer. (If using water, salt it.) Drop in half the canederli, then cook very gently for about 7–10 minutes. If the stock boils it will break them up. They will rise to the top when they are done. Scoop out with a slotted spoon and drain well on kitchen paper to soak up excess water.

4 Serve in soup plates with melted butter (you can flavour it by frying rosemary or sage in it) or in hot chicken stock, with shaved Parmesan sprinkled over.

ALSO TRY...

Serving canederli with the same topping as used for Viennese Potatoes (see page 92). Hardly surprising that this works, given that canederli are made in an area of Italy that borders Austria. They are also good with a soured cream and cucumber sauce: sauté chopped cucumber in butter, add soured cream and heat through. Spoon over the canederli then scatter with ground paprika or poppy seeds. Chunks of both roast beetroot and roast squash are lovely dotted among the canederli.

Beetroot, goat's cheese and caper pizza

The mark-up on pizza is astounding. Make your own and you won't look back.
I learnt this recipe on a course at River Cottage and the dough is the best I've tried.
Get the oven as hot as possible well before cooking.

makes 2 x 30cm (12in) pizzas

FOR THE DOUGH

5g (⅙oz) dried yeast
350ml (12fl oz) lukewarm water
250g (9oz) strong plain flour
250g (9oz) plain flour, plus more to dust
1½ tsp salt
slug of olive oil

FOR THE TOPPING

4 tbsp olive oil, plus more to drizzle
4 large red onions, very finely sliced
about 10 thyme sprigs
250g (9oz) goat's cheese, in chunks
500g (1lb 2oz) roasted beetroot, chopped
salt and pepper
3 tbsp capers, rinsed

1 Dissolve the yeast in 1½ tbsp of the water and mix in 2 tbsp flour. Stir to make a smooth paste and leave under a cloth, somewhere warm, for 30 minutes to form a 'sponge'.

2 Put the flours in a bowl and make a well in the centre. Pour in the sponge, salt, oil and remaining water and mix, gradually bringing in the dry ingredients, to form a wet dough (don't be tempted to add too much flour). Knead for 10 minutes until satiny and elastic. Put in a clean bowl, cover with a cloth and leave somewhere warm for 1½ hours, or until doubled in size. Preheat the oven to 250°C/480°F/gas mark 9 and put in pizza stones, unglazed terraotta tiles or baking sheets.

3 Meanwhile, for the topping, heat the oil in a saucepan and add the onions. Turn them in the fat, add 1 tbsp water, cover, place over very low heat and sweat for 15 minutes. Add the thyme and set aside.

4 Plomp the dough on to a lightly floured work surface and knead for 2 minutes. Divide into two and roll each piece into a 30cm (12in) round. Put on well-floured baking sheets or large pieces of cardboard to support them while you add the topping.

5 Top with the onions, cheese and beetroot. Season and drizzle with oil. Slide on to the hot stones or baking sheets (oil baking sheets at the last minute). Bake for 15 minutes, scattering with capers 5 minutes before the end. Serve immediately.

ALSO TRY...

Pizzas can go anywhere. Just remember your topping has to cook, without burning, in 15 minutes. But keep a rein on things. Don't go dreaming of pineapple chunks...

Fried onions, oregano and mozzarella cheese (for purists)
Potato, onion and taleggio cheese (partially cook and finely slice the potatoes)
Spinach, courgettes, ricotta and Parmesan cheese
Roast pumpkin, spinach and fontina cheese
Prosciutto, goat's cheese and figs

Brown bread and whisky ice cream

I just love this brown bread ice cream (laced with a bit of whisky) with raspberries.
A coarse-textured brown bread with seeds and grains is particularly good.

Serves 4–6

20g (¾oz) unsalted butter
75g (2½oz) brown breadcrumbs
50g (1½oz) dark soft brown sugar
400ml (14fl oz) double cream

75g (2¾oz) soft light brown sugar
1½ tsp vanilla extract
5 tbsp whisky

1 Melt the butter in a frying pan and add the breadcrumbs. Sauté until golden, stirring often, then add the dark brown sugar, pressing with the back of a wooden spoon to break up any lumps. Continue to sauté, stirring, until the sugar has caramelized the breadcrumbs. Be very careful not to burn the breadcrumbs or sugar. Pour on to a plate and leave to cool.

2 Whip the cream until loose peaks form, adding the soft light brown sugar as you go. Add the vanilla and whisky and stir in the caramelized breadcrumbs.

3 Put into a broad, shallow container and freeze, beating the mixture about 3 times during the freezing process to break down the small crystals and make the ice cream smooth (some people bung it into the food processor to blend it up, but that would ruin the breadcrumbs in this recipe). If you have an ice cream machine, churn it in that.

ALSO TRY…

Brown bread and coffee ice cream Make exactly as above but add 2 tsp instant coffee granules dissolved in 1 tbsp boiling water (and left to cool) along with the whisky.

Wine-soaked autumn pudding

Even better, to my mind, than the summer version. I love the texture of dried apples, but you don't have to use them. If you don't have a source for blackberries – they're so expensive you really have to go blackberrying for them – increase the quantity of plums. It may seem extravagant to make this with wine but you don't need a fantastic bottle. A passable Chilean merlot (or similar) or something left over from the night before is perfectly good enough.

Serves 8

75g (2½oz) dried cranberries
50g (1¾oz) dried apples
300g (10½oz) cooking apples, peeled, cored and sliced
200g (7oz) eating apples, halved, cored and sliced
450g (1lb) plums, halved, stoned and sliced

600ml (1 pint) red wine
225g (8oz) caster sugar
2.5cm (1in) cinnamon stick
300g (10½oz) blackberries
75ml (2½fl oz) crème de cassis (optional)
400g (14oz) white bread, sliced 2cm (¾in) thick, crusts removed

1 Put the dried fruit into a bowl and add just enough boiling water to cover. Leave to plump up for about 15 minutes, then drain. Put the remaining fruit, except the blackberries, with the wine, sugar and cinnamon into a saucepan. Heat gently, stirring to help the sugar dissolve, and simmer until almost tender. Add the blackberries (keep some back for the top) and dried fruit and cook for another 5 minutes. Strain through a sieve (reserving the cooking syrup) and add the cassis to the syrup.

2 Cut 1 bread slice in a circle to fit the bottom of a pudding bowl with a 1.5 litre (2½ pint) capacity, and cut the rest into broad fingers. Line the pudding bowl with the bread, dipping it in the reserved syrup before you lay in each one. Fill in any little gaps by tearing off smaller bits of bread to fit.

3 Now spoon half the fruit into the bowl (discard the cinnamon stick when you find it). Put another layer of bread, again dipping it, halfway up the pudding, then add the remaining fruit and finish with a layer of bread on top. If any syrup remains, pour it over the pudding.

4 Put a plate on top and weigh it down (use cans or a heavy bottle) then refrigerate for 24 hours (I've sometimes made this in the morning for that evening, but it tastes better the next day). To unmould, run a very fine knife round the edge and invert on to a plate.

5 Decorate with a small cluster of berries. Pour some more cassis over if you're feeling flush; it gives a nice gloss and tastes good. Serve with whipped cream or crème fraîche.

Eggs is eggs

Eggs must be one of the most beautiful ingredients: those lovely porous shells, that rich interior (I often think eggs and lemons are all you need to furnish a kitchen). They are perfectly packaged yet very cheap, and perhaps that's why we take them for granted. We turn to eggs when we can't think what else to make – I bet your heart sinks when someone says, 'Not much food in the house, I'm afraid. Could always scramble you a couple of eggs' – and we usually cook them badly. But many of our greatest dishes wouldn't be possible without eggs. They perform so much culinary magic. Their yolks provide the base for rich unguents, such as mayonnaise and hollandaise and their various offshoots. They can hold on to air as they set in a hot oven, giving clouds of meringue and light-as-a-feather cakes. The eggy filling of a properly cooked quiche can be so delicate it trembles, and a teetering soufflé is a thrill.

Eggs mostly provide humble treats, though. When I was ill, my mum used to ask me if I wanted 'a nice boiled egg'. That phrase still fills me with warmth. A perfectly boiled egg – white set, yolk soft and running down the side of its cup – is a joy. Give me a boiled egg when I'm in the right mood and I'll enjoy it as much as any fancier dish. But eggs require careful cooking. I always think it's funny that the egg is how we judge someone's culinary competence. 'She can't boil an egg' is not the worst thing you could say of a cook. You have to be gentle with eggs. Attention must be paid, for example, to the point at which you stop cooking an omelette. It should never be cooked all the way through, but left *baveuse*, as the French call it, slightly uncooked in the centre.

I have to confess to problems with poached eggs. I always lost half the white in the saucepan as it disappeared in little strands. It wasn't until I was taught to poach eggs in a frying pan (where the water is shallower, so there is less room for your egg to splay out) that I got it right. Thank goodness for the *oeuf mollet*, or soft-boiled egg, the treat on many a homely French salad. Once it is broken and its warm yolk runs over warm lentils or hot bacon and bitter salad leaves, you're in bliss.

Just a word on what to buy. Please go for free-range. Eggs are a really cheap source of protein, so buying free-range or free-range *and* organic eggs isn't going to break the bank, and battery hens have a miserable life. Free-range eggs from farm shops don't cost much more than battery eggs from supermarkets.

There are recipes in this chapter that should give you an appetite for these everyday staples. Think all you can do with an egg is scramble it? That's just the beginning...

306 EGGS IS EGGS

Eggs and vegetables with two mayonnaises

When I was an au-pair in Bordeaux I went to the same café each Wednesday evening for *oeufs mayo*. It was all I could afford, but I loved its richness and simplicity and looked forward to it every week. Saffron isn't cheap, but you only need a smidgen.

Serves 6

FOR THE MAYONNAISES
2 large egg yolks
½ tsp Dijon mustard
1 small garlic clove, crushed
150ml (¼ pint) olive oil
150ml (¼ pint) sunflower oil
2 tbsp white wine vinegar
salt and pepper
good squeeze of lemon juice
good pinch of saffron threads
30g (1¼oz) sorrel leaves

FOR THE EGGS AND VEGETABLES
2 chicons of chicory (red or white or one of
  each)
about 30 French breakfast radishes
25g (spare 1oz) watercress or lamb's lettuce
12 Tenderstem broccoli spears
9 eggs
cooked ham, poached trout or salmon (only
  if you have some left over), to serve

1 To make the mayonnaises, put the egg yolks in a bowl with the mustard and garlic and mix well. Start beating with an electric beater or wooden spoon, then gradually add a few drops of the oils. Increase the stream of oil as you are whisking, making sure the mixture is thickening. If it separates, put a new yolk in another bowl and start again, adding the curdled mixture to the fresh egg. (You'll need to double the quantity of other ingredients.) Add the vinegar, seasoning and lemon juice then taste; you may want more vinegar, salt, pepper or lemon. Divide between 2 bowls.

2 Put the saffron in a glass with 1 tbsp just-boiled water. Stir to dissolve, then slowly add it to half the mayonnaise. Put the sorrel into a food processor and add the other half. Whizz. Taste each mayonnaise for seasoning. Cover and refrigerate until needed.

3 Divide the chicory leaves, radishes and watercress or lamb's lettuce between plates. Prepare the broccoli and eggs at the last minute so they're bright and fresh and your guests can have both hot and cold elements. Boil the broccoli in water for about 3 minutes and the eggs for about 8 minutes.

4 Put the warm broccoli and eggs on the plates with ham, trout or salmon (if using) and add a pool of each mayonnaise. Serve with bread.

ALSO TRY...

The Provençal olive paste, tapenade, is a knockout with hard-boiled eggs, French breakfast radishes, unsalted butter and French bread. Or try cured anchovies and black olives with hard-boiled eggs, bread and olive oil. Try other mayonnaises such as basil and sun-dried tomato – purée basil leaves with the mayonnaise and add sun-dried tomatoes, chopped – or black olive and anchovy (chop and add to plain mayonnaise).

Buckingham eggs

I have long since forgotten where I read about this dish. I fancy it is called 'Buckingham' because it uses a few toff ingredients (I always think anchovy paste and Worcestershire sauce are the aristocrat's equivalent of Marmite and HP) but don't know for sure. Anyway, they are amazingly good. Scrambled eggs should be cooked over a medium to low heat until creamy and just set, not cooked to rubber on your highest gas ring. That's really all you need to know.

Serves 1

1 slice of bread	2 eggs, lightly beaten
1 tsp anchovy paste	salt and pepper
smidgen of English mustard	15g (½oz) mature Cheddar cheese, grated
knob of butter	Worcestershire sauce

1 Toast the bread on both sides, then spread it with the anchovy paste and mustard. Melt the butter in a nonstick pan and add the eggs and a little seasoning.

2 Stir over medium-low heat until the eggs are just holding their shape (don't over-scramble or they'll be like rubber once you grill them). Pile the eggs on the toast, then scatter on the cheese and a little Worcestershire sauce. Put under a *very* hot grill until pale gold and just bubbling. Eat immediately.

ALSO TRY...

With smoked haddock and Parmesan Cook 50g (1¾oz) smoked haddock (see page 225). Leave it in big flakes. Scramble 2 eggs as above (a slug of cream doesn't go amiss with smoked haddock) and gently stir in the fish and 15g (½oz) Parmesan cheese, finely grated, towards the end of the cooking time. Scatter parsley, finely chopped, on top, grind on some black pepper and serve immediately.

With chorizo and wilted spinach Cook 75g (2½oz) chorizo, sliced, in the fat that runs from it as it cooks. Scramble a couple of lightly beaten eggs as in the main recipe and, at the same time, quickly wilt 75g (2½oz) baby spinach leaves in a frying pan with 1 tbsp olive oil. Put the spinach on a plate, the scrambled eggs on top scatter over the chorizo.

Alpine soufflés

There's no mystery to soufflés. Just remember these key points: dust the dishes with breadcrumbs so the soufflé has something to cling to as it rises; make sure your base sauce is thick and add the egg whites to it while it's warm; season well; beat the egg whites until stiff but not dry; place the soufflé on a heated baking sheet so it starts rising immediately; don't open the oven before a soufflé has cooked for 20 minutes. Finally, soufflés should be slightly soft within, so don't cook them until they are totally set. They continue to cook once they're out of the oven.

Serves 6

60g (2oz) butter
dry white breadcrumbs, to dust
45g (1¾oz) flour
1 tsp dry mustard
good pinch of cayenne
435ml (¾ pint) full-fat milk

150g (5½oz) Beaufort or Gruyère cheese, grated
6 heaped tbsp grated Parmesan cheese
6 eggs, separated
salt and pepper

1 Preheat the oven to 200°C/400°F/gas mark 6 and put in a metal baking sheet. Melt a good knob of the butter and use it to brush 6 ramekins. Dust lightly with breadcrumbs. It isn't absolutely necessary, but you can make little collars of baking parchment, which should rise 5cm (2in) above the rim of each ramekin, and tie them with kitchen string. They just look nice.

2 Melt the remaining butter in a heavy pan and stir in the flour, mustard and cayenne. Cook for 45 seconds. Take off the heat and add the milk, a little at a time, stirring constantly to remove any lumps. Return to the heat, stirring, and bring to the boil. It will thicken. Cook gently for 2 minutes, then remove from the heat. Stir in the cheeses, egg yolks and plenty of seasoning.

3 Whisk the egg whites until stiff – they should stay in the bowl if you hold it upside down – but not dry, and fold a large spoonful into the warm mixture to loosen it. Fold in the rest of the whites, then divide between the dishes. Run your finger round the inside of each ramekin: this will give each soufflé a 'top hat' look when it puffs up.

4 Put the ramekins on the baking sheet and bake for 25 minutes until risen and golden brown. Don't open the door until they've cooked for 20 minutes or they will fall. Then just open the door wide enough to give the soufflés a shake. If they wobble a lot, cook for a further 5 minutes. Serve immediately.

ALSO TRY...

Once you've mastered the technique you can turn almost anything – spinach, potato and anchovy, courgettes, roasted red peppers, mushrooms, leeks, fish – into a soufflé. Try making the soufflé above with blue cheese and walnuts (use half Cheddar and half blue cheese), goat's cheese or smoked Cheddar.

Menemen

A Turkish dish and a fantastic supper (great for when you have a mate over and don't think scrambled eggs quite cuts it). It's chilli-hot but you have cool yogurt and emollient egg yolk to offset it. Great with very cold beer.

Serves 4

FOR THE EGGS
4 tbsp olive oil
1 large onion, quite thickly sliced
4 red, yellow and green peppers, deseeded and quite thickly sliced
2 green chillies, deseeded and finely chopped
400g can tomatoes in thick juice
salt and pepper

2 tbsp chopped coriander, flat leaf parsley or mint
4 eggs
extra virgin olive oil
ground chilli or cayenne
crumbled feta cheese, (optional)
flatbread, to serve

FOR THE YOGURT SAUCE
8 tbsp Greek yogurt
2 garlic cloves, crushed

1 Heat the oil in a large frying pan and cook the onion, peppers and chillies over medium-high heat until the onion is golden. Add the tomatoes, season and cook until the peppers are soft and the mixture not too runny, though still like a sauce. Stir in the herbs. Break the eggs on top and cook over medium heat until they are set but the yolks are still runny (15–20 minutes). The mixture underneath will become thicker.

2 Sprinkle the eggs with salt and pepper, add a drizzle of extra virgin olive oil and the ground chilli or cayenne. Scatter with feta, if using. Stir the ingredients for the yogurt sauce together and serve on the side with flatbread.

ALSO TRY...

Oven-roasted ratatouille with baked eggs Preheat the oven to 200°C/400°F/ gas mark 6. Thickly slice and deseed 1 red and 1 yellow pepper. Cut 4 courgettes into 5mm (¼in) slices, and 1 aubergine into chunks. Cut 2 red onions into wedges. Halve 700g (1lb 9oz) plum tomatoes. Put the vegetables, 2 garlic cloves, crushed, 8 tbsp olive oil, the leaves from 3 thyme sprigs and salt and pepper into a large roasting tin or wide cast-iron sauté pan. Toss everything around and roast for 45 minutes. When the vegetables have 15 minutes to go, stir in 450g (1lb) passata, mixing well and seasoning. Five minutes before the end of cooking, reduce the oven temperature to 180°C/350°F/gas mark 4 and break 4 eggs into the vegetables. Drizzle 2 tbsp olive oil and sprinkle seasoning over the eggs and cook until they have set but the yolks are runny (this should take the remaining 5 minutes, but do check as ovens vary).

Smoked Cheddar and apple omelette

Cook omelettes in butter and serve as the centre is just setting (*baveuse* as they say in France), not cooked to rubber. Make sure your filling is properly cooked before adding it. Mushrooms, for example, need to have exuded all their liquid – and that liquid needs to have evaporated – or your omelette will leak pale grey water. Cheese should be added in time to allow it to melt.

Serves 2

30g (1oz) butter

1 eating apple, cored and cut into slim wedges (no need to peel)

leaves from 2 thyme sprigs

4 eggs, beaten and seasoned

75g (2¾oz) smoked Cheddar, grated

1 Melt half the butter in a small frying pan and sauté the apple over medium heat until golden on both sides and tender. Set aside. Add most of the thyme to the eggs.

2 Heat the remaining butter in a frying pan and, once it is foaming, add the eggs. Tilt the pan, gently scraping up the bits of omelette which set in the middle and allowing the uncooked eggs to run into the spaces left behind. When the omelette is still soft on top but set underneath, put the apples and cheese on one half. Fold the other half over the filling, let the cheese melt for 20 seconds or so, then turn the omelette on to a warmed plate. Scatter with the remaining thyme and serve.

ALSO TRY...

Fill your omelette with the lovely, nutty-tasting Alpine cheese Beaufort or, if you can't find that, Gruyère, and shreds of ham. Goat's cheese and finely chopped soft herbs – chervil or basil, for example – make another good cheesey omelette. Flaked smoked haddock with grated Cheddar is delicious, or add chopped dill to the eggs and fill the omelette with flakes of hot smoked salmon or off-cuts of smoked salmon (you can get these in packets and they are always cheap).

Leeks vinaigrette with bacon and poached egg

Poaching eggs well is a skill that eluded me for years, so here's how. Put about 5cm (2in) water in a frying pan and bring to the boil. Use really fresh eggs (or the white will spread out like a disintegrating octopus) and have a teacup handy. Reduce the heat so the water is just shuddering. Crack the egg into the cup and slide it into the water as gently as you can. Cook for about 4 minutes. Remove with a slotted spoon and let the egg drain really well, without allowing it to become stone cold. If you're having trouble with poaching, for this recipe try soft-boiling the eggs for 4½ minutes, then carefully shell them, without breaking into the yolk, set them on top of the leeks and gently break so the yolk runs out.

Serves 6

FOR THE LEEKS AND EGGS
600g (1lb 5oz) slender young leeks, or
   medium-sized leeks
6 bacon or pancetta rashers
olive oil
6 eggs
balsamic vinegar (optional)

FOR THE VINAIGRETTE
½ tbsp white wine vinegar
salt and pepper
½ tsp Dijon mustard
8 tbsp extra virgin olive oil
¾ tsp caster sugar, or to taste
1 tbsp finely chopped parsley

1 Trim the leeks, removing the dark green bits and any tough outer leaves if you are using larger leeks. Wash thoroughly. If you are using small leeks, simply trim the ends; if using larger leeks, trim the ends and cut the leeks into 8cm (3½in) lengths. Steam or boil the leeks until tender. The length of time this takes depends on the thickness of the leeks you are using. If you boil them, make sure you drain them really well.

2 Make the vinaigrette by whisking all the ingredients together. As soon as the leeks are cooked, put them into a dish and cover with the vinaigrette.

3 Cook the bacon or pancetta in a little olive oil. Divide the leeks between 6 plates, put a rasher of bacon or pancetta on each serving and keep them warm while you quickly poach the eggs. Make sure each egg is well drained, then set on top of each serving. Grind on some black pepper, drizzle a little balsamic vinegar over, if using, and serve immediately.

ALSO TRY...

You can top the leeks with a slice of cured ham (such as Parma) or cooked ham, or replace the leeks with purple-sprouting broccoli when in season. If you use broccoli, you can scatter shavings of Parmesan on top and omit the bacon.

Peach and lavender honey clafoutis

Clafoutis is a batter pudding in which the fruit really shines. It's also cheap – especially when summer fruit gets plentiful and you can pick up punnets of peaches or apricots for a song – and makes a great Sunday lunch pud. Cherry is the classic, but go where you will... plums, nectarines and greengages are all good, though soft berries are best avoided as they collapse.

Serves 4–6

FOR THE PEACHES
800g (1lb 12oz) peaches, halved and stoned
4 tbsp caster sugar
juice of ½ lemon

FOR THE BATTER
150ml (¼ pint) double cream
150ml (¼ pint) milk
2 big tbsp lavender honey

2 sprigs fresh lavender, if in season
3 eggs
100g (3½oz) caster sugar
pinch of salt
25g (1oz) plain flour
toasted almonds (optional)
icing sugar, to dust

1 Put the peaches, sugar and lemon juice into a frying or sauté pan and heat gently. You want to soften the fruit slightly; it should be tender but not collapsing. Cool.

2 To make the batter, mix the cream, milk, honey and lavender in a saucepan. Bring to just under the boil, then leave to infuse for 20 minutes or so. Preheat the oven to 180°C/350°F/gas mark 4. Whisk the eggs, sugar and salt together until the mixture triples in volume and is pale and fluffy. Fold in the flour, then the milk mixture.

3 Arrange the fruit in a gratin dish and pour over the batter. Cook in the oven for 30 minutes, or until set. Scatter on the toasted almonds, and sift over a little icing sugar.

ALSO TRY...

Apricot and orange blossom Make as above but replace the peaches with the same quantity of quartered apricots, replace the honey with 2 more tbsp caster sugar, omit the lavender and add 1 tbsp orange flower water to the cream.

Cherry and almond Make as in the main recipe, but replace the honey with another 2 tbsp caster sugar, omit the lavender and add 1–2 tbsp kirsch or amaretto liqueur (if you have it) to the batter. You'll need 600g (1lb 5oz) cherries, pitted.

Apple, honey and rosemary Make as in the main recipe, but heat the milk and cream with 3 tbsp plain honey and a rosemary sprig. Leave to infuse for 20 minutes. Remove the rosemary and make the batter with the milk mixture, 40g (1½oz) flour and 75g (2½oz) sugar. Peel and core 600g (1lb 5oz) Bramley apples and finely slice. Toss with 25g (1oz) sugar. Put in a gratin dish, pour over the batter and bake for 30–40 minutes or until set. Scatter on toasted hazelnuts or walnuts and sift a little icing sugar over.

Index

Acknowledgements

For Ben, with love

Food from Plenty
by Diana Henry

First published in Great Britain in 2010 by Mitchell Beazley, an imprint of Octopus Publishing Group Limited, Endeavour House, 189 Shaftesbury Avenue London WC2H 8JY
www.octopusbooks.co.uk

© Octopus Publishing Group Limited 2010
Text © Diana Henry 2010
Photographs © Jonathan Lovekin 2010

A CIP catalogue record for this book is available from the British Library.

ISBN 9781845335076

Commissioning Editor: Rebecca Spry
Art Director: Pene Parker
Designer: Miranda Harvey
Photographer: Jonathan Lovekin
Project Editor: Georgina Atsiaris
Copy Editor: Lucy Bannell
Proofreader: Ruth Baldwin
Home Economist: Sonja Edridge
Production Manager: Pete Hunt
Index: Hilary Bird

Typeset in Baskerville
Printed and bound in China

All 'also try' recipes serve the same number as the main recipe, unless otherwise stated.

Writers stay at home most of the time, typing and working and hoping that somebody will bother to read what they spend their life doing. If you don't have readers your work is pointless, so huge thanks to *The Sunday Telegraph* who give me space, every week, to share recipes and passions with my readers. I am very grateful to Anna Murphy, the editor of *Stella* magazine, Ian MacGregor, the editor of the newspaper, and Elfreda Pownall, the Food and Interiors Editor, for their unfailing support and enthusiasm. In fact I am totally spoiled at the ST. Elfreda, along with Katie Drummond and Amy Bryant, make a wonderfully knowledgeable team who try out every recipe (and give me feedback) and provide me with a very caring office (albeit one I usually only experience on the phone and on-line). Every writer needs this kind of 'home'.

Thanks to my best and oldest friend, Jenny Abbott, for allowing me to take over her kitchen for recipe testing while my own kitchen was a building site. (She's a harsh critic, though – the roast squash lasagne on p81 is to her exact specifications. You had better make it often, Jen...).

Mitchell Beazley really believed in *Food from Plenty* and have put an enormous amount into it. My commissioning editor, Rebecca Spry, showed her usual incisiveness and she and David Lamb helped me to shape a book for changing times, and one that cooks would want to have in their kitchen. A big thanks as well to project manager Georgina Atsiaris (who nearly took the proofs on her honeymoon) for going well beyond the call of duty.

The wonderful Jonathan Lovekin did his usual amazing job. His pictures are always brilliant and we love having him around for his wry sense of humour as much as for his talent.

Food from Plenty wouldn't have been possible without three women who have worked with such passion and dedication that it makes me feel humble.

Sonja (Edridge), I couldn't have had a better partner in the kitchen. You're about the only person who'd get up at 5am to cook too many dishes in one day and still be smiling at the end of it (and uncorking a bottle of wine).

Lucy (Bannell), you are an editor among editors. You have worked on my words for so many years that you can cut my text and I haven't a clue what's missing. You keep me buoyant too.

Miranda (Harvey), your designs are simple and beautiful and you have given my books a style and identity all of their own. And you always make me laugh. Thanks and love to you all– my kitchen is your kitchen and there is always a bed for you upstairs.

My lovely boys – Ted and Gillies – thank you for your patience (they said I had to write that), and for eating new dishes when you would rather have had pasta with tomato sauce.

Lastly, thanks to Ben – for everything.